When Police Unionise

the politics of law and order in Australia

Mark Finnane

Sydney 2002

Sydney Institute of Criminology Monograph Series No 15

Sydney Institute of Criminology Monograph Series No 15

Series Editors: Chris Cunneen, Mark Findlay, Julie Stubbs
University of Sydney Law School

Other titles in the Monograph Series

Aboriginal Perspectives on Criminal Justice, Chris Cunneen (out of print)
Doing Less Time: Penal Reform in Crisis, Janet Chan
Usefulness of Psychiatric Reports in Court Proceedings, Peter Shea
The Man in White is Always Right: Cricket and the Law, David Fraser
The Prison and the Home, Ann Aungles
Women, Male Violence and the Law, Julie Stubbs (ed)
Fault in Homicide, Stanley Yeo
Anatomy of a French Murder Case, Bron McKillop
Gender, Race & International Relations: Violence Against Filipino Women in Australia, Chris Cunneen and Julie Stubbs
Reform in Policing: Lessons from the Whitrod Era, Jill Bolen
A Culture of Corruption: Changing an Australian Police Service, David Dixon (ed)
Defining Madness, Peter Shea
Developing Cultural Criminology, Cyndi Banks (ed)
Indigenous Human Rights, Garkawe, Kelly and Fisher (eds)

Published by
The Institute of Criminology
University of Sydney Faculty of Law
173–175 Phillip Street
Sydney NSW 2000
Ph 61 2 9351 0239

Distributed by
Federation Press
PO Box 45 Annandale
71 John Street
Leichhardt NSW 2040
Ph 61 2 9552 2200

National Library of Australia Cataloguing-in-Publication data
Finnane, Mark. When police unionise : the politics of law and order in Australia.
ISBN 1 86487 464 3.
1. Police - Australia - Political activity. I. University of Sydney. Institute of Criminology. II. Title. (Series : Sydney Institute of Criminology monograph series ; no. 15).
363.20994

Cover Design by Pro Bono Publico P/L
Printed by Printing Headquarters
Typeset by Four Eyes Editing

Contents

Introduction **1**

1: Politics and the police in Australia **5**

1.1 Law and order elections 5

1.2 An international story 18

2: Organising the police **27**

2.1 Before the unions 29

2.2 Combinations and aspirations 31

2.3 Police strikes 45

3: The politicisation of police **57**

3.1 Defining the game 58

3.2 Political campaigns 69

3.3 Wages and conditions 74

3.4 The developing political role 81

4: Industrial battlefields **91**

4.1 The uses of law 92

4.2 Matters of appeal 100

4.3 Commissioner–union conflict 107

4.4 Implications for policing: ministers, commissioners and unions 114

5: Alliances and conflicts **126**

5.1 A national union? 127

5.2 Political rights 130

5.3 Using the media 134

5.4 Are police workers? 142

5.5 Fractured relations 151

6: Political interventions **159**
6.1 A thousand more police, or two 163
6.2 Damage control — commissions and inquiries 174
6.3 Law reform — the unions for and against 186
6.4 The politics of victimhood 192

7: The politics of change **197**
7.1 New agendas and old responses 198
7.2 Discipline and the commissioner's powers 206
7.3 Operational issues — policy and practice 212

8: Law and order **219**
8.1 Political choices 219
8.2 Taking stock 225
8.3 Conclusion 235

References **239**

Index **246**

Acknowledgements

My interest in the subject of this book goes back to 1987 in the early days of the Fitzgerald Inquiry. I am grateful to the Queensland Police Union of Employees for granting me access at that time to the invaluable collections of union journals and executive minutes that are held at its headquarters. Subsequent research in those records by Jenny Fleming developed the first thorough account of the early formation of a police union in Australia and I owe much to her valuable research now published in a number of articles.

This book is largely the product of extensive data collection made possible by an Australian Research Council Large Grant, 1998–9. This enabled me to organise research on the primary data of the book, the union journals in the different Australian jurisdictions. It is regrettable that complete collections of these are so difficult to access — but between the various state and university libraries, and the union holdings in a number of places, this study has accessed most of them. I owe a platoon of researchers a great debt for their work on these records, and in some cases, on state archives and other materials as well. They include Margaret de Nooyer and Jonathan Richards in Brisbane, Iris Petrass in Victoria, Katie Hall in Sydney, Barbara Baird, Bernard O'Neil and Greg Tostevin in Adelaide, Wade Matthews in Perth and David Coombes in Hobart. In a number of cases their work involved access to otherwise closed collections and I am grateful for their diplomacy in that cause — as well as to the staff of the respective police unions and libraries in the various states who have provided that access.

Thanks are due to my scholarly colleagues in a number of places for discussions and suggestions, for sharing their own work, and responding to queries and requests for help. They include Clive Emsley and Robert Reiner in England, Phillip Stenning in Canada, David Brereton, Darren Palmer, David Dixon, David Baker, Karl Alderson, Janet Chan, Charlie Fox, Stefan Petrow and Steve James in Australia. It has been a somewhat unexpected but pleasant experience in the course of this work to find a great deal of interest in the research among a number of people in the police unions in Australia and elsewhere. In particular I have benefited from the assistance and interest of Greg Chilvers at the NSW Police

Association and Andy Dunn at the Police Association of South Australia. Unsolicited but helpful distribution through the police unions network of some of my lectures or conference papers on the subject of the book has brought in turn correspondence and current research materials from Ron DeLord in Texas and Dale Kinnear in Canada. The importance of the international networks and benchmarking in policing has been brought home very powerfully to me in researching and writing this book, and I hope to follow up some of the issues raised here in the future.

I am very pleased to see this book appear in the Institute of Criminology Monograph Series and want to express my thanks to the co-editors of the Series, Chris Cunneen, Mark Findlay and Julie Stubbs and to those who have seen the book through production, answering my queries promptly, Tessa Boyd-Caine and Dawn Koester. Thanks are due also to Juanita Marris for preparing the index at short notice.

Mark Finnane, Griffith University
February 2002

Introduction

In November 1976 the secretary of the Police Federation of Australia claimed that police militancy had resulted in police ministers in two unnamed states being sacked. Press speculation suggested they were from Queensland and New South Wales. In the former state the minister lost his portfolio after ordering an inquiry into allegations of police bashing, in the latter the minister had lost his preselection after a torrid time in charge of the police department. Around this time in another state, Victoria, the police union had gone to a work-to-rule campaign in confronting the government over the threatened prosecution of police involved in a corruption inquiry, while in South Australia police unionists were in repeated conflict with their management and the government through the later 1970s. By 1979 a review of police industrial disputation was concluding that 'police industrial militancy is the highest for more than 50 years'.[1]

In the 1980s police unhappiness with changes to complaints legislation and summary offences powers in New South Wales resulted in sustained public conflict between police unionists and the Labor government. In retrospect after his ten years in power, ex-premier Wran announced that the biggest regret of his time in government was 'disobedience by Police'. He was not alone in being burned by police action. In South Australia and Victoria in this same decade governments were forced to back down over complaints legislation, in the latter case disbanding an already established police complaints authority. Throughout the decade police unions mounted public campaigns for more police, and against legislation they considered soft on criminals or hard on police. Only in Queensland finally, and surprisingly, did the unions seem to face a significant reverse — in 1989 the Fitzgerald Inquiry into police and political corruption in that state suggested that police unions should stick to industrial business and keep out of politics.

By the early 1990s the spectre of police union campaigns seemed to haunt most governments facing the polls. Having played the police numbers game in his ride to power in New South Wales Liberal premier Greiner was himself confronted by a hostile police union campaign at a by-election in 1992. He was gone from office not long after, his term marred by repeated conflict between his police ministers and the police department (headed from 1991 by an ex-president of the Police Association) and unions. In Tasmania in 1991–2, and Queensland 1995–6, Labor premiers were to find the police unions no friendlier — in Queensland the Mundingburra by-election in February 1996 was fatal to the Goss government, and the police union's role in that election reverberated in the state's politics for two years after.

Was the Victorian Police Association's deep and well-publicised conflict with the state government in May 1999 a factor in Premier Kennett's shock loss of power at the state election a few months later? Quite possibly — and if so, we might wonder whether that turn of events had been brewing from the government's earliest days, when it made clear that the police would not be sheltered from Kennett's winds of change, cutting the public sector and neutering the unions. As early as February 1993 the Victorian Police Association had gestured rhetorically that 'we do not take political sides', while attacking Kennett for subjecting the Association to the *Public Sector (Union Fees) Act 1992* which removed the facility of payroll deduction of union dues.[2] By the end of his time, the conflict was so deep that the Victorian Police Commissioner was describing the Association as those 'defenders of mediocrity'.[3]

How have police unions come to play such a role in politics today? How have organisations of workers who once were denied the right to organise come to deploy significant power in shaping, or seeking to shape, public policy over crime control and prevention, resource allocation in policing, the size of police budgets, the rights of other citizens to complain about what happens to them in policing situations? Is the police union story one of expanding power and influence — are there never any setbacks, or balances? All these questions are worth considering. Answers to them help us to understand how policing is organised today in Australia, and what are its limits. Answers to them may also tell us something about the history of public provision of services to the community, and what is happening to it now. For it is striking that many of the pressures that have shaped police union dispositions and activities in recent decades are also those that affect other areas of social policy and services — in teaching, health, public utilities and so on.

The method of this inquiry is historical. Much commentary on the role of police unions, or the development of criminal justice policy in Australia today is unhistorical, or ahistorical. Being historical means more than giving a description of what happened in the past. This book starts instead from the position that the contemporary institutions and practices of policing are historically formed — i.e. they are made possible by distinctive histories which result in particular arrangements of the major actors in political domains or other social settings. In addition, we cannot assess the power of police unions to shape and influence policing today unless we know how different is or was the position in other places and/or other times. It is precisely the absence of such an understanding that seems to characterise public debate about the roles (what are they?) and responsibilities (do they exist?) of police unions today. Such a lack of understanding does not characterise this field alone of course — but the issues raised for example in the Mundingburra case, leading to a change in government, do call out for special attention.

This book is far from a comprehensive treatment of the subject. There will be other more specific studies, of particular jurisdictions, or of particular episodes, or smaller time periods. It is in the nature of public debate (in the media, in parliament, in academic and other journals) to focus on the most recent past, and much can be gained from examining events in one's own time. But this book does draw attention to the significance of a longer history. Police unions are relatively youthful in the ranks of labour movement organisations, but in Australia they are drawing on nearly a century of influential activity. I intend to show that many of what are seen as their contemporary characteristics (encapsulated so frequently in the phrase 'politicisation') are in fact of very long standing. Indeed it is difficult to estimate today just how *political* the first attempts at unionising police really were, how challenging to government, law and administration of this arm of criminal justice.

In brief then my focus will be on police unions as players in the determination of criminal justice policy and administration. This is not primarily a history of organisations. It is a history of how choices are made in criminal justice administration, under what influence of which players, and with what demonstrable effects. 'Demonstrable effects' is itself a challenge to orthodox commentary on police unions. The opponents of police unions are frequently stronger at articulating what might be an ethical position to adopt on criminal justice matters, than in assessing concretely what the police and police unions do. This history can inform both sides of the public debate about the role of police unions by making visible how police unions have helped shape, but also have been shaped by, the forces of political power in law, justice, government and industrial relations.

The primary source for this book is an extraordinarily rich source of information — the union journal. From them we can glean the priority law and order issues as seen by the unions over many decades. There are of course other sources, and these play their part in filling out the story — law reports, parliamentary debates, selected newspaper reports, archival evidence. The last is often the most useful — but is also either very resource-intensive, or else closed to the researcher. I have been able to make up for some of the deficiencies of limited archival access with the invaluable insights occasionally provided by the evidence given at royal commissions and other official inquiries.

Such are the sources — but what of the themes? I intend that the book will provide readers with a better understanding of the following issues. The primary task is to explore how far the politics of law and order has been affected by police unionisation in Australia — but essentially exploring this issue from the police unions' perspective. A number of subordinate themes flow from this. The first is to comprehend the conditions under which unions were formed. A second is to assess what impact unionisation had on the internal management of police forces. Especially I am concerned to show what changes in the relation between commissioner and constable were wrought by police union struggles to establish mechanisms such as appeal boards, as well as through arbitration on industrial conditions issues. A third concern is the changing engagement of police unions with the political sphere — including not only the policy and law-making process, but also the vitally important domain of the media. Finally, I want throughout to reflect on the implications of these changing themes for our views of what constitutes good government, and of the mechanisms that foster it.

Notes

1 *The Australian*, 23 Nov 1976, p2 for report; Bruce Swanton and Robert W Page, "Police industrial dispute resolution processes and their implications for militancy," *Journal of Industrial Relations* 21 (1979).

2 *Victorian Police Journal* (*VPJ*), Feb 1993, p5.

3 *The Age*, 19 Jul 1999.

1: Politics and the police in Australia

I regard law and order in this State to be far too serious a matter to be the subject of political rhetoric.
Barrie Unsworth, New South Wales Labor Premier, 1986

Labor's a crook vote.
Police Association election ad, 1991, Tasmania

What GOSS, BRADDY, MOONEY and their cronies didn't realise, is that we're coppers and we're confronted with filth and dirty tricks every day of the week. They thought they'd get the better of us, but trust me when I say (and I won't go into details), they didn't. ***We won, and they lost in all departments*** *...*
Queensland Police Union branch newsletter, 1996

1.1 Law and order elections

It is not only the accident of the author's time and place that explains why the Mundingburra by-election of February 1996 might be taken as a leitmotif for this book. Mundingburra was the most successful intervention of a police union in Australia in the electoral process, up to a point. We can take it in the Australian context as representing the culmination of a century of aspiration by police to shape criminal justice administration and policy to the mould preferred by a representative union. At the same time its repercussions in the political sphere necessarily provoke a consideration of political rights and responsibilities which, while inevitably having no definable outcome, might be seen in the longer term as part of a continuing renovation of those standard elements of democratic politics in a liberal state. The defeat of the Labor government at Mundingburra was seen as the essential condition for achieving specified outcomes — but victory for the police union cause turned out to be somewhat pyrrhic in the short term. And in the longer term? The prelude to this episode, and its outcomes, deserve some extended analysis here.

The Mundingburra by-election came less than a decade after the momentous events of the Fitzgerald inquiry into police corruption (1987–9) which became an inquiry into a whole political system that had dominated Queensland for the previous two decades. Political and institutional change accompanied the recommendations of Fitzgerald — a Labor government under Wayne Goss replaced the National-Liberal coalition which had been deeply implicated in the corruption and maladministration disclosed in the inquiry. Electoral and administrative reform were the tasks of a temporary commission established in these years. In policing crucial changes were instituted by the establishment of a new body, the Criminal Justice Commission (CJC), with statutory functions affecting senior police appointments, complaints hearings and disciplinary proceedings, as well as research into policing and criminal justice policy and practice. Accompanying the political and institutional changes were others affecting police work and conditions — managerial reform, alterations in promotion systems, a new focus on education and training. The early 1990s were years of constant change, much of it consistent with what was happening elsewhere in Australia, but inflected with the tones of a new order associated with the conditions that had brought to power the Goss Labor government.[1]

The notoriety of the Mundingburra by-election came to centre on a Memorandum of Understanding (MOU). This 14-page document was signed on 10 January 1996 by the president of the Queensland Police Union, Senior Sergeant Gary Wilkinson and the National Party leader of the Queensland Opposition, Rob Borbidge, as well as the Opposition's spokesman on police, Russell Cooper, himself a former police minister. Subsequent inquiry concluded that the document had been negotiated by Wilkinson and Cooper, and that Wilkinson had consulted with a majority of his union executive in its preparation. Coincident with the secret negotiation and signing of the document, the union executive committed $20,000 to funding a law and order publicity campaign during the running of the Mundingburra election.

The MOU's 14 pages detailed a wide-ranging agenda of policing issues, a wish-list of the executive's priorities for addressing the union's apparent grievances about the staffing and resourcing of Queensland's 5,000-strong police force. Under subheadings of Staffing, Promotion, Discipline, Enterprise Bargaining and Industrial Matters, the union's proposals were set out in greater detail, together with statements of the aspirant Coalition government's responses to the individual proposals. Many proposals were 'agreed', some qualified or elaborated in detailed policy positions, a couple of matters were 'partially agreed'. Only one of the more than 40 matters was 'not agreed', while a couple of important issues were to be the subject of detailed review. The scope of the items was wide-ranging. While the union executive was subsequently to defend its position as 'industrial' rather than 'political',[2] the issues clearly covered some matters that were central to the policy direction and resource priorities of a future government — especially matters of the size of the police force, the selection of a future commissioner, and the powers and operation of the Criminal Justice Commission. As will be shown throughout this book the division between industrial and political is by no means a clear one. Moreover the union's ambitions, as expressed in any one of its 'wish-list' objectives were also by no means unprecedented in union initiatives, in Queensland as elsewhere. Even on the controversial matter of the naming of six senior officers as 'unsuccessful', and therefore ripe for redundancy, there have been earlier, if more public, precedents — in particular in a 1952 dispute over punitive transfers, and what was seen as political interference in police administration.[3]

From the point of view of the politics of policing what made the MOU vitally important was its secret nature, its linkage to a union strategy capable of shifting the balance of power through the result in a democratic by-election, and the ambit of its wish list. In retrospect the production of the MOU was not surprising. The political context was crucial, and the union's disposition increasingly hostile to the government of the day. What was mandated in the public proceedings of the union, through its annual conference decisions and their publication in the freely available union journal was however somewhat different from the burden of the secret MOU. To understand the difference it is instructive to review the union journal coverage of the political context in the year leading up to Mundingburra.

The focus of the police union campaign was signalled by a decision of the 1995 annual conference. The motion was to become the umbrella for the union executive's approach to the 1995 state election and 1996 Mundingburra by-election. Conference had moved:

> That the Executive under the direction of the General President commence a protracted advertising campaign to highlight the serious staff deficiencies throughout the State and make the public aware that the Government is not taking the appropriate steps to solve those shortages or ensure the safety of the general public.[4]

Subsequent issues of the journal developed the campaign theme. By the July issue the thrust of the campaign was inspiring some comment within the union to the effect that the journal's editor was 'mounting a campaign against the Labor Party'. This was denied in a predictable defence:

> The Government is our employer. This Union has an obligation to comment on the statements and actions of our employer — the Government. Unfortunately Union statements which highlight issues affecting the well-being of police officers are likely to appear to be politically biased. Nothing could be further from the truth. This Union and, in particular, this Editor do not endorse or support any political party.

Rather, it was explained, the appearance of political favour was an accident arising from the union's right to comment on performance and promises of both government and the opposition parties.[5] In perhaps too defensive a posture this same issue of the journal, appearing in the month of the pending state election, featured a front-cover photograph of the Labor premier Wayne Goss, addressing unionists at a May 1995 Labour Day function.

The potential of the conference motion to develop as a broad-stroke law and order campaign was also by July too evident. The issues were becoming not just those of police numbers but 'law and order issues' which, it was claimed, the opposition was continuing to raise while the government 'was being exceptionally quiet'. The July editorial page signalled another matter that lurked in the background of the union's law and order agenda. Under the heading 'Shades of Fitzgerald', the editorial referred to the current proceedings of the Wood Royal Commission into the New South Wales Police Service. Police unionists were asked to 'spare a thought for our colleagues in New South Wales ... As survivors of the Fitzgerald reforms and the PSMC recommendations we offer our full support to our fellow officers in the trying times ahead'. A parenthetical note asked rhetorically: 'did anyone notice the former Queensland Superintendent and strong advocate of the Fitzgerald reforms who appears to be assisting the New South Wales Inquiry?'[6]

Quite publicly then the Queensland Police Union was already drawing attention to the range of issues that would engage its attention in the next six months of political jockeying over the future complexion of government in Queensland. Police numbers were on the agenda, linked to matters of public safety and 'law and order' generally. An underlying complex of grievances was linked to the Fitzgerald reform process and the establishment of the Criminal Justice Commission and the Public Sector Management Commission. Both these Commissions had effected substantial change in personnel practices within Queensland policing — the former through its powers of investigation of misconduct and corruption, the latter through its public sector reforms which embraced merit in promotion criteria as well as opening up the police and other public sector departments to lateral entry from outside the agency, and even outside the state.

In the MOU these elements of a long-developing police union antagonism towards government policy were brought together to great effect. Police staff numbers have become a union perennial around election time. The appearance of police numbers on the MOU was nothing exceptional — and the union was doing nothing in the lead-up to Mundingburra to hide the fact. As union president Gary Wilkinson told members in the February 1996 issue of the union journal:

> Very early in the Campaign, it became known that your Union intended to involve itself in the By-Election. This of course forced both sides of the political spectrum to up the anti on police numbers and the law and order issue./ The Union's prime objective was to embarrass the Government over operational staffing numbers and force an increase in those numbers from whatever party gained power in Queensland.[7]

The MOU however had a number of other objectives. It sought to return to Queensland police the *status quo ante* in matters of discipline and promotions, with the re-establishment of an appeals board on a model that had been achieved in the 1920s. It sought a police union veto over the appointment of senior police, including the commissioner and senior officers. It demanded a substantial change in the mechanisms of misconduct and discipline investigation by the Criminal Justice Commission — on these matters not all the executive's demands were agreed by the Opposition which commented that some proposals 'would interfere with the investigation of disciplinary offences'. Later the new police minister, and signatory to the MOU, Russell Cooper, was to claim that 'my use of the word "agreed" in my responses indicates only an agreement to have the matter reviewed'.[8]

The union's further achievement, to a degree which stood at odds with the industrial relations disposition of the non-Labor parties by this time, was to secure a number of 'union preference' matters, including continuity of rights of union access to members, payroll deductions of union dues and no legislation interfering with 'the QPUE operating as Trade Union representing its members'.[9] The union's desire here has to be read against a background of industrial relations reform that from the 1980s on has challenged the security of Australian trade unions in their previously hard-won freedoms to organise.[10] The capacity of the Queensland body to achieve consent by a non-Labor political party to such matters is striking evidence of the success of a police union. Yet even here the MOU had its limits, with the opposition politicians refusing to agree to a union demand for the repeal of the non-strike clause of the 1990 Police Regulations. As Cooper's commentary in the MOU stated:

> this would be difficult to agree to. The Police Service is regarded as an essential service in maintaining peace, law and order and security for the people. Any withdrawal of that service could place the people at risk and this would have unacceptable consequences. The Coalition believes that attention to and resolution of matters of concern existing within the Police Service and its systems should negate any need to debate Section 5.3.[11]

Revelation of the existence of the MOU came only in the aftermath of the by-election, lost by Labor and leading shortly after to the replacement of the Goss government by the Borbidge-led National-Liberal Coalition. In subsequent events, the document was referred by Cooper himself to the Criminal Justice Commission, whose powers and responsibilities had been specifically targeted in the MOU. The CJC sought legal advice on whether 'the creation and execution of the MOU enlivened the CJC's jurisdiction to investigate'. That concluded that the CJC had jurisdiction to investigate a possibility of misconduct by officers of the Queensland police, and that the investigation would best be carried out by an independent person, given that the MOU's content created a perception that the CJC might have a vested interest in such an investigation. A retired judge of the New South Wales Supreme Court, Kenneth Carruthers QC, was appointed to undertake an investigation under the 'official misconduct' provisions of the *Criminal Justice Act*.[12]

The Carruthers Inquiry, as it became known, began public hearings in April 1996, receiving extensive coverage in a political climate that continued to provoke debate over the politics and ethics of the MOU and its implications. While the inquiry proceeded as one into possible official misconduct of the police officers concerned in the making of the MOU, the possibility of criminal charges involving a breach of the *Electoral Act* (s155 relating to 'Bribery') also emerged, possibly implicating politicians and others who had been party to the MOU. Over the following months some matters which had been the subject matter of the MOU were pursued by the new government. A review of the police service (the Bingham Review) was established, with broad participation including the police department, the CJC, and the police unions.

But a more ominous note was sounded when the government announced an inquiry into the CJC itself, appointing to head the inquiry two retired judges of the Queensland Supreme Court. The government's announcement came shortly after the Carruthers Inquiry had been furnished with a legal opinion by Cooper's counsel that exonerated Cooper and the union from any wrong-doing. That legal opinion had in fact been prepared by Peter Connolly QC, one of the two retired judges now appointed by the government to inquire into the CJC. By this stage the Carruthers Inquiry had finished its public hearings, and Carruthers was preparing his report. Given the potential conflict between the authority of a commission of inquiry (the Connolly-Ryan Inquiry into the CJC) and the Carruthers Inquiry (being conducted under the powers of the CJC), the government legislated by 15 October 1996 to render Carruthers and his staff answerable to the Connolly-Ryan Inquiry. A week later the Connolly-Ryan inquiry senior counsel demanded of Carruthers and the CJC all materials relating to the Carruthers inquiry, including drafts of the report. In turn Carruthers sought legal advice, which concluded that it had become impossible for him to conclude his report — and he resigned shortly after.[13]

The government was not alone in seeking to bring the Carruthers Inquiry to a conclusion. Some months earlier the union executive had itself taken legal action to restrain Carruthers from reporting to the CJC on his investigation in so far as it related to them. The basis of the action was an allegation of bias against the Chairman of the CJC, Frank Clair, who had embarked on his own public defence of the CJC against union attacks. In particular Clair had claimed that the union was attempting to de-rail the reform process: its 'political activity in the Mundingburra by-election was designed to recreate the same highly unsatisfactory situation that existed prior to the Fitzgerald inquiry'.[14] The sought injunction was refused, with the judge concluding that there was no implication that Carruthers would not act impartially in preparing his report, whatever the opinion of the head of the CJC.[15]

Carruthers' later resignation was far from the end of this extraordinary saga. The CJC resolved to continue some of the work done by Carruthers by engaging independent counsel to consider whether the materials gathered by Carruthers contained evidence sufficient to warrant charges of official misconduct or breaches of the *Electoral Act*.[16] That advice was submitted and published by the CJC in December, with recommendations for certain charges to be brought against some union executive members, and against Cooper, now the police minister. In the meantime the Connolly-Ryan Inquiry pursued its wide-ranging review of the CJC's powers and conduct of investigations over a number of years. While the union was delighted, regarding it as 'an excellent opportunity for the QPUE and every member of the Queensland Police Service to have input into the future role and structure of the CJC',[17] the CJC Commissioners were increasingly concerned about the Inquiry's proceedings, especially about perceptions of bias on the part of Connolly. It was Connolly who had prepared legal advice back in September 1996 exonerating Cooper and the union from any wrong-doing. The matter was raised by the CJC's counsel in chambers during the early stages of the Connolly-Ryan Inquiry. Nevertheless the inquiry proceeded during 1997 to explore the conduct of the Carruthers investigation. In June however both Carruthers and the CJC took action in the Supreme Court seeking a declaration of bias on the part of Connolly and a consequent termination of the inquiry. After a short trial the matter was a decisive victory for Carruthers and the CJC. Judge Thomas concluded that Connolly had disclosed strong evidence of bias and that both commissioners should be disqualified from proceeding with their inquiry into the CJC.[18]

It will be evident that the union-initiated MOU had profound political effects, but what were they? If the wounding of a government which had disappointed the QPUE was an objective, then Mundingburra was a triumph. Yet it may be questioned whether the union's involvement in the by-election was decisive — and no election is ever determined by one factor alone. In this case, the Labor Party had been limping along since its disastrous performance in the state election six months earlier, and the by-election itself was an outcome of a very public falling out with the former Labor member for the area.

Symbolically however Mundingburra was something else. It represented an increased tempo in police union activity, deploying all the scare tactics of a prototypical law and order campaign. An internal union newsletter, prepared by the police union's Cairns region delegate, highlighted for local police the import of the campaign.[19] Mundingburra signified the 'coming of age of the Police Union'. Precluded from going on strike, the union had looked instead to the by-election:

> Mundingburra was a "backs to the wall" fight for the Union and therefore all of us. The Labour Party had pushed and pushed until we would not be pushed any more ...
> Never before has the Police Union fought the Government with such vigour. But now was the time, and so we fought back and we fought back well ...
> I've just watched the 6.30pm Channel 7 Current Affairs Program (7/2/96) where GOSS blamed his Mundingburra loss, in part, on the "INSIDIOUS CAMPAIGN OF THE POLICE UNION". Thanks for the compliment Wayne, but if there was any insidiousness involved, then it was what the Labour Party was doing to, not only the members of this Union but also to the people of Qld. ...
> What GOSS, BRADDY, MOONEY and their cronies didn't realise, is that we're coppers and we're confronted with filth and dirty tricks every day of the week. They thought they'd get the better of us, but trust me when I say (and I won't go into details), they didn't. **We won, and they lost in all departments.** ...
> Before we decided to embark on our Mundingburra campaign, we considered what ramifications there may be if Labour won ...
> If they stay in Government, then Mundingburra is just the start, not the end!!!!!!

The newsletter ('Union News', Issue 5, 1996) spelled out what had been done in the $20,000 campaign — a series of 15-second TV ads in the fortnight before the election; a letter box drop of 11,000 leaflets; full page ad in the local paper; radio ads; a visit from the president and vice-president of the union for interviews and radio talk-back, a local union branch meeting with politicians invited; and the use of a mobile billboard (3m x 8m) driven around the electorate, fitted with loud speakers and ads which proclaimed 'Lack of police numbers is the real crime!!', 'Vote 1 — More Police', and 'Dial "000" and make a wish'. Press ads advised voters of things they might need 'if the Queensland Government doesn't strengthen your police service', things such as a baseball bat, a trained German Shepherd dog, perfume spray or stiletto heels.[20]

Were greater police numbers the heart of the union campaign? That was the import of the press advertising and the mobile billboard. The

MOU told a different story — as we have seen. Increased numbers were indeed listed at number one on the agenda, but there were more than 40 separate items making up the Wilkinson-prepared and Coalition-signed wish list. Apart from the matters touching directly on the senior administration of the police (the six named assistant commissioners targeted by the document and the demand for a union say on the future commissioner), there was an extended array of union demands for a review of CJC matters, including discipline, as well as pay and various operational issues, not to speak of union demands for protection of its organisational privileges. These were scarcely likely to be matters likely to sway a volatile electorate — and the lack of disclosure of the MOU helped to ensure that the electorate would focus on the simple law and order message.

Subsequent disclosure of course did not change the election result. It did set back the union's cause, and subjected the executive in particular to a sustained and very public scrutiny under media and quasi-judicial auspices. The early termination of the Carruthers Inquiry precluded a more formal consideration of the ethical and political issues involved in this kind of political-industrial campaign. On the other hand the termination of the Connolly-Ryan Inquiry limited the potential for a writing down of the CJC's powers that seemed inherent in the directions of the MOU. More seriously, it might seem, at least for the longer-term aspirations of the union, the political furore surrounding the MOU tactic helped bring an early end to the Borbidge government.

That may be to look at the events in too short a time frame. For it might be argued that a more enduring effect of the union's noisy and provocative intervention at Mundingburra was to build a new wall around criminal justice policy. Going into the 1998 state election from opposition, the Labor Party was keen to avoid any suggestion that it might be soft on law and order. The changes were subtle, and a bi-partisan rhetoric had also emerged around the wisdom of crime prevention. But both government and opposition now competed on which might employ more police, and which might be demonstrably tougher on criminals. At the 1997 Queensland Police Union annual conference the Labor shadow minister for police had already signalled that the union had an 'absolute right as a Trade Union to take the action that was taken' at Mundingburra.[21] In the Beattie Labor government's first budget a big winner was 'law, order and public safety' with a growth of nearly 20% in outlays compared to 13% overall for the total budget. The strong outcome for law and order compared to other major policy areas was evident in the increases in education provision of only 5.4% and health of 8.4%. While the second budget did something to adjust this balance, we see in the shaping of law and order priorities after Mundingburra a desire to limit the possibility of another outbreak of union militancy.

Mundingburra was in a line of Australian elections around 'law and order' that have developed in recent decades. The secrecy of the MOU made it special. But that was a matter that was arguably superfluous to the core business of the police union's campaign — shaping the outcome to effect an increase of resources to policing. The mobile billboard was the highlight of a campaign that sold the electors the urgency of attending to their personal safety.

What have become known as 'law and order' elections have their origins in Australian politics in the 1963 election bringing the Askin government to power. We will examine that election in context later in this book. But the recent past has been perhaps more directly affected by the way in which governments as well as oppositions have sought to construct their political security behind a law and order defence. In this respect a typical example was the 1988 New South Wales election, which brought a Greiner-led Liberal-Country Party coalition to government.

The lead-up to the New South Wales election was one in which law and order had played a prominent part, led by the police union, and willingly engaged by both sides of politics. In July 1986 a decade of political reform, much of it focused on policing issues, was brought to an end with the resignation of Labor premier Neville Wran. His immediate successor was Barrie Unsworth, a former head of the New South Wales Trades and Labour Council, to which the New South Wales Police Association (NSWPA) was affiliated. The Association was an early enthusiast. It had already launched its own political campaign calling on the government to 'Reinforce the Force', leading to the premier's commitment of an extra 2,000 police over the next three years. Further public demands by the Association for detail sought to lock the premier in. Unsworth came quickly to the party — a meeting with the union brought forth a commitment to 'law and order' as a first priority. In a statement that sums up the way in which this slogan can be deployed as a populist device to distance its user from narrow political purposes, Unsworth declared to the union that 'I regard law and order in this State to be far too serious a matter to be the subject of political rhetoric'.[22] The public rhetoric did not signal abandonment of private political calculation. A year later, with a state election in prospect, the premier signalled to his police minister that in spite of the pressure of a number of backbenchers to do something about street prostitution in Sydney, the issue was 'not to be brought forward until after the election'.[23]

Not all police union militancy has been focused on election campaigns. There are other industrial union tactics that can be extended to the policing arena. But inevitably they can become closely tied to electoral fortunes — and police unions in the modern era are quick to develop the potential. An unprecedented action in Tasmania in the early 1990s flowed from broken election promises and probably had electoral consequences. But the immediate tactic was a piece of classic industrial pressure — a work ban. On 17 April 1991 members of the Police Association of Tasmania (PAT) commenced a six week long campaign of bans on police work at courts. The withdrawal of police services at the courts reduced security for other court officials and soon led to further industrial action from public sector unions responding to what was seen as an increased security risk. After unsuccessful informal negotiation involving government and senior police the industrial bans of police were lifted in early June after a court order, and commitment to hearing the desired pay claim.

The confrontation developed out of a reversal of government commitments. The political context was one of relative weakness of the government in any case. The 1989 Tasmanian election had resulted in a unique, and unstable, outcome — a coalition of the Labor Party with the Greens. Economic difficulties limited the capacity of the government to deliver on the promises of the majority party in this coalition, i.e. the Labor Party. The rising expectations of police were fed before the election by the Labor Party's crime policy, *Tackling Crime Together*, which was welcomed by the PAT 'as it reflected the organization's wish list regarding police salaries and superannuation'.[24] Disillusion followed over the succeeding years, typified by the mixed reaction to severe financial cutbacks in the 1990 budget. Voluntary redundancy was taken up by a number of police as the department sought to reduce its establishment by 10%. Police were further alarmed by a proposed reduction in police functions to accommodate a fall in numbers of personnel.

The chief issue however, as so often, remained primarily that of pay. The Victorian police extracted a significant pay concession from the Labor government in early 1991, following threatened industrial action and significant Australia-wide support from the ACTU and the Police Federation.[25] Police Federation policy was increasingly encouraging a national standard for police pay and conditions. And the Tasmanian Labor Party before the election had promised parity of pay and functions with the mainland police forces. In the early months of 1991 there were increasing demands from union branches for the PAT to pursue a 25% pay increase, if necessary through industrial action. A ballot of members resulted in overwhelming support (96.5% of returns) for industrial action and bans were commenced on 18 April. The most significant and well publicised were those affecting police attendance at court, causing magistrates to adjourn matters 'that required higher levels of security'.[26] The bans continued throughout May as government ministers resisted the pressure, but were eventually brought to an end when referred to the industrial court. An order to lift them was accompanied by a commitment to inquire into levels of pay. Damage to the government's reputation as a committed defender of law and order was likely sustained by a sophisticated advertising campaign — a TV ad with a masked crook selling the virtues of voting Labor, was reinforced by press ads that were explicit in targeting Labor, with text drawing the moral:

> Labor's Law & Order Policy
> It's criminals who belong in handcuffs, not Tasmanian police officers
> Protecting our community from crime has always been tough but by slashing funding and cutting police numbers, the Labor government has made it just about impossible.
> They've broken their promise to make Tasmania a safer place for your family.
> They'll be sorry. As crime increases, we'll all be sorry.
> Labor's a Crook Vote.[27]

The outcome was less than satisfactory to the union, with a hearing and determination lasting nearly two years from December 1991 to September 1993. The Industrial Commission ruled that there was no case for parity with Victorian police, and that Tasmanian conditions and circumstances would determine the pay rates of Tasmanian police. While substantial pay rises, to be paid in two stages, were awarded, a final frustration was faced as payment dragged into 1994.[28] The larger political context was however much changed by this time. There had been a change of government, and a major industrial dispute in which the Tasmanian police had been accused by some of limiting their policing interventions, perhaps through aggravation at the pay dispute.[29] The political effects of the PAT's dispute of the early 1990s are difficult to gauge, but a reflection by the union secretary nearly ten years on has summarised the context:

> The PAT went further in its dispute with the Labor Government than any other union would at that time have dared to go. This established its credentials as an apolitical organization that should be taken seriously when resolute.[30]

We will have reason repeatedly to interrogate the semantics of the adjective 'apolitical'. But it is clear that the Tasmanian dispute, involving one of the country's smaller unions and the smallest state, was another significant demonstration of the capacity of police unions to assert their autonomy and political weight.

1.2 An international story

The contemporary activity of Australian police unions is by no means exceptional. Over recent decades the international picture has been one in which police labour unions have played a similar kind of politics, and frequently around similar kinds of issues. Indeed recent years have seen some aggravated cases of police violence attracting international media attention and police union response. In 1999 the European Court of Human Rights found France guilty of human rights violations following its hearing of a case involving repeated police violence against a detainee, Ahmed Selmouni. The police concerned in the beating, sexual assault and torture had already been tried and convicted for their actions — but not without provoking a national campaign by French police unions protesting their 'unfair treatment'.[31]

In the same year New York city police were at the centre of enormous controversy after four white police were charged with murder following the shooting of an unarmed West African immigrant man, Amadou Diallo. Almost simultaneously other officers were charged with the brutalisation of Abner Louima in a Brooklyn police station. Both events contributed to divisions in the local police union, with a particularly virulent campaign being waged among contenders for the presidency of the NY Patrolmen's Benevolent Association, the first time the election had been contested since 1980. The Association's leadership was challenged by dissidents, one of whom won the election to head the 29,000 member union after a campaign dominated by concern over demoralisation and lack of leadership. Notably one concern appeared to be a contrast between the mid-1980s mass police protests over the indictment of one of their number for a fatal shooting, and the much more muted response to a call for a demonstration of support for the police charged over the Diallo shooting. Indifference appeared to be fostered by the failure of the union leaders to secure pay increases in a new contract.[32]

Elsewhere more traditional concerns dominated police union business in 1999. The well-known tactic of blue flu struck the Irish police, the Gardai, in May 1999, as they struggled for pay increases in the midst of a booming economy. Their radicalisation was the more striking in so far as their representative 'Association' was a non-union, modelled since the 1920s on the Police Federation of England and Wales. But the latter was already well known for its militancy, a transformation noticed by Robert Reiner in the 1970s, and enhanced since then.

A mass meeting of some 20,000 police in London's Wembley Stadium in 1993 was prompted by police opposition to reforms proposed by a government committee, reforms including performance-related pay and engagement on contracts reportedly based on innovations in the management of the Australian Federal Police.[33] The rally was attended by about one in six of the 125,000 members of the Police Federation, and reported to have cost £250,000. The Federation by this time had supplemented its parliamentary advisers, engaged on a retainer, with the services of a public relations company. Under the slogan 'Keep the Blue Lamp Burning', the mass police protest was yet another sign of the police adopting the tactics of those they had long been used to policing, in pursuit of a range of objectives, not all of them limited to the core concerns of wages and conditions of service.[34] The anger of the protests could not disguise the fact that they were also provoked by an attempt to bring police into line with other public services administration. As one commentator put it, reflecting on more than a decade of Thatcherite reform: 'The last public sector service to face government imposed change, the police have had a remarkable capacity to resist unpopular reform'.[35]

As if bearing coals to Newcastle leaders of some British and American police unions have in recent years come to Australia advocating a new political militancy. From an Australian perspective it might be considered that police unions here had more than a thing or two to teach their colleagues in other countries — as we will see the Australian police unions were clearly well ahead of others in English-speaking countries in achieving legitimacy and engaging in the political system. But in recent decades police unions in Britain and North America have engaged in new levels of militancy. Hence the head of the Police Federation of England and Wales, Fred Broughton, brought to Australia in October 1999 the message of his organisation's determination to fight government cutbacks in police services. Its tactics have included mass rallies (as at Wembley in 1993), getting to the centre of decision-making by acting on professional issues (such as 'crime and powers') before pay and conditions, retaining three Westminster politicians as political advisors on salaries of £20,000. All these tactics, it should be noted, were known to Australian unions from the 1920s.[36]

Similarly visiting American police union chief, Ron DeLord, president of the Combined Law Enforcement Associations of Texas (CLEAT), could scarcely have surprised Australian police unionists with his advice in the same year (1999) that 'Australian police associations must become feared and disliked in political circles' by adopting an 'in-your-face' style of political lobbying.[37] In the light of the histories discussed in this book, the response of some Australian police unionists to such advice, to the effect that traditionally Australian police unions have been conservative in their approach, seems either disingenuous or historically ignorant. In Australia, as in other comparable countries, police unions have been militant, and political, unions for some time.

While there has been limited scholarly consideration of the most recent incidents outlined above, a flurry of research followed the development of a very activist police union politics during the 1960s and early 1970s. In the United States a sequence of political interventions in municipal politics drew the considered attention of a number of researchers interested in police industrial relations as well as the politics of policing. In Britain the major scholarly intervention was that of Robert Reiner, whose extensive work on the Police Federation would deserve the appellation pioneering if it had been followed by any comparable research in other jurisdictions. Instead it might be concluded that Reiner's work established an understanding of police unions and politics that has become an almost singular authority.

Reiner's theses on police were developed in his major study *The blue-coated worker* as well as in a number articles and a later book *The politics of the police*. In a 1980 article he argued that a class analysis of police politics offered the best possibility of understanding the increasing interventions of police unions in the political process, especially in what was being characterised by the 1970s as 'law-and-order politics'. Police, argued Reiner, occupy a contradictory place in the class structure:

> While their social and political role underlines the political ideology and initiatives described above, at the same time their conditions as wage-earners subject to managerial control exerts contradictory pressures towards unionism and in some conjunctures identification with the labour movement.[38]

In understanding why the police had become an 'independent police force' during the 1960s–70s, a class analysis of the position of police in different countries would offer more explanatory power, suggested Reiner, than some other explanations of police political interventions, such as police ideology (e.g. their activity as particular types of moral entrepreneurs) or bureaucratic self-interest (e.g. in expanding the police domain).

Reiner's self-description of his own comparative analysis of police law and order politics in the USA and England as a *class* analysis may read today as too simplistic and in fact belied by the complexity of his own historical accounting for the different dispositions of the English and American police unionists. His account in fact attributed these different styles of intervention to the foundational histories of policing in each country. In England, suggested Reiner, the police had been established in an atmosphere of intense class conflict, their acceptability depending on their role as embodiments of law, not agents of government. In America by contrast the 'enfranchisement of the working-class and the absence of serious political crises allowed the police to be trusted with a personal authority without the framework of controls from above which were imposed in London'. We may allow some debate about the solidity of these very generalised historical contrasts without denying that they highlight the very different institutional locations of the police in these two countries.

Reiner related these different constitutional histories of police to the development more recently of different kinds of law and order interventions. In the United States in the 1960s the police labour unions had in many cities sided with a working-class resentment of liberal reform and sympathy to minorities, a resentment in the case of police which found its expression in antagonism to the authorities governing the police (i.e. the urban municipal governments). In Britain, on the other hand, the police unionists through their Federation had more commonly been found supporting the police hierarchy and national government in a combative approach to the trade union militancy associated with the developing British economic crisis of these decades. In the light of this identification with the objectives of the police hierarchy Reiner concluded that English police ideology reflects the peculiar concerns of the petty bourgeoisie, rather than as in the USA the working class.[39]

In the wake of this analysis it remains unclear what purchasing power is exercised in the analysis of police union politics as something best understood through a *class* analysis. If fundamental structural change is effected at some historical point in the past it becomes part of the conditions under which later generations become social actors. In this case the important structural conditions framing police union activity in the United States and Britain were only in the remote instance a matter of class politics. The fundamentals of the scene described elsewhere in the 1980 article by Reiner are those of the freedoms and constraints exercised by police labour unions within a political structure of policing which was expressive, popular-democratic but illiberal in the American case and constrained and hierarchical in the British case.

The *class* analysis of police politics advanced by Reiner is therefore suggestive, but not conclusive. Its limits are reached when we look at the selective historical account he gives of the policing roles of the forces in the two countries. No less than in Britain police in the United States have played vital, indeed historically perhaps even more bloody, roles in the policing of industrial militancy. Conversely, no less than in the United States, police in Britain can be found historically and more recently playing the political game in the policing of racial conflict and against the intrusions of civilian oversight.

A different kind of reading of the United States police union experience has been advanced by another scholar of policing writing with a police union official. In a brief study of 'Police unions, police culture, and police use of force', George Kelling and Robert Kliesmet lament first of all the dearth of research on American police unions, almost completely absent since the 1970s. Their account has something of a tendentious flavour, seeking to find a place where police labour unions will come to play a more effective and legitimate part in policy making and the development of a professional policing approach across the whole range of police duties. Instructive indeed is their interpretation of the context that has shaped American police unions. For in contrast to what we see later in this book with respect to Australia, American police unions struggled for legitimacy.

> Opponents of police unionism were so successful in forestalling it — primarily by firing anyone who attempted to organize until well into the 1950s and early 1960s — that police unionism, in contrast to other public sector unionism, remains inchoate, fragmented and immature.[40]

The model of police unionism that gained some toehold in American policing was thus one in which police were workers subordinated to management, and the objects of unions became 'wages and benefits; job security; hiring, retention, promotion, and disciplinary processes; access to "good" jobs, shifts, assignments, overtime, etc: and regulation of work practices by rules'.[41]

The vital element constraining acceptance of police unions, suggest Kelling and Kliesmet, was the police reform movement in early twentieth century cities. A preoccupation of this movement was to distance policing from political interests, an ambition that was pursued through a focus on redefining policing as a subject for scientific management. Conceding a role for police unions would open up policing again to the play of political influence — the quality of policing services, their organisation and delivery, were matters for management, not unions. Hence in some cities with strong and well-reputed police chiefs, police labour unions found extraordinary opposition. An abiding element of this tradition was the exclusion of unions from a role in policy debate or consideration of operational policies. Reviewing the experience and attitudes of a number of urban police unions in respect of policies regarding police use of force, Kelling and Kliesmet found by the mid 1990s an overwhelming desire to be playing a role in policy formation, an aspiration they endorse as part of a move to a more professional and community-responsive policing. In other respects short of policy making, it emerges from their survey that the police unions had little to say in public media about a major incident such as the Rodney King beating.[42] The idea of an 'independent' police voice in the USA appears more constrained in this light than implied in Reiner's earlier analysis.

How do the Australian police unions fit into this international comparative picture? One value of inquiring into the Australian case is that it can enable some further testing of arguments such as those developed by Reiner to explain the emergence of police as an independent force, or of Kelling and Kliesmet to explain the limited role of police in the United States with respect to policy formation. Police forces were established in Australia in a context of weak local government and strong central government. The substantive historical influences on the organisation of Australian police forces were those of both London and Ireland. On the other hand it might be said that the culture of Australian police forces has historically been closer to that of American urban police — except that a substantial portion of the force also comes from rural areas, and serves in the country, at least for part of the typical police career. Working class can describe the origins of most Australian police historically, and especially before the 1980s — but that term obscures the importance of other ethnic, religious and cultural distinctions that the aspirant police officer brought to the job. Among police officers, almost all of them police unionists, could be found a great variety of capacities for and attitudes to their work — and debates within police unions frequently allow us to hear some of those differences come alive. The particular conjunction in Australia of a very centralised policing structure and a police workforce with sometimes surprisingly strong labour identity suggests important differences from other countries. Historically this resulted in an early legitimation of police unions, as we will see in the following chapter.

It will be the task of this book to develop an understanding of the emergence of an 'independent' police voice in Australia. It is arguable that those features of law-and-order politics which emerge quite differently (in Reiner's analysis at least) in the USA and England can be present at one and the same time in Australia during the same decades. If the 1960s and 1970s are those decades in which this independent police voice emerges (a timing we will question anyway for the Australian case), then we find evidence in Australia of both kinds of police activist disposition. There was during these transition decades evidence both of opposition to civilian control initiatives and the intrusions of liberal reform agendas; *and* aggressive policing of the industrial militancy associated with Australia's own changing economic order, and in which police unions and police hierarchies were usually driving in the same direction. The evidence in addition will suggest that the development of a police union political voice is not only much older than might appear the case in the USA and England, but also less unified, more historically contingent, than Reiner's analysis of the police role in law-and-order politics might lead us to expect. In so far as a collectivity like a police union brings together a wide variety of personal dispositions then it is scarcely surprising that this be so — and indeed Reiner's invaluable insights into the variety of archetypes in his research force helps us to appreciate the potential of these to produce different outcomes in the varied political and social circumstances that structure policing.[43]

Notes

1 Colleen Lewis, *Complaints against police: the politics of reform* (Sydney, 1999), ch9.

2 See Criminal Justice Commission, "Report on an Investigation into a Memorandum of Understanding between the Coalition and QPUE and an Investigation into an alleged deal between the ALP and the SSAA, December 1996," (1996).

3 Queensland State Archives (QSA) A/44888 – QPUE newsletter of 1952 on the 'Police Dispute' in which he attacks the competence of the Minister, Commissioner, and other senior officers, and calls for a royal commission or a ballot for a strike.

4 *Queensland Police Journal (QPJ)*, Feb 1996, p7, in a 'President's Report' by Wilkinson.

5 *QPJ*, Jul 1995, p3.

6 *QPJ*, Jul 1995, p3.

7 *QPJ*, Feb 1996, p7.

8 Criminal Justice Commission, "Report on an Investigation into a Memorandum of Understanding between the Coalition and QPUE and an Investigation into an alleged deal between the ALP and the SSAA, December 1996".

9 Memorandum of Understanding (MOU), p13 (copy in CJC Library, Brisbane).

10 David Peetz, *Unions in a contrary world: the future of the Australian trade union movement* (Sydney, 1998).

11 MOU, pp13–14. The relevant part of Section 5.3 relating to 'Withdrawal of services' provided that an officer must not 'do any act or make any omission which, if done or omitted to be done by two or more officers, would constitute a strike within the meaning of the Industrial Relations Act 1990' — *Police Service (Discipline) Regulations 1990, Queensland Government Gazette*, No.57 (16 Jun 1990): 924–942.

12 Criminal Justice Commission, "Report on an Investigation into a Memorandum of Understanding between the Coalition and QPUE and an Investigation into an alleged deal between the ALP and the SSAA, December 1996".

13 Kenneth Carruthers, "Carruthers Inquiry Statement 29 Oct 1996 and appended legal correspondence and opinions," (1996).

14 As cited in Queensland, "Re Carruthers v Connolly, Ryan and Attorney-General of Queensland; and Re CJC and Le Grand v Connolloy, Ryan and A-G," (1997).

15 Ibid.

16 Criminal Justice Commission, "Report on an Investigation into a Memorandum of Understanding between the Coalition and QPUE and an Investigation into an alleged deal between the ALP and the SSAA, December 1996".

17 *QPJ*, Dec 1996, p29.
18 Queensland, "Re Carruthers v Connolly, Ryan and Attorney-General of Queensland; and Re CJC and Le Grand v Connolloy, Ryan and A-G".
19 Mundingburra matter, CJC Legal File 519.
20 Ibid.
21 *QPJ*, Oct 1997, p6.
22 *New South Wales Police News (NSWPN)*, Aug 1986, p6.
23 Mitchell Library, George Paciullo Papers, ML Mss 5288, Add-on 1956, Box 13, note on file copy of letter from Paciullo to Unsworth, 26 Aug 1987.
24 Mark Kadziolka, "Masked man revealed," *Association News (PAT)*, Jun 2000, 11. My account draws generally on this decade later reflection on the events of 1991.
25 *VPJ*, Feb 1991, p7.
26 Kadziolka, "Masked man revealed," 13.
27 Ibid, 14.
28 *South Australian Police Journal* (*SAPJ*), Apr 1994, p16.
29 David Baker, "Police, pickets and politics: the policing of industrial disputes in Australia" (PhD, Monash, 2000) is a major study; see also David Baker, "Avoiding "War on the Wharves": is the non-confrontational policing of major industrial disputues "Here to Stay"?," *International Employment Relations Review* 5 (1999) and David Baker, "Trade unionism and the policing "accord": control and self-regulation of picketing during the 1998 Maritime Dispute," *Labour & Industry* 9 (1999).
30 Kadziolka, "Masked man revealed," 17.
31 *Sydney Morning Herald (SMH)*, 3 Apr 1999, p18. See Case of Selmouni v France, European Court of Human Rights, 28 July 1999, http://www.dhcour.coe.fr/hudoc/.
32 *New York Times*, 3 May, 7 Jun, 1999.
33 *The Times*, 15 Feb 1993, p7.
34 *The Times*, 21 Jul 1993, pp1–2.
35 Jane Goodsir, "Loitering with intent to reform", *The Times*, 20 Aug 1993, p14.
36 *SAPJ*, Dec 1999, (http://www.policejournalsa.org.au/9912/19a.html); also in *Territory Police Journal* (*TerrPJ*), Dec 1999, pp10–11.
37 *TerrPJ*, Jul 1999, pp4–5.
38 Robert Reiner, "Fuzzy thoughts; the police and law-and-order politics," *Sociological Review* 28 (1980): 403.
39 Ibid: 400–403.
40 George L Kelling and Robert B Kliesmet, "Police unions, police culture, and police use of force," in *Police violence: understanding and controlling police abuse of force*, ed. William A Geller and Hans Toch (New Haven and London, 1996), 196.
41 Ibid, 198.
42 Ibid, 199.
43 Robert Reiner, *The Blue-Coated Worker: A sociological study of police unionism* (Cambridge, 1978), 234–235. Variously the Bobby, the uniform-carrier, the new centurion, the social worker, the professional and the Federationist.

2: Organising the police

Everything that can heighten in any degree the respectability of the office of a policeman adds to the security of the State, and to the safety of the life and property of the individual.
South Australian police addressing the Chief Secretary, April 1911

The association had always adhered to constitutional methods. They were on the eve of another election, and would probably again be the "political rags" to be torn to pieces and then get nothing for it. The association had been accused of Bolshevism, but the only Bolshevism it possessed had been created by the manner in which it had been treated by the authorities.
Constable reported in *The Advertiser*, Adelaide, 12 March 1927

The right to unionise is not a God-given inheritance, nor an essential human right, but one dependent on government policy and legal mandate. Looking elsewhere helps to highlight the point. In the early 1990s, following the admission of Greece to the European Community, the country's police remained the only ones in Europe without a representative organisation. Although constitutionally protected, the Greek police right to a 'trade union' was in practice hindered by governmental tactics which have been well known in Australia as well — in the Australian police media it was reported that the Greek government had transferred the putative Police Federation executive to remote country locations, and that the general secretary had been fined a month's pay after speaking to the press.[1]

In 1999 the Canadian Supreme Court delivered a final judgment on a claim by a Mountie that a ban on unionisation of the Royal Canadian Mounted Police (RCMP) constituted an infringement of his Canadian Charter rights. A series of court challenges extending back to 1986 failed to establish the right to unionise under the framework of collective bargaining in the Canadian public service. The unique constitutional position of the RCMP makes this case a less than likely moral lesson for assessing the issues associated with the powers, rights and responsibilities of police unions in Australia. Nevertheless the judgment, emerging as it does in a legal system sharing a common heritage with Australia, constitutes something of a benchmark against which to measure Australian distinctiveness.

The Mountie's appeal was founded on the rights protected by the Canadian Charter of 1982 — there is no Australian equivalent. The Supreme Court however found no breach of individual rights since the RCMP members were not prohibited from joining together to advance their collective claims: it was just that they were not entitled to access the normal bargaining framework enjoyed by other public servants. The more developed industrial relations structure of the *Public Service Act* that (like the framework of industrial relations in Australian arbitration systems) was predicated on the institutional legitimacy of unions was something not available to the Mounties. On analogy with the armed forces, it was held that a national force like the RCMP, should not be rendered vulnerable to the potential threats to national or domestic security seen to be entailed in unionisation. The judgment stood in line with the uneven development of Canadian police unionism, activist from the 1970s, but constrained into the 1990s by constitutional and legislative limitations on their freedom of action.[2]

The rights of workers to unionise were established over a long time, and through many bitter disputes. Police were no pioneers in such an arena, and their attempts at unionisation in the years around the Great War, followed in the wake of victories already won by the labour movement in arduous political and legal struggles. Australia was a leader in such successes of the labour movement. And the recognition of a police right to unionise was closely correlated with political hegemony of the Labor Party in much of Australia after the Great War. Conversely, the most memorable battle of all in this struggle of the police unions versus resistant governments was that waged in Australia's most non-Labor state, Victoria. The consequences of the Melbourne police strike of 1923 were so striking (popular disorder, the loss of jobs of the striking policemen) that they continued to influence the state of industrial relations in Australian policing for many decades after.

At the same time, the police strike may be seen as a lesson in the stabilising functions of police unions in the Australian context. For the strike was essentially an action of the non-unionised, of those who were profoundly disillusioned with the inaction of the existing collective body, the Victorian Police Association (VPA). Before and long after 1923, some police in Victoria and other states would threaten strikes. But those who argued that police could get what they wanted through other action would consistently take the initiative from the firebrands. The struggle to bring police into the fold of arbitration was crucial in this respect — its advocates claimed that the justice of the police case for improved wages, reduced hours, and other improvements in working conditions would emerge once there was an independent umpire and police were no longer dependent on the whim of unreliable and parsimonious governments. That at least was the ambition of the Australian police unionists from their earliest days.

In tracing the origins of the police unions we do well to remember not only the local but also the international context. In this chapter we will see that the Australian experience shared much with that of police in other countries. But we will also be driven to understand why Australian police unionisation was relatively more successful and an early achiever of legitimacy.

2.1 Before the unions

Prior to the Great War employment as a police officer was one of the solid occupations of Australian life. Police departments were among the more significant employers of labour — and police officers, like railwaymen, or teachers, could be found even in quite small towns and villages throughout the country. Only in Tasmania, and even there only until 1898, was policing a responsibility of municipalities. Police were employees in large organisations, administered with varying degrees of bureaucratic efficiency from the respective commissioners' offices in the colonial and then state capitals.

The attraction of policing was its relative security, especially in the fickle labour markets of a colonial economy. Every town and every rural hamlet wanted a policeman, and governments were generally impelled to provide them. Policing could be an occupation for life, for those who accommodated themselves to mostly tedious but sometimes dangerous work, and to the demands of the police bureaucracy. Policing was still a man's work — only during the Great War would women start to be employed as police. And it was in the earliest years of employment a job for single men only. Only as the labour market changed and other occupations became more attractive would police departments start to relax the rules on constables being permitted to marry.[3]

Police work was for working men. And the wages were those of working men.[4] In contrast to the fate of a labourer however, police work offered some prospects of social advancement to those who stayed long enough, and who moved through the ranks. A modicum of comfort, and an improvement of status, was however under constant threat, especially from the risks entailed in life as a subordinate in a bureaucracy occupied by senior officers with a wide degree of discretion. The level of police salaries was thus only one of the work relations issues that underlay developing police grievances in the decades before the war. The perpetual grievances of police during the decades since unionisation — wages, promotions, transfers, discipline — were also the preoccupations of police before then. Chafing under the arbitrary rule of sergeants and inspectors, the ordinary constable was a potential unionist for other reasons besides money.

Those reasons included their vulnerability to being transferred at whim, or to being dismissed without being heard in their own defence. Under the statutory provisions governing their appointment since the 1860s police constables in Australia were appointed by the commissioner of police, and could be dismissed at pleasure. Legal authority was firm in support of the commissioner's authority in such matters. In 1873 Judge Redmond Barry in the Victorian Supreme Court was emphatic in concluding that the engagement of police by government was unilateral, binding the constable to serve but not obliging 'Her Majesty to retain him in her service beyond the period which circumstances may render necessary'.[5] Barry's statement of the law was re-affirmed by the High Court of Australia in 1906 when the Queensland police commissioner's dismissal of Constable Foley was supported. Not only did the High Court overturn the Queensland Supreme Court's conclusion that it was necessary for the Governor in Council not just the commissioner to exercise the dismissal power. The three judges, Griffith, Barton and O'Connor were unanimous in rejecting the notion advanced in the lower court that constables had a right to be heard before being dismissed. Hence engagement in the police force entailed suspending one's right to be heard as an element of natural justice in any proceedings within the police department.[6]

Low pay, the weight of discipline and a liability to be transferred a thousand miles and more from the capital, the aggravations caused by inspectors and commissioners — such were some of the burdens weighing on police at the turn of the century. In addressing them police were not completely without voice, or power. Like other workers, or more accurately, like other public servants in the civil service bureaucracies, police would seek to make their grievances heard through petitions and letters, protests on the parade-ground or elsewhere, and even occasional strikes. In the neighbouring colony of New Zealand there were strikes over wages by the small numbers of police in Wellington in 1852 and Dunedin in 1872, the latter resulting in the dismissal of the men concerned.[7] Pay cuts imposed by the colonial government in Victoria in 1862 resulted in widespread police industrial action, with many police refusing to accept their smaller pay packets for up to three months.[8] In Queensland in 1904, a different issue altogether provoked a strike of detectives — the appointment to head them of an officer who had not previously worked in the crime investigation unit. The strikers were punished with demotion, transfers and reprimands.[9]

There were other less visible actions through which non-unionised police sought to have grievances addressed. The frequent inquiries into police administration allowed some ventilation of the wide range of issues that would come to concern unions in later years — including not only wages and other conditions, but promotions, transfers, discipline and the inspection system. Such were the subject of royal commissions in New Zealand in 1898 (which heard evidence from 500 witnesses), Queensland in 1899 and Victoria in 1906.[10] No such inquiry however produced the kind of change in police conditions that would put to rest the incipient moves to collective action. This was to be the task of the first two decades of the twentieth century.

2.2 Combinations and aspirations

Unionisation of police was seen by its advocates as the necessary step to address the grievances which have been discussed above. By 1914 there were already in place two unions in Australia, in South Australia and Western Australia, and murmurings of others. The developing Australian movement took its inspiration from the achievements of trades unions over the previous three decades, but there was also an international dimension to police collectivism. Moreover in the case of police, as with some other public sector workers such as nurses, there was an element of professionalisation evident in the impetus behind some of the new unions. Over the years 'professional' would struggle with 'worker' and 'employee' as terms with which to characterise the identity of members of police unions. In the beginning however, the police unionists were at one with their time — in the year of the Russian Revolution a formal appeal of the South Australian Association for non-members to join up was addressed to 'Dear Comrade'.[11] As we will see in many episodes later in their history, the ardent police unionist for the first half century of the movement would often be found appealing to working class solidarity in defence of police rights to fair pay and conditions.

Yet historically police and union were two words that more commonly could be found in opposition. The remarkable successes of Australian labour unions were built on a combination of vigorous industrial actions, including strikes that had brought the country to its knees in the 1890s, and a broad-based appeal to the collective interests of workers. The craft unions of the 1850s which had been responsible for early successes like the eight-hour day were displaced from the 1880s by the new unionism — organised across industries and mobilising labourers as well as the more skilled. The historic decisions of the union movement to build a political party capable of influencing and even taking over the reins of government resulted by 1914 in Labor governments taking office in a number of states and most importantly in the Commonwealth itself.

A vital element of the political culture of Australia was thus introduced in these years — the idea that unionisation was not only legal but that it was capable of contributing actively to the transformation of working people's welfare through government policy. Unions were legitimate, and increasingly the leading institutions of Australian life found a place for them — not only in parliament of course, but in those special branches of the judicial apparatus known as conciliation and arbitration (or later, industrial) courts.

In such a context police attitudes and self-image were bound to be affected. In the 1890s especially, the police had been expected to play a central and often violent role in the repression of strikes in the pastoral districts and ports of Australia. By the 1900s unionists were not as easily reviled, especially since Labor was moving towards a place in government, first achieved briefly in Queensland in 1899. Police authorities were now counselling their subordinates to take a softer line in the policing of labour disputes and meetings.[12] In such a changing environment it was predictable that the strong collective identities of police themselves might prompt a review of their exclusion from the ranks of the unionised.

These transformations were not by any means unique to Australia. The international environment of policing was changing by 1914 — and was accelerated by the Great War, which broke out in that year. In spite of the very different jurisdictional contexts we can see similarities in the patterns of police grievance and police activism in many countries. In Ireland for example in 1882, a petition by more than 80 constables stationed in Limerick city forced police grievances into national media attention and on to the political stage. The police, non-unionised, but collectively determined to pursue their concerns, used the newly available telegraph to quickly spread word of their campaign around the country. The tactic made a harsh disciplinary response almost impossible, especially in the disturbed state of Ireland at the time. Indeed the grievances originated in the failure of government to reward or even reimburse the police for the extraordinary service they had performed in the years of the Land War, defending sheriffs and landlords against boycotts and worse. It was an advantageous moment at which to raise the stakes for addressing police grievances, and in the end police were rewarded. The historian of the episode concludes that this decisive agitation propelled government into pay increases and service reform that helped turn the constabulary into a worthwhile career.[13] It is also striking that at a time of great political crisis in Ireland the police should seek to exercise their undoubted potential to set out their demands and confront governmental complacency. It was a *sine qua non* that police were non-political — but their centrality to the maintenance of basic internal security delivered them great political power should they ever choose to use it.

In Ireland the police had extracted improvements by industrial action, in advance of unionisation, and seeking advantage from their special relation to government during a time of social and political crisis. In other places grievances were more consciously expressed in a framework of identity with the status of workers. This was notably the case in France. There police activists from the end of the nineteenth century promoted the cause of police 'syndicalism'. The term evoked the passionate cause of aggressive and highly organised industrial unionism that took hold in France from this time. While the legitimation of French police unionism was as protracted as in many other jurisdictions the determination of the activists saw significant affirmations of police grievances — as well as the emergence of conflict within police ranks. French police unionism, concludes one of its historians, affirmed Republican political ideals, especially the notion that police should serve the interests of all, not just a particular social interest. At the same time this affirmation was qualified by the reality of strong identification of some police with conservative and even reactionary political movements. And when 3,000 police demonstrated in Paris for wage rises in December 1923 their protest was in turn brutally dispersed by some of their colleagues aided by the Republican Guard. Institutional and ideological divisions within policing in France did not however obscure the similarity of police grievances to those of police in other countries — salaries, allowances for lodging or housing, the oppressive conduct of overbearing superiors, all the subject of the first police strike in Lyons in 1905.[14]

As with any other collective movement the development of a capacity for unified action was one of the most challenging of tasks for police agitators. Standing solid was a requirement for success but achieving solidarity against the demands of personal interest was no easy task. Police interests across the organisation were by no means identical — young and single and newly enrolled had much less at stake than those who were long-serving, married, institutionalised in the culture, and in some places entitled to pension and leave entitlements should they survive in the service long enough. Jurisdictional restructuring and changing entitlements attending on them might expose these differential interests, as they did in the course of producing South Africa's first and only police strike in 1918.

In the wake of the Union of South Africa in 1912 the many police forces of the provinces were united in a single force. Yet differentiated policing continued, with much higher policing numbers concentrated in the industrial Transvaal than in the Cape province. Moreover Cape police grievances were aggravated by a system of 'local allowances' which were available to police in interior stations but not to themselves. Government failure to address the petitions of aggrieved police resulted in a strike by about a fifth of the urban Cape's 500 police in January 1918 — non-unionised but given some collective purpose by a formal 'local allowance committee' that had failed to persuade government of the justice of their case. While the strike was not comprehensive, its historian notes that it did involve a majority of the white constables in the force, agitated by low pay forcing them into housing in coloured areas — and the action was confined to younger, single men on tactical grounds. Government readiness to respond with kid gloves, as in Ireland in 1882, was evident in the outcome — after confinement in barracks, imprisonment and then prosecution, the strikers were given suspended sentences on condition they returned to duties, which they all did. Wage increases followed — but the wider significance of the episode was its unveiling of the racial divide in the police force, with this strike being embedded in what Nasson describes as a 'white populist police campaign'. The racialised character of both Cape and South African policing would help avert the emergence of a unified police action in future.[15]

Taking these few examples we can see that even well in advance of unionisation the police in many jurisdictions were shaping themselves as a collective interest, adopting tactics that were common in the struggles of other workers, and seeking to advance their mostly mundane but very concrete demands at times of strategic advantage. In the political sphere the expansion of the suffrage in many democratic countries had already added another pressure to review the status of police as essentially non-citizens. While police administration and government were fearful of a unionised police they were increasingly compelled by circumstance to recognise the coming reality of police demands for a say in the conditions governing their working lives. But whether these changing times might diminish conventional opposition to the unionisation of police was another matter.

So in many countries the formalisation of police combinations gathered momentum in the decade preceding the First World War. Like many craft unions before them one impetus for the developing police unions was the need for collective defence against the fates of life — especially illness, old age and death. Police in many jurisdictions were already the beneficiaries of pension schemes — and it is notable that one of the most compelling issues in the push to unionisation, and a provocation of police strikes in Australia and abroad, was that of fair and equitable access to pensions. The fundamental drive towards unionisation however was the desire to improve fundamental working conditions — wages and working hours were to prove solid and enduring concerns throughout the early years of all the unions. As these two incentives to collective action drove the activists on, broader issues of political and industrial rights inevitably emerged — sometimes to sink the cause of unionisation for decades.

Both stimuli, pensions and wages, can be found on the agendas of the earliest associations formed in Australia, which ranked among the earliest in the world. But there was also present in the ideas of those forming the early unions some aspiration to a collective ideal that was both democratic and professional. This is particularly evident in the South Australian case. In the euphoric tones of a later observer writing in the 1920s the early founders of the Association had aspired to 'form the police into a huge social democracy which, by its combined action, would procure for its members the fullest share possible of every advantage given to the public service generally'.[16]

The steps by which the South Australian police approached the formation of their Association were in truth more tentative than suggested by this retrospective account. In the first place the early meetings had to be authorised by the commissioner if they were not to result in disciplinary action. The approval was forthcoming under a sympathetic Labor administration and the first meetings were held in January 1911 at the City Watchhouse. A committee of nine members elected by ballot prepared an agenda of issues to discuss with the chief secretary and the commissioner of police — increased wages throughout the ranks, three months sick leave on full pay instead of 14 days, establishment of a Police Pension Fund as in New South Wales, and the granting of 'the right of Association'.[17]

The mood of aspirant police unionists is however better captured in the rhetoric of their claims, than in their prosaic nature. Indeed the rhetoric is less labourist than professionalising, less appealing to the justice of the cause, than to the state's need to secure a dependable and honest police. As put in their address to the chief secretary in April 1911, the case was made for a recognition of the distinctive nature of the police, one which reached beyond thief catching and mob restraint.

> A well maintained Police Force would not require the friendship of the bookmaker, spieler, or publican, nor the applause of the rabble. It would seek only the respect and approval of all good citizens, who would recognise the police as their friends and protectors. Everything that can heighten in any degree the respectability of the office of a policeman adds to the security of the State, and to the safety of the life and property of the individual. The police, we contend, not only enforce compliance with the definite law of the land, but also encourage a general recognition of the unwritten code of manners which makes for social progress and good citizenship. The police occupy a position of vital importance in the Commonwealth. The restraining influence exerted by a good policeman is as necessary to the welfare of society as are self-imposed moral and physical restraints to the health of the individual. Upon the

> impartiality, efficiency and intelligence of the Police Force depends the estimation in which the law is upheld by the masses.[18]

The challenge held out to this model of a respectable police was the reality of low wages, below those of an unskilled labourer, and inadequate provision for post-service pensions. Aggravating the poor conditions at the bottom of the organisational ladder were the dim prospects of a police career — lack of compulsory and early age retirement meant limited promotion through the ranks, a sore point in South Australia as in other police forces through these decades. The question was confronted openly by the founding committee addressing the chief secretary — 'We ask —"Do the Government and Parliament seriously believe that a Police Force can exist and keep honest and be free from corruption in present conditions?"'. Driving the point home, the committee implied that past governmental indifference might be breeding undesired outcomes, those such as police could achieve by 'adopting some of the American police tactics, which are read about, but which would not appeal kindly to the South Australian public'.[19]

With government backing the Association was formally established at a meeting in Adelaide's Co-operative Hall on 18 October 1911, the first meeting being held on 7 December. The South Australians were fortunate in their chief secretary at this moment — F S Wallis had once been sacked after going on strike with fellow printers at the Adelaide *Register* newspaper.[20] Nevertheless the responsibilities of his office were attended to with care — and the negotiation of the rules of the Association was pursued with evidently one eye on the commissioner of police and another on the approaching state election, after the Labor premier had obtained a dissolution of parliament. Exception was taken at the outset to the inclusion in the proposed rules of an objective that was copied from those of the Public Service Association. The offending clause sought 'to afford opportunity to discuss matters affecting the welfare of the Service, and to provide means for combined action in matters affecting any members thereof'. This conveyed more than a hint of collective action, even a strike should circumstances demand. Over a couple of weeks prior to the change of government the Association executive negotiated with Wallis to revise this clause. The afternoon before the state election which ended Labor's 20 month stay in office, the chief secretary approved the rules, now without reference to combined action.[21]

The objectives of the new Association were ambitious, mixing appeals to the 'esprit de corps' of the police with promises to address grievances that could not be satisfied through the normal channels of the police force. The rules respected the constraints of a working police force, but also reached out to 'afford opportunity for the full discussion of any subjects having relation to the general welfare of the Police Force, and to provide for the use of all reasonable and constitutional means in dealing with any matters affecting any members thereof'.[22] The reach of 'reasonable and constitutional' might be great, although the South Australian body was not to pursue its possible limits in the foreseeable future.

The politically contentious nature of police unionism at this point in time was highlighted almost immediately. Wallis' determination to see the Police Association established is evident in the fact that he then took the rules to a final cabinet meeting, held after the election and two days before the new government was sworn in — the minute of approval was signed off in cabinet by the out-going premier. The commissioner of police had to date acted as little more than an intermediary, evidently under direction from the Labor minister to facilitate the formation of the union. His response to the political change following the election was swift. Two days after the new government was sworn in the commissioner forwarded the file to the new chief secretary with a minute: 'In view of the change of government I feel that you should be afforded an opportunity of perusing this correspondence and suggested rules of the proposed police association'. These rules of course were not by this stage 'suggested' but established by cabinet decision. Three weeks later cabinet responded in kind by asking for the commissioner's opinion 'as to whether the proposed rules contain anything which is likely to interfere with the discipline of the force under his control'.[23]

Commissioner Raymond's response was disingenuous, barely disguising the deep opposition to police unionisation which he shared with commissioners of the time. In brief he challenged the formation of the Association as an organisation which intruded on responsibilities of his own office, with a 'great danger of friction and disorganization':

> I pointed out to the late Chief Secretary that such an Association in connection with a semi military body was an unknown thing, and might lead to an interference with discipline. He admitted that it was an experiment, and they would have to be very careful, and under no consideration would they be allowed to affiliate with any other organization.

The government's response was more measured. After further consideration the Liberal chief secretary told the commissioner that he did not wish to interfere with the previous government's approval of the rules. But he did agree that 'any combination of the Members of the Force should have been discountenanced, and not encouraged as appears to have been done in this case'. Nevertheless the government policy at this point appears to have been to do nothing further on the matter, hoping possibly that the movement might wither on the vine.[24]

Hence the early success of the South Australian Association was limited to the brief reign of Labor in government. Once a non-Labor ministry returned to office in 1912 the mood altered, and in 1913 the commissioner was emboldened to ignore the Association's request for a 'day off' per month. His attitude continued his earlier stance — such an Association request was said to be undermining the administration and discipline of the force.[25] When the executive persisted with its request by arguing the point over roster allocations, the response from the commissioner was sharp:

> I am not aware of any changes having been made other than necessary for the good government of the Force. I also desire to add that I think the Police Association will be well advised not to attempt to interfere in the discipline and administration of the Police Force.[26]

The ambivalent stance of the Liberal government enabled the commissioner to exercise his supervisory and discipline powers to keep the Assocation under control. When the secretary of the Association, Mounted Police Constable George Downing, wrote direct to the chief secretary asking for copies of the proposed Police Pensions Bill he was reprimanded by the commissioner in a communication that took advantage of policy ambiguity over the status of the union:

> The present Government have never recognised the Police Association, and though the Chief Secretary stated in his minute of 22/3/1913 that he had no desire to interfere with the action of the previous Government he at the same time made it very clear that he was not in sympathy with the movement. Under the circumstances therefore I think the less the Police Association is in evidence the better, and I trust it will not again be necessary to deal with any breach of discipline by M.C Downing.[27]

Two years later however, the swing of the political pendulum brought the Association back into the fold. With a Labor government back in power, the Association was again able to meet with the chief secretary; and by following due process in its communications with government, sending them through the commissioner, the union was able to provide suggestions for amendments to a pension bill in 1915.[28] Accelerating tension over salary issues was soon to envelop the union in a new round of contention with senior police and government. The negotiated outcome of that tension would in good part be a result of the accommodation already made by government to the reality of unionisation.

In other states the path to legitimacy was always a negotiated one, more rocky in some than others. The more radical labour state of Western Australia provided much less hostile ground for aspiring police unionists and from 1912 the union was established as a representative body with a capacity to deal with the commissioner and government — by 1916 it even had a journal, later boasted to be a world first.[29] Dissatisfaction over pay and promotions (especially the dependence of promotion on vacancies in the ranks above) led to agitation by the 'Second Class Constables' in 1910. The election of a Labor government in 1911 was the catalyst for more confident moves to the establishment of a permanent collective voice. By January 1912 the approval of the minister of the formation of a Police Association was secured and the first conference of the Association was held in July 1912.[30] Early support from a Labor government did not always translate into effective advantages in bargaining position —as we will see later, the Western Australian union would wait for some years for access to the industrial relations framework enjoyed by other unions.

The mixed success of the South Australian police unionists was more of a kin with the Victorian developments before the war. There an early stimulus to collective assertion of police demands was brought on by an issue that has remained as an aggravation for most of the past century – promotional opportunities. An objectionable and self-serving police commissioner, having attained his post in part through a lowering of the retirement age to 60 years, succeeded in getting the government to then raise the officers' retirement age to 65 years. This ensured he and others would remain in office to the detriment of promotional opportunities for those below them. As described by Haldane, this policy almost immediately provoked a large protest meeting by police in Melbourne in

March 1903. The protest meeting came to the notice of the press and resulted in the repeal of the retirement at 65 policy. Encouraged by their success the police agitators followed up with a proposal to form a Victorian Police Association, having for its aims 'to guard the interests of its members individually and collectively. To instil in them the need of mutual improvement, and for the interchange of opinions in respect to police matters generally'. It was a proposal in advance of its time — and repelled by the police administration which regarded it as 'designed with a view to not only exercise political control but also to support its members in any conflict with constituted authority'.[31]

By the outbreak of the Great War then police unionism was already a reality — duly constituted police associations, though with limited rights, had been approved by government in South Australia and Western Australia, while stirrings in other jurisdictions were challenging the old order. Statutory foundations that underlay the establishment of a neutral police at the service of the state in the nineteenth century, purposely constituting them as bodies of non-citizens subject to strong executive authority, were showing signs of decay — but not in all jurisdictions. And in the decade from 1914 the success of aspirant police unionism would vary greatly.

The nature of change between the pre-war position and later is exemplified in the developments in Queensland. The negative response of the Victorian commissioner in 1903 was not unlike that of the Queensland commissioner a decade later. The notion of an autonomous, or even simply a representative, body of police was at odds with the constitutional and statutory formulae governing police. Police regulations typically prohibited combinations of any sort, and the statutes delivered extensive and unilateral authority to the commissioner over his subordinates, though typically in Australia subject to a minister or the governor-in-council. Rule 20 of the 1869 Queensland Police regulations was explicit — 'all combinations, and as a general rule, any petition signed by members, for any purpose, will subject those who sign it or join such combination to punishment'.[32] Hence attempts by the Queensland police to develop an association during the last years of Commissioner Cahill's office (1905–1916) were initially strongly opposed. But after a new Labor government repealed the anti-combination clause of the regulations, Cahill took a stance from a passing age. The police commissioner found his direct links to government increasingly challenged by the privileged access to Labor ministers seemingly gained by aspiring police unionists. Protesting that his authority was being undermined by rising police unionism Cahill told his minister, the home secretary that 'the rank and file of the Police Force ... manifestly desire to ignore discipline and invert the order of things as they ought to exist'.[33]

Cahill's stand was just a dying splutter of protest against the inevitable for the Labor government in Queensland had already determined its position in favour of the union and after his replacement in 1916 the Queensland Police Union (QPUE, 'of Employees' as it was later known, to distinguish it from an Officers Union that was later established) was quickly established as a permanent body with a developing role in the negotiation of police pay and conditions.[34] This seems to suggest, following the South Australian and Western Australian examples, that having Labor in government was a guarantee of success in the legitimation of police unions. Yet the political identity of the government of the time was not always a predictor of attitudes on unionisation in other places — in New South Wales it was a Labor minister, George Black, who objected in 1915 that 'a police union would be as indavisable as a military union',[35] even though the government had already signalled a year before that no objection would be made to the formation of an association.[36]

All the same within a few years in New South Wales a Labor government prompted the development of a registered trade union for police, in spite of commissioner reluctance. Already prior to the Great War there had been significant advocacy of the need for a police association by an ex-police officer and Labor parliamentarian, Ted Larkin — his promotion of the necessity of a police representative association in connection with a Police Appeals Bill in 1914 was in advance of its time on an issue (discipline and promotion decisions) that would be a rallying point for the police unions in all jurisdictions from the 1920s.[37] After the war there were signs of an informal police union with a report in July 1920 already speaking of a New South Wales Policeman's Union.[38] The Labor government's mandate of the new body was signalled by the appearance of the chief secretary, James Dooley, at a mass meeting at the Police Depot shortly after, and the publication of his speech in the first issue of the Association's journal in January 1921.[39]

The approval of the New South Wales body only followed after some anxious consideration by the inspector-general (the New South Wales equivalent of a commissioner). He telegrammed his Victorian counterpart in June 1920: 'Would be glad to be furnished with a confidential letter as to whether the police association your state has hampered police administration in any way'. A reassuring reply came back — the Police Association in Victoria was formed of the 'most reputable and level-headed Members of the Force, and it is found that they have a steadying influence upon the younger Members who are inclined to be extreme in their views'. This spoke volumes for the incorporation of the Victorian Police Association as a virtual sub-department of the police, a kind of advisory body whose agendas had to be approved by the chief commissioner. The moral was drawn: 'I may add that it is recognised that, if the Executive and Council of the Association were differently constituted, the position would not be the same'.[40]

The somewhat exceptional status of the Victorian Police Association in the Australian context, effectively a company union, should not be allowed to cloud a more general message arising from this exchange. Even the more radical police unions proved to be bodies that would contain police frustration, channelling grievances through institutional provisions designed to address them, with negative as well as positive outcomes. It was vital for the unions to present a respectable front, especially in the early years when resistance to their very legitimacy had been deep. Ironically New South Wales anxiety to hear about the lessons from Victoria was of a mode with a Victorian request made to the South Australian police commissioner just seven years before, at a time when the Melbourne police were starting to agitate for a union. Victoria's Chief Commissioner Sainsbury was reassured by his South Australian counterpart in 1913 that 'when first formed it rather looked as if the Association was to manage the Department but now of course all that is a matter of the past'.[41]

In Victoria in fact it was not until well into the war that government attitudes had softened. The reasons are instructive. In the first place police demands themselves built up over time, and even in spite of some government decisions to address wages and conditions — the protest meeting of 1903, a 1912 deputation for increased wages, secret meetings in 1915 and then a large meeting of 200 police in the Guild Hall in Melbourne in July 1916 which elected a secretary to approach the commissioner for permission to form a 'non-political' association. Second, the changing political disposition of government itself facilitated a more receptive response to rising police expectations. Although under a Liberal government (and thus not as predictably favourable as in the increasingly

Labor states), in December 1916 the Victorian constitution was altered to give public servants a right to participate in political affairs. It took some years for this enhancement of rights to be tested in respect of police — yet the implications for formation of an independent Police Association were almost immediate. In any case the government had already shown itself prepared to go further than the police commissioner had in consenting to the police request for an association. A third factor was pressing on government — the support of other labour unions, including both Trades Hall and other public sector unions.

The agreement of the chief secretary to the formation of some kind of police association followed in 1917. The moment was celebrated by the 600 police who gathered on 10 May, but notably under the presiding authority of the chief commissioner. Sainsbury had been brought reluctantly along the path to the formation of an Association, having been the source of the enquiry to South Australia in 1913 and a refuser of desired meetings in 1916. As it would be in later years after the trauma of the 1923 strike, the Association's eventual formation under the wing of the chief commissioner made it more like the police federations of Britain, and less like the police unions of the other Australian states.[42]

At the same time we do well to note how similar were some the features of the Victorian union's formation to those in more Labor-leaning states. The legitimation of Victorian police unionism shared its timing with that of the quite different political culture of Queensland and was well in advance of New South Wales. Victorian anxieties about police unionism, as we have seen, were no different from those patently evident in South Australia, Queensland and New South Wales. Police commissioners in all states it seemed were very conscious at the moment of police union formation of the potential challenge of unions to their administrative authority — presciently so, for they could not rely on their ministers to observe protocol by referring union representations first to the commissioner. In Victoria indeed the Association showed from 1917 to 1922 that it was able to seek and gain audiences with the government without the commissioner being present.[43] Australian governments by 1920, whether Labor or Liberal, exercised a countervailing force by acknowledging the demands of police to enhanced status, to the extent at least of having a right to express their collective demands on some fundamental conditions of work and service. By the time the last state police representative body was established, in Tasmania in 1922, the legitimacy of police unionisation in Australia was assured.[44] But as history often turns, so was this assurance almost immediately challenged by the events in Melbourne in 1923.

2.3 Police strikes

The international incidence of police strikes during the decade after the outbreak of the Great War suggests how important is the context of the times in shaping political options. Strikes were the last resort of police frustrated both by their worsening relative socio-economic condition, and their lack of power to shape the conditions of their employment. It is symptomatic of this period that the most drastic expression of this frustration in Australia came in the state where the aspirant police union was most constrained by the governing authorities.

The police strike in Melbourne was an anomaly. Like most strikes it was the consequence of a failure in management, but in addition it signified a failure in the local police union. Australian governments had gradually accommodated themselves to the idea that police were not only much like other workers, but were entitled to have grievances addressed through a representative association. In spite of these changes over the previous decade we will see that the strike in Melbourne was in many ways a movement of the non-unionised. It was solid enough in its limited arena to demonstrate to government and populace alike that the long-held fears of what would happen if the police went on strike had some substance. The consequences were two-fold. The local effect, in the wake of the defeat of the strike, was the enactment of statutory controls over the Victorian Police Association, modelled on those used in England and Wales. A second and symbolic effect was of national significance — the reality of a police strike had been engaged, and thereafter would be a benchmark of police agitation. Would it, could it, happen again? For the remainder of the century police agitators would invoke the strike as the benchmark of what might happen if demands were not met.

The Melbourne strike appears an aberration in an otherwise quiescent history of industrial conflict. But in many respects it was of an order in its time and place. To what degree this was so may be viewed through attention to police strikes in other jurisdictions. And although there is reason to look abroad to understand the mood of the times, an important precursor of the Melbourne events took place in South Australia five years before this. The action of South Australian police in 1918 in forcing a government to arbitrate on their pay claim amounted to a strike, one long forgotten, but more organised, purposeful and successful than the Melbourne one in 1923.

Aggravated by the lack of a pay increase since 1911 a revived South Australian Police Association took advantage of the return of a Labor government to press their case from early 1917. Divisions within the Association limited the impact of the campaign at the outset, as did a change in government back to a Liberal administration in July. But with support in parliament leading to a resolution in November 1917 to increase police pay to a minimum of 10 shillings a day the Association campaign strengthened over the following months. Inter-state comparisons and international example such as the news of the August 1918 London police strike prompted political warnings to the South Australian government in September 1918 of the dangers of a discontented police. When the Liberal-National coalition government responded with a decision below the level of the 1917 parliamentary resolution the Association executive sought a meeting with the chief secretary. The government refused, advising instead that it was willing to receive a deputation from 'each branch of the Police Force'. In response the Association organised a mass meeting of police on 14 September 1918 at the Co-operative Hall in Angas Street. The meeting voted unanimously for a motion that pledged members to take 'individual action in accordance with conscience'. Individual action was collective action — a large number of police immediately resigned from the force and within a month one-third of the force had sent their resignations.

The response of the government was initially conciliatory — but hardened over the succeeding days to an insistence that the resignations be withdrawn before an arbitrator was appointed. Advice to municipal councils that they should appoint 'vigilant committees' and employ special constables appears to have had limited effect. The brinksmanship resulted eventually in agreement to the appointment of an arbitrator from the Industrial Commission, with the Association's assent to this being taken as a simultaneous withdrawal of the resignations. The recommendation of the arbitrator was for a substantial increase in pay, which was back-dated following further negotiation between the government and the Association deputation.[45]

To all intents and purposes the mass resignation of about 300 police in South Australia in 1918 was a strike — and the government's concession of an arbitration inquiry constituted de facto recognition of the Association's strength, even at a time of government hostility. Yet in spite of the drastic step involved by resigning their posts (presumably in some expectation that this would eventuate in their re-employment) the South Australian constabulary were proud in the claim that they were a police that had never gone on strike.[46] In retrospect the Association would tend to view the events of 1918 as evidence of police moderation. Reviewing the position in 1920 the newly-established *Police Journal* pondered whether recognition of the Association as an industrial union was being denied because of early sponsorship by a Labor government, and then contested arguments for non-recognition because of the special nature of the police. Fears that the South Australian police might strike were groundless, since (it was interestingly observed by the editor of the journal) police were well aware of the limited impact that a police strike would achieve: 'probably a few minor traffic accidents and a few more burglaries, but the community would hardly miss a stride in its daily routine'.[47] Perhaps this reflected the peaceable disposition of the citizens of Adelaide, for events in Melbourne in 1923 were to challenge such a perspective. If Adelaide in 1918 typified an Australian moderation and resort to institutional mediation of industrial conflict, then Melbourne in 1923 pointed to the possibility of less happy outcomes.

In two countries with police systems of long-standing the end of the Great War brought momentous police strikes that had substantial local and long-term effects. In the United States the Boston police strike of 1919 was decisive in turning back the rising tide of police unionism. The conditions provoking the strike were shared by many countries at the time. The end of the war brought with it waves of industrial unrest over the need for wage rises to match rampant inflation. In Boston the environment was one of quasi-revolutionary demands by the labour movement, but also of urban unrest including racial riots. Conditions within the police department were not conducive to stability. A successful police chief who had cleaned up the Boston police had been replaced by a former Mayor of Boston, with no experience of police administration. Police Chief Curtis was also a hard-line opponent of the recent and spreading enthusiasm for police unionisation. Following a 20 year ban the American Federation of Labour (AFL — the peak union body) had begun in 1919 to allow the chartering of police unions — legitimating them as members of the general labour movement. When the Boston police were granted an AFL union charter in August 1919, Curtis responded by immediately banning police from affiliating with any outside organisation, other than veterans' bodies.

When the police refused to disband their union Curtis prosecuted the office-holders and some others — 19 were dismissed from the force. The dismissals were followed by a near unanimous vote to strike. In the course of the action, and in the absence of an effective response by the city authorities, there was widespread rioting, looting and the deaths of seven people. The governor of the state of Massachusetts, Calvin Coolidge, then assumed control of the city's police. His resolution of the strike was ruthless — 1,200 striking police were dismissed without entitlements and never reinstated. The effects of the strike on the police union movement in the United States were widespread. In spite of the general pre-strike enthusiasm of police in many cities for affiliation to the AFL, the charters of those affiliated were soon dissolved. City administrations adopted strong anti-union stances — but also in many cases sought to avoid future confrontations by granting pay rises.[48]

Long-term, the effects of the Boston police strike were evident in the weakness and lagged development of American police unionism. A number of states forbade police unions and even when such attitudes were relaxed police were slow to organise. Twenty-five years after the Boston strike there were only 15 police unions chartered by the AFL in the largest 168 American cities (over 50,000 population) and only three were recognised by city officials. Attempts after the Second World War to organise a national police union were unsuccessful. Most notably there were no more police strikes in the United States before the rise of a new militant police unionism in the 1970s.[49]

Across the Atlantic the effects of the war on social conditions and labour activism were equally evident in Britain. The police in England had engaged in both wages agitation and proto-unionisation before the outbreak of the First World War, in spite of specific directives by the home secretary threatening dismissal for membership of a police union. Opposition to the unionisation of police was as firm in the upper reaches of government as it was in other countries.[50] The war however was a catalyst to the union cause in England. In August 1918 the right to form and belong to a union became the underlying cause of a widespread police strike in London involving both the Metropolitan and city police forces. The precipitating cause was the dismissal of a constable active in the cause of the union. Like their contemporaries in South Africa, the authorities gave way during this war-time strike, the constable being reinstated and various grievances addressed. Opposition to the formation of a union continued, but confronted by evidence of covert unionisation: thus a 'representative association' established at Scotland Yard had elected to it delegates mainly associated with the union.

The aftermath of the 1918 strike saw an increase in union support in some of the big cities. A mass meeting of the fledgling union was held at Albert Hall in London in January 1919. The Lloyd George Liberal government responded in the same year by moving to assert control over the movement. Following a major inquiry into police pay and conditions, which recommended a formal representative body, the home secretary prepared legislation providing for a police federation free of any links to the labour unions or other bodies. This challenge to the independent police union was met by another strike in London, Liverpool and Birmingham in August 1919. The outcome was as fatal to the strikers as the almost contemporaneous action in Boston. The strike was not solid, involving only 2,400 out of the union's claimed 50,000 police — but its consequences, including costly rioting in Liverpool, brought it to international attention. Almost all of the strikers were dismissed and never reinstated to the police service. A campaign for reinstatement continued into the 1920s, but without success, even under a Labour government.[51] Such a story was to be replicated in Melbourne a few years later.

The endorsement of the British Labour government for its predecessors' 1919 actions in establishing the Police Federation was a striking sign of consensus around a notion of the police as an exceptional occupation whose services could not be compromised by the extension to them of the standard industrial rights enjoyed by other workers. The statutory provisions governing the Police Federation were to have more than an echo in Australia — when it came time to mop up after the Melbourne strike the Victorian government adopted almost *in toto* the constraints on external association and political freedoms that had been enacted at Westminster.

In contrast to the earlier actions of the Irish constabulary in 1882 or the Cape Town police in 1918 the Boston and English police strikes of 1919 were struggles over the very right to unionise, a claim given sustenance by the post-war conditions. Government in both places responded swiftly and without mercy — anxious above all about the potential of police strikers to establish alliances with a rebellious labour movement. The Melbourne police strike was different in origin, but the tactical response of government was much the same as in Boston or London. It may be a moot question whether government response might have been different if the strike was more solid — but that was far from the case.

Recent research on the Melbourne strike has shown just how far this action was from being the last resort of a frustrated union. In fact the strikers were largely non-unionised, and were more likely to be little acculturated to the police, a large number of them being recently recruited cadets. The causes of the strike, like most industrial disputes, were complex — but they centred on some long-standing and familiar grievances. In the first place there was great resentment in the Victorian police over differential access to police pensions, which had been abolished in 1902 for those enlisted after that date. Entitlement to a pension was a factor distinguishing strikers and non-strikers in Melbourne — only two of the 636 striking police in 1923 had pension rights. A second and precipitating issue was the mode of police discipline, with the chief commissioner having reintroduced a surveillance system involving inspectors who quickly became known as 'spooks'.[52] The abolition of the spooks' system was the sole objective of the strike, so its leaders insisted, but the structure of support suggests the pertinence of more general issues of wages, conditions and pensions.

The strike has received much research attention over the years, but its most recent historians have provided the clearest account of the events in the context of the history of the Victorian Police Association. Unlike the other Australian police unions, which had by this time proved remarkably successful in recruiting members, the Victorian body was in something of a decline prior to the strike. Being something of a company union its effectiveness as an industrial union was muted and there seemed little prospect of such notable advances as had been won in Queensland or were in prospect in other states. One result of this lack of legitimacy as an effective organisation was its poor membership base — on the eve of the strike while nearly 90% of police in some districts were Victorian Police Association members, membership was as low as 35% at the Police Depot in Russell St, 56% in Melbourne and 62% across state. Only 59% of constables were members of the Association.[53] These patterns were reflected inversely among the strikers. A minority of strikers were financial members of the Association, and only a minority of the Association executive joined them. Notably there was a high proportion of strikers among non-unionised new recruits, still in training at the Depot, and Brown and Haldane also identify a relatively high number of ex-servicemen among the strikers.[54] In essence the strike was by those most aggravated by differential rights — those who went on strike did not have access to pensions, those who did *not* strike were those most secure in the organisation, and with most to lose, since their pension rights would be lost if they were dismissed.[55]

The events themselves are well described elsewhere and need not detain us.[56] Brown and Haldane have characterised the event as a 'wild-cat' strike, an event which got out of hand after the incendiary leader Brooks persuaded 29 men at Russell Street to refuse duty. The combative attitude of the chief commissioner and a fumbling Police Association executive did not help resolve matters. City rioting on the day after the strike commenced was not avoided by the appointment of General Sir John Monash to coordinate the recruitment and deployment of special constables to make up for the absence of the mainly city-located strikers. What had initially been a small action located at Russell Street escalated within a couple of days to involve over 600 men and the aid of Trades Hall. But the dismissal of the strikers quickly turned the dispute into a campaign for reinstatement, again with the support of the Trades Hall, and anticipated support from the Labor Party. Over the rest of the decade the campaign for reinstatement was to continue but without any success and in spite of Labor obtaining government briefly in 1924 and then 1927.

Had labour conditions been more opportune government and commissioner attitudes to reinstatement might have been different. But in the 1920s there seemed little difficulty in recruiting sufficient police. And the opposition of the chief commissioner to reinstatement called up reasons that had long informed the fears of opponents of police unions. By availing themselves of the strike weapon and allying with the Trades Hall the strikers were seen as having compromised their autonomy as police officers — no longer could they be viewed as credible witnesses, and they would have a 'perceived bias towards the Trades Hall in future industrial disputes'.[57]

The results of the strike share much with those of the English events just four years before. All strikers were dismissed — and the government responded almost immediately by establishing in statute a representative association. This 'company union' would have responsibility for the advancement of welfare and other issues in the police service but would be precluded from any active or indirect role in politics or the wider labour movement. A pensions bill introduced almost immediately after the strike was enacted from 1 January 1924 and re-established a comprehensive pensions scheme. Over subsequent years other conditions were improved — especially the standard of accommodation in police barracks and stations, and an increased annual leave provision.[58] But almost identical with the English response was the Victorian government's enactment of restrictive conditions on the freedom of association of police or their union. In 1919 the British government's police statute was revised to ensure that the Police Federation, which it had established, could not affiliate with political or other external bodies. The clauses were adopted wholesale in Victoria's 1923 *Police Pensions Act*. For the next 70 years they were to stand as a reminder of the days when governments decided that police could not be entrusted with a right to unionise like other workers. The difficulties of enforcing such provisions, like any legal regulation, were another matter and would be encountered in later decades.

The memory of the Melbourne police strike runs long in Australian policing. Over the years many articles on the events have appeared in the union journals. And the lessons are drawn on in varying ways by union officials, rank and file and politicians as well as the media. The ways in which the strike was received and remembered are worthy of comment.

In the first place other Australian police unions were divided in their response to the strike. The Queensland Police Union signalled its sympathy very quickly when the executive forwarded a sum of £100 to the strike committee within three weeks of the strike. In the less hostile political climate of Queensland a police union had already achieved much — and its sympathies with the cause were also shaped by an eye to the advantage it saw in this lesson on the dangers of civil disorder. Within weeks, Fleming shows, the union executive in Queensland had decided that 'now was the time to growl' — and over the next 12 months the union pursued pay claims and other improvements from a government shaken by intimations of a 'strike'.[59]

Quite different was the response in New South Wales. Threats of industrial militancy could not come at a worse time for the New South Wales union, which was grinding away at government over access to arbitration and appeal rights. The result was a hostile reception to the appeal of the Melbourne strikers. The mood was signalled by the *Police*

News in December when it concluded that the strike had been an 'unwise step' — and that while New South Wales police sympathised with the women and children they did not with the 'agitators'.[60] Behind the scenes the response had also been less than friendly. As we have seen a strike committee had been set up in Melbourne with Trades Hall support. When a delegate from this committee attempted to present a case for support to the New South Wales Association executive at its November 27 meeting the meeting refused to admit him. One executive member told the meeting that while 'they as an Executive might be in sympathy with the men in their requests, they could not endorse the method they had adopted of striking to obtain redress for their grievances'. The immediate concern of the executive was that they did not want to 'jeopardise the Appeals Bill'. Only one person supported the right of the Victorian delegate to be heard — and the latter was subsequently told to leave the room before being able to speak. As in Queensland however there was some suggestion in New South Wales that the strike had prompted a government into action. Another executive member dissented from the view that the strike might have frustrated the prospects of getting through their Appeals Bill. The contrary could be argued — 'Thanks to the strike that bill would be brought on early. It was only when a crisis came that anything good was done for police'.[61]

The moral lessons of the strike, in some variety, continued to be told and reinvented for later generations. There were at least two, and contradictory, lessons drawn from the strike. While there were those police who considered the Melbourne strike had been a catalyst for changing police conditions there and elsewhere, there were others who regretted it as reprehensible. From South Australia, prominent police unionist Foot Constable Alker, warned in March 1924 that 'the organised state of civilisation ceases without a police force' — and confessed his pride that the South Australian police had avoided the temptation to strike.[62] Outside the police the media remembered the strike down the years as a symptom of what might happen if the shackles of policing were loosened. 'Black Saturday', when Melbourne had gone on a rampage, was a symptom of what happened to a city deprived of police protection.[63] As a limit case the Melbourne strike had its uses in the symbolic constructions of social order — and it would be useful in the future as a signal to governments of what damage might flow from too complacent an attitude towards their police.

Notes

1 *SAPJ*, May 1992, p10.
2 *The Globe and Mail* (Toronto, Ontario), 3 Sep 1999. On the status of Canadian police unions see the illuminating discussions by R Jackson, "Police labour relations in Canada: a current perspective," in *Conflict and cooperation in police labour relations*, ed Bryan M Downie and Richard L Jackson (Ottawa, 1980). and Philip C Stenning, "Police and politics: there and back and there again?" in *Police powers in Canada: the evolution and practice of authority*, ed R Macleod and D Schneiderman (Toronto, 1994).
3 On wages and conditions in the nineteenth century see Robert Haldane, *The people's force: a history of the Victoria Police* (Carlton, 1986), 101–113, W Ross Johnston, *The long blue line: a history of the Queensland Police* (Brisbane, 1992), 27–35.
4 For a recent comparative overview of this dimension of policing see Clive Emsley, "The policeman as worker: a comparative survey c. 1800–1940" *International Review of Social History* 45 (2000).
5 As cited in Ryder v Foley, [1906] 4 *Commonwealth Law Reports*, 422–454.
6 Ibid, See also Fletcher v Nott, [1938] 60 *Commwealth Law Reports*, 55 affirming the Commissioner's power to dismiss at will, which was exercised against 13 police officers by Commissioner Mackay following the Markell Royal Commission into Starting-Price Betting.
7 David McGill, *No Right to Strike The History of the New Zealand Police Service Organizations* (Wellington, 1992), 7.
8 Haldane, *The people's force: a history of the Victoria Police*, 64–65.
9 Johnston, *The long blue line: a history of the Queensland Police*, 158–159.
10 McGill, *No Right to Strike The History of the New Zealand Police Service Organizations*, 8–9, Johnston, *The long blue line: a history of the Queensland Police*, 104–107, Haldane, *The people's force: a history of the Victoria Police*, 128.
11 South Australia State Records (SASR), GRG 24/6/568/1917.
12 Mark Finnane, *Police and government: histories of policing in Australia* (Melbourne, 1994), 55–58.
13 W J Lowe, "The constabulary agitation of 1882," *Irish Historical Studies* xxxi (1998). See also Fergus D'Arcy, "The Dublin police strike of 1882," *Saothar* 23 (1998) for an account of the contemporaneous strike in Dublin, focused on pension and supervision issues.
14 Jean-Marc Berliere, " "Quand un metayer veut etre bien garde, il nourrit ses chiens" La difficile naissance du syndicalisme policier: problemes et ambiguites (1900–1914)," *Le mouvement social* (1993): 50–51, 26.
15 Bill Nasson, " "Messing with coloured people": the 1918 police strike in Cape Town, South Africa," *Journal of African History* 33 (1992).
16 *SAPJ*, Nov 1929, p25.
17 From a circular of 26 Jan 1911, *SAPJ*, Nov 1929, p25.
18 *SAPJ*, Nov 1929, p26.
19 *SAPJ*, Nov 1929, p29.
20 See entry 'F.S. Wallis', *Australian Dictionary of Biography*, vol 12, p368.
21 SASR, GRG 5/2/1912/68 contains the documents negotiated through this period.
22 *SAPJ*, Oct 1920, p6.

23 SASR, GRG 5/2/1912/68, fol 35.
24 SASR, GRG 5/2/1912/68, fol 38.
25 Police Association South Australia web site 'History' — http://www.pasa.asn.au/organisation.htm#history.
26 SASR, GRG 5/2/1913/137 — Commissioner to Secretary SAPA, 10 Feb [actually March] 1913.
27 SASR, GRG 5/2/298/1913, Comm of Police minute, 18 Jun 1913.
28 SASR, GRG 5/2/1915/1734 (deputation to Chief Secretary (6 Dec 1915); GRG 5/2/1916/223 for correspondence over the Pensions Bill 1915.
29 *The Police News* (*WAPN*), Oct 1929.
30 *WAPN*, Oct 1929, pp10–12.
31 Haldane, *The people's force: a history of the Victoria Police*, 126–127.
32 Jenny Fleming, "By fair means or foul? The impact of police unionism in Queensland, 1915–1932" (BA Hons, Griffith University, 1991), 17.
33 Mark Finnane, "Police rules," *ANZ Journal of Criminology* 22 (1989): 104, 106.
34 Jenny Fleming, "Shifting the emphasis: the impact of police unionism in Queensland, 1915–1925," *Labour History* (1995), Johnston, *The long blue line: a history of the Queensland Police*, 129–133.
35 Kevin Seggie, "Aspects of the role of the police force in New South Wales and its relation to the government 1900–1939" (PhD, Macquarie University, 1988), 187.
36 Bruce Howe, *The Blue Collar Workers' Union: a history of the Police Association of New South Wales* ([Sydney], 1988), 2.
37 Steve Brien, *Serving the Force: 75 Years of the Police Association of New South Wales* (Sydney, 1996), 12–15.
38 Howe, *The Blue Collar Workers' Union: a history of the Police Association of New South Wales*, 3. Citing *SMH*, 1 Jul 1920.
39 Brien, *Serving the Force: 75 Years of the Police Association of New South Wales*, 18; *NSWPN*, Jan 1921, pp3, 25.
40 Victorian Public Record Office (VPRO), VPRS 807 Unit 2637, Act Chief Commissioner of Police, 30 Jun 1920 (courtesy of Helen Harris).
41 Haldane, *The people's force: a history of the Victoria Police*, 154.
42 This account draws principally on Ibid, 153–158.
43 Peter Sadler, "Sir John Gellibrand and the Victoria Police: a short, unhappy association," *Victorian Historical Journal* 66 (1995).
44 *Tasmanian Police Journal (TPJ)*, Aug 1947, p3.
45 This account draws on a history of the early years of the Association by F A King, published in *SAPJ*, Jan 1969–May 1969. See also the unpublished account of Bruce Swanton, "Police employee representation in South Australia 1911–1963," ([unpublished], 1983) which draws principally on King's articles and the union journal, as well as some early executive minutes; and SASR, GRG 5/2/1918/440.
46 P Higgs and C Betters, *To walk a fair beat: a history of the South Australian Women Police, 1915–1987* (Lockleys, SA, 1987); *SAPJ*, Sep 1929, pp3–13; Mar 1924, p6.
47 *SAPJ*, Oct 1920, p5.
48 Francis Russell, *A city in terror: 1919, the Boston police strike* (New York, 1975), Allen Z Gammage and Stanley L Sachs, *Police Unions* (Springfield, Ill, 1972), *The Boston police strike: two reports*, (New York, 1971).

49 Russell, *A city in terror: 1919, the Boston police strike*, 234–235, William D Gentel and Martha L Handman, *Police strikes: causes and prevention* (Washington, 1980).
50 Clive Emsley, *The English police: a political and social history* (Hemel Hempstead, 1991), 94–95.
51 Ibid, 124–127, Gerald W Reynolds and Anthony Judge, *The night the police went on strike* (London, 1968).
52 Gavin Brown and Robert Haldane, *Days of Violence: The 1923 police strike in Melbourne* (Melbourne, 1998).
53 Ibid, 36–37.
54 Ibid, ch6.
55 Haldane, *The people's force: a history of the Victoria Police*, 174.
56 Ibid, Jacqueline Templeton, "Rebel Guardians: the Melbourne Police Strike of 1923," in *Strikes: studies in twentieth century Australian social history*, ed John Merritt, John Iremonger, and Graeme Osborne (Sydney, 1973), Brown and Haldane, *Days of Violence: The 1923 police strike in Melbourne.*
57 Brown and Haldane, *Days of Violence: The 1923 police strike in Melbourne*, 97.
58 Haldane, *The people's force: a history of the Victoria Police*, 188.
59 Fleming, "By fair means or foul? The impact of police unionism in Queensland, 1915–1932", 46–47.
60 *NSWPN*, Dec 1923, Supplement 11.
61 *NSWPN*, Jan 1924, p20
62 *SAPJ*, Mar 1924, p6.
63 "When Melbourne police went on strike", reprinted from *Man*, in *NSWPN*, 1 Aug 1945, pp5–6.

3: The politicisation of police

... the doings of Governments are matters that directly concern every member of the Police Force, in as much as the Police give their allegiance to whatever Government is in power and expect to better their conditions through that allegiance.
New South Wales Police News editorial, 1926

I say this, when our destinies are shaped politically we must think politically.
New South Wales Police Association conference delegate, 1930

This occasion was unique in as much as it was the first occasion in the British Empire that the whole of the ministry had been present at a police picnic.
Labor Premier's speech, Tasmania, 1936

Having won the battle for recognition, the Australian police unions spent most of the succeeding years of the inter-war period consolidating and extending their reach. The achievements were substantial. Recognition was not only formal — increasingly it meant that police union conferences were places where government ministers and even premiers should be seen. With their status rising the unions found doors open for discussion on key issues in police administration and even law reform. The capacity to address individual cases remained vital, and the integration of some unions into structures like appeal boards, doubtless facilitated the capacity for informal resolution of some complaints and grievances.

At the same time the institutionalisation of the police unions brought its own problems. The strength of the union was frequently tied to the energy and resilience of its chief administrative officer, the secretary. In many cases this was a non-police appointee. An element of intolerance of criticism and contempt for those who questioned union priorities crept into some unions — and created ructions lasting often years. Externally the achievements of the unions were usually less than the members, or the executive, wished for — a matter almost in the nature of things in industrial relations, but aggravated during these years by the catastrophe of the Great Depression. At the same time, the protection offered to police by full-time employment, and increasingly under conditions that were more like those of other workers, could not be gainsaid.

In this chapter we explore some of these themes. In particular we explore the industrial relations context in which the unions were encouraged to grow, but also to conform. We look at the effects of these regimes on some of the fundamental objectives of the unions, and their members, especially wages, conditions, and employment rights. But we see also in these decades the development of an increasing sophistication of the unions in their role in the public political sphere, extending in some cases to strong interventions in law making, and in others to attempts to influence electoral outcomes. Yet with power come limits — and the very real limits on what police unions could achieve must be recognised if we are to appreciate the precise role of the unions in the field of policing and criminal justice.

3.1 Defining the game

The formal rules of police unions were usually organised around a standard list of ambitions to improve the conditions of working police officers. Later some would add more expansive concerns, such as those of the Queensland union regarding all matters pertaining to policing and the rule of law. To understand the aims and objectives however requires going beyond a formal legalistic statement to consider the range of matters and the mechanisms used to pursue them. In this respect it will be useful here to give an overview of the objectives as they developed down the years.

We can summarise the range of concerns in a formulaic way as these. First the unions have been concerned with direct benefits — above all pay, but as time went on attached to this were matters such as leave, overtime, uniform allowances, housing issues including rent, transport and car allowances and so on. As we will see later in this chapter the fundamental mechanism through which these matters would be addressed became that of arbitration, though much earlier in some states than others. And as Australian workplace relations have been reformed in recent years the police too have been required to enter the world of 'enterprise bargaining'.

Second there was also from the beginning much attention paid to delayed benefits — including such matters as pensions, superannuation, sick leave, workers' compensation. We have noted already that a matter like pensions was enough to provoke substantial disaffection in the background to the Melbourne police strike. In the future arbitration would frequently be invoked to resolve such issues.

Third we must count the importance of workplace relations issues. These are of particular interest to any study of policing and its context since they bear on the way in which the police organisation was shaped in its management of policing. Just as much as wages and pensions, the conditions under which authority was exercised in police departments became a central concern of the emerging police unions. Disciplinary matters such as charges over breaches of police rules, punishment, transfers, dismissal, and in general the powers of the commissioner and supervising officers over the lower ranks — a large part of the union's business and at times many of their most costly campaigns and defensive actions have attended to these.

Last we can note the significance of police union interest in the policing environment more broadly conceived. Here we can discern a whole range of concerns covering legal reform, penal and social policy. Police unions were vocal from the 1920s on matters of legal reform affecting police powers, and their liabilities, for example in relation to the danger of civil suits against them. From time to time they also attacked what they saw as the lenient treatment of offenders in the courts, including those who had assaulted police. Protecting police territory was the source of another kind of union concern — with the threat of private policing, again a concern from the 1920s on. But protecting one's territory was not just a matter of threats to jobs — police unionists could also become agitated about how police themselves were seen. This reflected a disposition supporting an important dimension of police unionism — its aspirations to respectability. Attacking the figure of the 'Stage Policeman' of popular entertainment, the *Queensland Police Union Journal* in October 1917 captured this aspiration perfectly:

> *We are entitled to proper respect and protection from the silly, slighting shafts of the would-be funny man; we claim it as citizens; we are doubly entitled to it as policemen.*[1]

A vital step on the road to respectability and citizenship in the Australian context was access to those institutions that for most of the twentieth century defined wages and working conditions, epitomised in the arbitration courts, but complemented in the public service context by appeals boards. Campaigns for access to such institutions defined the ambitions of police unions from the 1910s to the 1950s and in turn underlay their political entanglements. In turn, as we examine in the following pages, arbitration brought with it issues of affiliation with the labour movement. This became evident in the aspirations of some police unions to close involvment with the Labor Party, and in their interest in such collectivist policies as preference for unionists.

The most important institutional motor for the Australian labour movement in the inter-war years was industrial arbitration. These were decades in which the relative success of the labour movement in achieving office coincided with a consolidation of arbitration as the Australian mode of handling industrial issues. Union power was sometimes enhanced by access to state arbitration — and constrained by it. In turn arbitration was a political incendiary of some consequence, a focus of major political confrontation during the 1920s in particular.

For the police unions access to arbitration became a core aspiration. Their belief in the justice of their wage and other claims encouraged their faith in arbitration mechanisms as an answer to their long-frustrated demands. The Queensland union was the first to achieve satisfaction. Its path was smoothed by the support of Australia's most radical Labor government. In June 1917 the union was registered as an industrial organisation under the state's 1916 *Industrial Arbitration Act* and an industrial agreement between the commissioner and the police union was determined in April 1918.[2] Other states were less forthcoming. As we have seen in South Australia the Police Association membership had secured an ad hoc arbitration of their wages claim by a co-ordinated mass resignation in 1918. Formal access to arbitration would be some years away, dependent on the Association agreeing to register as an industrial organisation — eventually this was agreed by a large majority of the membership at a meeting in January 1925, but only after due expression of the usual worries about identifying too closely with Trades Hall.[3]

In the other states matters moved more slowly. By 1951 the Tasmanian annual conference was told that only New South Wales and Tasmania lacked access to full arbitration rights or a police classification board where all conditions of service might be adjudicated.[4] The complaint reflected the limitations on the jurisdiction of the Tasmanian Classification and Appeals Board, established only in 1950, and dealing mainly with salaries issues, leaving large amounts of 'conditions of service' to government or commissioner discretion. By this stage Labor in federal government had also overseen the establishment of arbitration in the territories of the ACT and Northern Territory, both of which now had their own police associations.[5] In New South Wales a succession of Labor governments appeared unable to bring the police into the arbitration system — wage increases for police were addressed in that state by government decision (as through the Labor government's extension to police of a basic wage increase to public servants in 1921, or its 1925 decision on a 44-hour week to police).[6]

Frustration with the lack of access to full industrial union rights led in one state to a strategic affiliation between a police union and the labour movement. In Western Australia the Police Association had achieved early recognition, but by the mid-1920s was finding only limited satisfaction in some of its key demands, such as improved police pensions. The assumption of Labor government in 1924 began a long period of labour movement ascendancy that was interrupted only twice (in 1930–3 and 1947–53) between 1924 and 1959. Already sympathetic Police Association leaders read the signs early. In June 1924, only two months after the Collier Labor government took office, the Association presented its case for a pay rise. Although Western Australia had introduced compulsory arbitration in 1901, the police did not have access to it — a grievance since at least 1921 when the Association had raised the matter with the previous government.[7] Earlier pay rises, such as that of 1920, had been won on the basis of approaches to the commissioner and thence to the government of the day. The new government's response to the June request was to establish a Police Board to review the case for a pay rise, and other matters. The Board supported the case and the government awarded a rise, though inevitably lower than the Association had expected.

Simultaneously the Association began to lobby government for access to the Arbitration Court. The Minister for Police was sympathetic and necessary legislation was prepared to allow the Association to register as an industrial union. In March 1926 members of the Association formally agreed to the necessary changes to enable registration. The formalities included a change of name — now the members would belong to an organisation known as the Western Australian Police Union of Workers.[8] The name change was not without controversy — the Association executive assured members that becoming a union did not mean that the police would have to support other workers on strike. The reassurance was necessary — as the meat in the sandwich in strikes such as those at the Fremantle docks in 1919 when they had read the riot act, police had mixed views on the merits of other workers' struggles.[9]

Becoming a union of workers did not guarantee satisfaction with Labor government nor with the outcomes of arbitration court decisions. But the first award to the police made under the new arrangements was substantial and appeared to vindicate the executive's advocacy of the trade union path.[10] More than other police unions in the 1920s the Western Australian body had solidly identified its future with a state in which the workers would get their entitlements, and adopted a name to suit the cause. For some police unionists there was, as there had been from the beginning, an invigorating sense of identity associated with labour politics. And they were not averse to appealing to this tradition in their struggles with the commissioner, or the government. When the police commissioner publicly attacked the arbitration court's award of a pay rise to the police in 1929, the union journal was quick to respond, calling on the Labor government to pull the commissioner into line, and appealing to its sense of 'working class solidarity' and traditional support of the labour movement.[11]

This labour movement ethos reached its apogee during the war when the Western Australian Police Union embraced Labor in government most fully, resulting in direct affiliation with the ALP. The flavour of the time is captured in the *Police News* editorial in December 1943 that asked the question 'What is a Policeman?' Prompted by a strike by police and firemen in Montreal over the issue of whether the Canadian Congress of Labour should be recognised as a bargaining agent for police and firemen, the journal argued that too often police were not considered ordinary members of society, possessing ordinary rights. Because police could not strike like other workers with the backing of the wider union movement, all their achievements were attained only through arduous struggle. Affiliation with the ALP would ensure that ' we shall lose our exclusiveness, and become one with fellow unionists, all striving for the same ends'. Unless the police union affiliated with the ALP and undertook a policy of cooperation with other unions they would continue to be seen as 'the plaything of governmental and departmental chicanery'. Moving forward with other unions economically, they would 'become cooperators with the public in their own interests'.[12] The article followed mounting pressure for affiliation with the ALP, following a motion on these lines which had come forward from the Fremantle branch, and strongly supported by the general secretary of the union. But its direction was consistent with political affairs in a state in which there was a very close link between the political and industrial wings of labour combined, as Sheridan notes, in a unique unitary structure in the ALP.[13]

With little general discussion in the union (a matter raised by a recalcitrant sergeant, whom the journal dismissed as 'an enemy of progress'), a ballot on affiliation was held in December 1943 and resulted in a vote of 390 members for and 59 against. Decisive as the mood seemed to be, the pragmatic element evident in the union journal's advocacy seemed to promise disaffiliation in the future if police found solidarity did not produce the right results. It was nevertheless a powerful signal about the potential political ramifications of police unionisation.

While the Western Australian union had gone farthest it was not quite on its own. In Tasmania the Police Association embraced Labor political hegemony in Tasmania from 1934. There was an underlay of political identity in this small state between the Labor Party and the police union leadership, expressed in numerous affirmations of union satisfaction with the government and vice-versa. Within two years of the Ogilvie Labor government's election in 1934 the premier attended the annual police picnic along with fellow ministers and the commissioner of police. Ogilvie enthused: 'this occasion was unique in as much as it was the first occasion in the British Empire that the whole of the ministry had been present at a police picnic'. Like other police unions the Tasmanian Association was constitutionally a 'non-political body'. But 'despite neutrality in matters political' the union journal could not ignore the return of the Labor Party with a greatly increased majority at the 1937 election. Its editorial went further than congratulating the government:

> we can say quite impartially that, on the record of the Labor Government, 1934–1937, a Party of such admitted strength of purpose and all-round ability of its Ministers would undoubtedly have weathered that storm of depression better than did its opponents ...[14]

The Tasmanian Association's identity with the Labor government was built less on a distinctive affinity with police and law and order issues than on the strong record of the government in welfare and state-directed economic development. As a Labor Party advertisement in the union *Journal* put it in 1946, police were 'workers' and the Labor government boasted a record of getting things done for workers and their families, things like housing and shorter working weeks, from both of which police were said to benefit.[15] The compact between police union and Labor in Tasmania was built on the intimacy of local politics and the immediacy of interests readily addressed by government.

Political contexts in some states made it less easy for other police unions to embrace Labor in government. The Victorian Association could only look with interest on an approach that was legally impossible to it, limited as it was by statute to non-political objectives. But even in Queensland, in a political climate quite as favourable to Labor as Western Australia, the police union was cautious, considering affiliation imprudent, in 1944, though considering the possibility again in 1955, and actually putting the issue to a referendum in 1957, with the motion for affiliation losing narrowly 663 votes to 691 opposed.[16] If we except the rather unique embrace of union and government in Tasmania, in the longer run the Western Australian move to formal affiliation appears an aberration — explained in part by the peculiar structure of the labour movement in WA, dominated as it was by the ALP, and without an independent trades union council until 1963.[17] Direct affiliation with a political party was hardly wise in the longer term in states likely to experience government at some point by a different political party — but the consequences of that possibility were not always evident in the early decades of Labor political hegemony in the states.

Where it was achieved, arbitration gave a distinctive legal identity to the police unions as they one by one registered with the different state industrial courts. Registration enabled the unions to lodge claims for improved wages and conditions. Yet the formalisation of union personality in this legalist way was not totally divorced from the underlying strength of unionism, its claim to represent the collective interests of a substantial body of workers. Many police unions achieved quite rapid coverage of their workforces — a vital point in sustaining their claims against their employer, the government. Yet coverage was never quite complete, and was somewhat less than this in some states, especially South Australia. The response of the police, like workers in other unions, was to look to further institutional mandate of their function. Above all this was sought from about 1920 on in a claim that government should give preference to police unionists in vital matters such as salary increases or promotions and transfers.

Preference to unionists in a range of employment matters was a standing item of the Australian labour movement policy agendas for many decades. Balnave's study of the only Australian instance of a state legislating for compulsory unionism, New South Wales in 1953, highlights the distinction between qualified and absolute preference to unionists in employment matters. In the former, weaker case, employers might be expected to give preference to a unionist over a non-unionist, other things being equal. In the second case, of absolute preference, the employer would be expected to employ only unionists. Moreover in Australia the achievement of union security through preference provisions could be achieved in one of two ways — through parliamentary legislation, as enacted in New South Wales in 1953, or through the provisions of the industrial arbitration mechanisms, as in Queensland before this and in New South Wales after 1959.[18] The New South Wales experiment, lasting only from 1953–9, was ineffectual and largely counter-productive, although some unions experienced spectacular growth in their core membership: the New South Wales Nurses Association increased its membership by 183% in one year from 1953, at a time when total New South Wales union membership expanded by only 10%.[19]

When police unions spoke of preference they were interested in a more limited range of concerns than those in the labour movement who advocated comprehensive unionisation. Preference to police unionists of course would help address the irritation of those unionists who resented the flow-on of benefits to non-unionists. Police union leaders however looked at preference above all as a way of consolidating claims and influence, and as a means of financial security. The union that could claim to speak for the whole police force was one that would have a powerful weapon in its hand. The union that could marshal significant resources was one that could combat unfair administrations, or defend police vulnerable to civil suits, disciplinary charges and other legal threats.

In the absence of comprehensive membership of the union, activists sought repeatedly in the early decades to bring moral pressure to bear on those who were not throwing their weight behind the wheel. In 1917 a threatening letter from Hugh Talty, the general secretary of the Queensland Police Union to a Brisbane sergeant who had resigned from the union warned that preference to unionists was being sought by the union — 'if same is effected, and I have no doubt it will be, it must necessarily hamper your welfare in the Service'. The letter prompted a refusal by the commissioner and minister to deal with Talty, in turn provoking a police union executive attempt to censure Talty.[20] Talty resisted censure and pursued comprehensive coverage through moral suasion in the pages of the union journal. The matter had the character of a religious cause. The first issue of the *Queensland Police Union Journal* claimed that only 19 men were not in the union, among them eight who had resigned — action was urged to bring about the 'conversion of those beyond the pale of Unionism'.[21]

Comments were frequently made at meetings and in correspondence condemning the backsliders and warning of their possible future exclusion from benefits won by the union — and on occasion sympathetic government ministers lent their moral support, criticising unfinancial members.[22] In later decades publication of names of non-unionists, or of unfinancial members, was contemplated by some in the Queensland union, but rejected in favour of the more impersonal but still targeted publication of the numbers of those who were unfinancial in particular branches.[23] The South Australian Association, also much agitated over the matter, appears to have indulged in a form of informal boycott of non-unionists. At the 1930 conference, it emerged that non-unionists were being refused a place on police cricket teams. The secretary, Constable L.B. Fenwick was frank — he would not play with, or against, men who were not Association members, adding that 'if he is not with us he is against us'. A voice from the audience proffered an alternative — 'Make them bat without pads'.[24] In 1932 it was suggested at the annual general meeting that members of the Association not associate with non-members except when on duty, and even that current non-members be prohibited from joining in the future. The anxiety over lack of coverage was by this time needless — there were only about 50 police who were not members, including all the women police, who were said to oppose arbitration, and many in the detective office who were said to be prejudiced 'against everyone but themselves'.[25]

In New South Wales preference was a persistent issue for police union advocates. The general secretary in July 1921 suggested that the executive should go into the question of preference for unionists because they had 'put their hands in their pockets and formed the Union'.[26] Appeals to solidarity were made — in 1923 the issue of preference inspired an appeal to the 'brotherhood' of police as a basis for motivating non-unionists to pull their weight.[27] Support for the possibility of preference came from a somewhat surprising quarter in 1924 — namely the Nationalist attorney-general, T R Bavin, but without result.[28] Several times in the following years the New South Wales Association would receive a sympathetic hearing from ministers in the Lang Labor government. Yet by the time Lang finally legislated in 1931 for compulsory unionism through the industrial award system, the political moment was too late and he lost office before the bill could be enacted.[29]

In Tasmania the recognition of police union membership as the basis of preference in a number of matters was a signal moment at the beginning of Labor hegemony in Tasmanian politics from 1934–1969. Within two months of attaining office, the new minister, attorney-general E J Ogilvie, announced in August 1934 a policy of 'Preference to Unionists' in the administration of promotions and transfers of police. It took some months for the implications to get through to other sections of the community — in the case of the *Launceston Examiner* the alarm bells were rung only in June 1935, when its editorial denounced the writing of this 'new page in the history of police organisation'.[30] The attorney-general was unmoved, expressing at the 13th annual conference a month later his appreciation of the Association, and complimenting the police generally 'for their support of the Government's policy for law and order'.[31] The promise was substantial, although its administrative effects were uneven — in 1941 the Association was calling on the Commissioner once again to implement preference for members of the Association.[32] Maintaining financial membership remained a problem in spite of the compact with government, a compact evident in the threatening notice of 1938 that after June 30 'the names of all unfinancial members are expected to be forwarded to the Commissioner's office', a notice highlighted in capitals with the warning 'DON'T LET YOUR NAME BE INCLUDED'.[33]

Nevertheless one demonstrable effect of the 1934 announcement was the stimulus to union membership — by March 1937 the Tasmanian Association was boasting 98% membership and in August that year the attorney-general was congratulating the body on having achieved 100% coverage. In such a context it was hardly surprising that before long a Tasmanian police commissioner had already been a president of the Association.[34] In spite of these favourable developments the preference policy appears to have been muted in application. Into the 1950s, as membership dropped to 'only 91.1%' the Tasmanian Association again focused on preference as a means of boosting full and financial membership. The weakness of preference policy unless bolstered by statute was evident when an ex-South Australian officer appointed as Tasmanian police commissioner rejected the Association's renewed call in 1953 for the policy to be implemented in promotions. Commissioner Delderfield noted that it was the 'prerogative of the Commissioner to select the person he considers most fitted by "efficiency" for these positions'.[35]

Other unions could only observe with envy the extent of the Tasmanian concession. The South Australian Police Association had languished with relatively low membership through the 1920s. Government ignored repeated calls from the Association to make preference for unionists a qualification in appointment and promotion decisions. Some succour appeared in sight in 1930 after a Labor government returned to power and a seemingly sympathetic chief secretary responded positively to the police union's case for compulsory membership of the Association.[36] But membership grew in any case over the following years, undermining the urgency of the case. By 1945 when the Association presented government and the commissioner with a long list of demands, the latter felt free to note that most police were Association members anyway — and those who weren't were more likely to be so junior that their promotion was hypothetical.[37] So too in Western Australia a new Labor administration was sympathetic in 1925 to the idea of preference for union members in promotion decisions — but coverage of the Western Australian union was already substantial so the gains of such a favour were likely to be limited.[38]

The Victorian Police Association, bruised by the struggles for survival in the early 1920s and then later, especially under Commissioner Blamey, appears to have been less focused on the preference issue. Not until 1945, in the changing political climate that brought the Labor Party back to office under John Cain, does the Association appear to have asked for preference in appointment, promotion and transfer decisions to go to financial members of the Association.[39] A nil result on that matter was probably of less import than the substantial gains won under the Cain government, in which the chief secretary and responsible minister was the former honorary solicitor for the police union, W J Slater. To the extent that preference was a matter of securing the financial viability of the union then, the government's agreement in 1946 to allowing Association dues to be deducted from pay was a vital step.[40]

As implied in the discussion above, preference was of decreasing importance to the Australian police unions. In a workforce where only one union for rank-and-file employees would be admitted, in which it was common for both sides of politics to embrace the cause of the union, and in which the work culture encouraged collective expressions of one's identity and frustrations, the membership rates were in any case very high. Financial membership was another matter — and there is little doubt that there were times when the failure to pay dues, or to come onside in support of special purpose levies, preoccupied the union administrations. The history of the preference demands are yet another instance then of the conformity of the police unions to the labour culture of which they were part. To a great extent the police unions achieved on their own behalf comprehensive coverage of their potential membership — and to that degree their capacity to become active political players was enhanced.

3.2 Political campaigns

For the most part the over-riding concerns of the unions in the first half-century of their existence were conventional industrial issues — wages, work hours, allowances, promotions, pensions. These matters could quickly spill over into the political arena, resulting in police unionists threatening political careers and the waging of an industrial war through the conventional weapons of strike and protest.

The definition of union business was nevertheless fluid enough even in these early decades to allow occasional sorties into other areas of interest, such as criminal justice policy and law reform. To appreciate the context of these developing interventions it is necessary to consider the way in which policy making took place in the policing and criminal justice domains. A conventional view would have it that the police simply act according to the powers and duties laid down in statute and common law. Yet it was clear by the 1920s that police in Australia and elsewhere were playing an active role in setting the agendas of law reform and policing policy. For the most part it might be assumed that this role would inhere in the office of a police commissioner, with direct accountability to the responsible minister. In reality, commissioners could advise ministers, and through them the government, of the necessity of legal reform and other policy matters, only on the basis of what they learned from their underlings. The evidence is clear that by the turn of the century police in Australia could be part of a policy-making process that flowed from the base of the police pyramid, i.e. from the station and district level. Thus, in

Queensland important changes in the administration of indigenous peoples had developed at the instance of serving police in North Queensland. In New South Wales the fundamental changes in the policing of street offences legislated in 1908 were significantly shaped by an iterative process involving the head of the police force and the sergeants and first constables in charge of various Sydney police stations.[41] There seems little reason to doubt that this was becoming a common means by which legal reform affecting police powers and duties was effected by the inter-war years.

What role, if any, would police unions have to play in such a process? To the extent that a quasi-union like the Victorian Police Association was explicitly prohibited from holding political affiliations or otherwise acting in a political manner it might be expected that the absence of specific prohibitions in other cases opened up the field of law reform to the police unions. The unions were nevertheless not preoccupied with such matters to any degree overshadowing their primary concerns. There are instances, and instructive ones, in which the unions became involved in pressing the case for a desirable legal change or other policy matter. In noting some of them the discussion following seeks to highlight what had already been opened up as a field of potential activity by the legitimation of the unions as bodies with most of the freedoms possessed by other institutions and associations in civil society.

The two instances in which it appears that police unions were most active in pursuing criminal justice law reform matters in the inter-war era occurred in Western Australia and Queensland. Some significance may be attached to this in that both these unions were most secure in their independent union identity. Both were also close to the ruling political party, i.e. usually Labor. But the unionising ethos of their members was perhaps most important. To the police union members of these two bodies, playing an active role in lobbying government for desirable changes came naturally.

The Western Australian Police Union was a prime mover in agitation at the end of the 1920s to reform firearms laws. Its motivation was simple — to limit the likelihood of police dying in the course of their duties. At least four police were shot dead in separate incidents in the late 1920s, two of them in circumstances that inspired construction of a memorial to the cost of which police all over Australia subscribed over £500.[42] An ancillary police interest in firearms law was the ambit of police work, in particular the police monopoly of arms.[43] The matter was first raised at the

15th Conference in 1928 when a motion urged the government to prohibit the use of weapons by unlicensed persons. A special committee of the union was appointed to the task of framing desirable amendments to the law, which were published in *The Police News* in July 1929. The government was scarcely pro-active on the issue — over a year later the union was still lobbying in demand of firearms restrictions. But by June 1931 the desired legislation had been passed, its terms representing a first successful foray of the union into public policy.[44]

The process in Western Australia was not unlike the proceedings in Queensland. Fleming has examined in some detail the development of police advice and lobbying of government for a change in a piece of legislation much more comprehensive of police work, i.e. the *Vagrants Act*. Under Queensland law, the vagrancy provisions were entailed in a nineteenth century act that empowered police to act with considerable effect against a wide range of people on the streets. But in a crucial provision regarded by police as impeding their street-cleaning work, an arrested person did not have to account for the possession of the money they had on them, and hence were able to contest a vagrancy arrest. The Queensland CIB complained that such persons included 'confidence men, card sharpers, spielers and bludgers .... with insufficient means of support still operating on the Public'.[45] The enactment over the previous three decades of deterrent legislation in other states had reportedly resulted in the migration of con men and criminals to Queensland.

As described by Fleming the police union campaign emerged from the April 1927 conference and was almost immediately followed by requests by the home secretary for police suggestions on criminal law reform. Over the succeeding five years the union input flowed especially from the CIB branch of the union — not an insignificant factor in Queensland where the district and other branches of the union appear to have been especially active. The difficulties allegedly faced by police were accentuated during a series of unsuccessful arrests in the late 1920s, leading finally to a disastrous Full Court decision against police in March 1929.[46] In this case the costs of the unsuccessful prosecution under the *Vagrants Act* went against the arresting police, whom the government refused to support. A crucial union and police objective in the achievement of successful law reform was highlighted — reducing the liability of police to a civil suit for wrongful arrest, and thereby potentially saving the union and its members money. Already in 1928 the QPU had been forced to abandon its 'Legal Defence Fund' in the wake of a series of suits against police.[47] Thereafter the union provided support through levies organised on an individual case basis — with always the danger of union branches or individual members contesting the worthiness of cases to be supported.

The lesson of the wrongful arrest cases was not lost on the union. Talking up Queensland's crime wave the union secretary Hugh Talty continued to urge government to act on the law reform suggestions that had flowed from the union branches, especially the CIB. The rancorous end of the Labor government in 1929 opened the required window of opportunity for the union. Over the following year the union pressed its case on a willing conservative government, one that showed increasing enthusiasm for legal amendments that would also facilitate police control of the restless and resistant unemployed and their political allies. By late 1930 the home secretary was forwarding drafts of the bill to the union for their comments. Not everything went the union's way in the processing of the bill through parliament — enhanced police powers of arrest and investigation were allowed through by the Labor opposition only on the concession of penal clauses directed at police using intimidatory tactics during questioning.[48]

The Queensland case is a striking early instance of the powers of a police union to play both sides of the political fence in pursuit of the main game, in this case enhancing police powers, or more exactly extending their legal immunities, which had been shown to be too limited for police liking in the 'wrongful arrest' cases. The activism of the CIB branch of the union drives home the moral of the tale — policy making in this jurisdiction at least was not something to be fashioned outside of the police department, but inside through a two-fold pressure. The success of the police union in building on the popular media's images of a Queensland under threat from southern criminals, forced out of their states and New Zealand by tougher vagrancy legislation was strikingly similar to stories familiar from later decades. The solicitous approach of governments in dealing with the union's representations was a final but very familiar feature. At the same time we must recall that the achievement of this legislation took a number of years, and that for the most part it repeated what had been enacted in other states already. For both reasons the story of the QPU's role in vagrancy law reform between 1927–1931 is also instructive on the limits of union power.

These two cases of significant involvement of police unions in law-making do not exhaust the modes of police union intervention in the policing and criminal justice domain by the time of the Depression. As the unions grew in confidence we find that they ventured occasionally onto other ground. An instance reported in the eastern press as well as in Western Australia was the 1928 objections of the police union to the release of prisoners sentenced under the habitual criminal provisions of the WA code. In this case the union was prompted by the murder of a policeman by a released prisoner. Such interventions were not likely to be decisive in shaping institutional practice — but they did signify the ambit of union concerns.[49] Sentencing policy and practice was certainly an easy target for police union protest — as when the New South Wales union contested lenient sentences given by magistrates in Broken Hill in 'assault police' cases in the mid-twenties.[50]

While such protests were directed at the practices of another criminal justice agency, there were also areas of police operational concern that frequently made their way into the media through police union publicity. In a case bearing on the commissioner's prerogatives in administration of resources, the New South Wales Police Association successfully opposed a 1925 decision to limit the issue of handcuffs. Attempts by the commissioner in this case to curb the outspoken union secretary who had gone to the press over the matter were counter-productive, at a time when the Labor government was making conciliatory gestures towards the union.[51] In the more fractious years of the Depression the union's protests against the uses by the police department of 'spooks' to monitor misconduct of uniformed police (e.g. non-payment of fares by police travelling on public transport) recalled an issue that had sparked the Victorian police strike.[52] A more public and contentious matter epitomised the era. With clashes between the police and unemployed leading to numerous assault cases in the lower courts, the Association decided to mount its own publicity campaign over the issue of lenient sentencing in such cases. Noting that some 'firebrands' were likely to take advantage of the government's tightening of the dole relief, discussion at the executive meeting of the Association contemplated 'that a little publicity in the press of the intention of the Association to seek heavier penalties would have a restraining influence on mobs controlled by disgruntled persons'.[53] Cosgrove, the general secretary, wrote to the newspapers, and a month later a self-satisfied item in the union journal noted that magistrates have 'lately taken a serious view of assaults on the Police, and the "sport" of kicking members of the Force should become less popular.' The journal claimed that Mr Cosgrove's letter protesting the inadequacy of punishment was already 'bearing good fruit'.[54]

Regardless of the verity of such a claim it is striking that within a decade or so of their founding the readiness of police unions to enter the public fray was already well developed. The press listened, and so too did government. While the public policy and general policing concerns of the unions remained subordinate to the primary matters of industrial rights, and wage bargaining, the standard tactics of political lobbyists were already well known, and the objects of possible influence ranged from internal matters of police administration through penal policies and sentencing discretions to the shaping of laws that governed police duties and powers.

3.3 Wages and conditions

The impact of unionisation in effecting positive gains in wages and other working conditions is a long-debated issue in industrial relations and labour history. Hypothetically, it seems unlikely that unions could ever effect unmitigated improvements that were substantially beyond what the economic state of the country allows and, in the public sector, what the government might raise revenue to cover. Moreover there is international comparative evidence that institutions like arbitration have had limited impact in achieving wage and conditions outcomes substantially different from those in non-centralised systems.

Regardless of these global comparisons it might yet be the case that there are marginal gains to be effected through the relative influence and effectiveness of a labour union. In considering what the police unions achieved in their first few decades we need to look therefore at what were simply relative shifts, or else the result of resistance to change, in wages and conditions that were sought by the employer, i.e. the government.

While wages and conditions outcomes might be seen as the purely industrial business of the police unions, it becomes clear on historical investigation that these have a distinctly political dimension. Already in the inter-war period it was becoming clear to governments in Australia that the extent of police grievance had the potential to undermine confidence in a government, or more seriously, threaten one of its fundamental structural foundations — or at least that was how police unions would represent the case, and politicians enough be found ready to agree with them. So we find that in times of civil quiet the police unions argue for improved wages not only on the grounds of wage justice, but of the effectiveness of police in keeping society in order; while in more disturbed times, the case would be made that police work was so necessary to controlling dissent and dealing with disorder and crime that police should be correspondingly rewarded, or protected from the rigours of the wages market.

The success of police unions measured by wages outcomes might be assessed in a number of ways — and in fact their determination was always subject to an equal variety of factors. Those unions that had entered the arbitration arena necessarily opened up the possibility of their member's work being subject to the same criteria as applied in some comparative industries. Just what those comparators should be was a moot point, and subject to extended debate by legal counsel for the unions and the government or department. The danger to the unions of being considered as just one part of the public sector was especially highlighted when pay cuts came onto the agenda during the Great Depression. Indeed in the case mounted by the South Australian Police Association against a pay cut in 1931–2 can be found many of the arguments about the distinctiveness of police work, and its political and social functionality.

Against the background of a deepening economic depression, a special conference of the Association was held in December 1930 to consider the issue of a reduction in pay. Speaking for government, the chief secretary drew attention to the reductions already in place for teachers, public servants and in the basic wage. Association executive members made conciliatory noises, but rank and file members were predictably opposed. A mounted policeman pressed the point that 'with all the industrial trouble and ever-increasing army of unemployed, it is necessary that the Police Force be maintained at a very high standard'. Others observed that Port Adelaide was 'the hot point of unemployment' which needed a police force 'that can combat it', and that in the 'troublesome time ahead for policeman … they will need all the loyalty they can muster to carry them through'.[55] The meeting's opposition to a reduction in pay was predictable but when the first proposed pay cut came in January 1931 it was only 10%, less than had been applied to the teachers and others.

Regardless of the comparative picture a large meeting of 190 police met on 4 February to protest the reduction, most of them doubtless agreeing with a constable that 'The Police Force cannot be classed with any other body of men, because nowhere has the danger to life and limb increased like it has with us'.[56]

An unsympathetic chief secretary nevertheless received a protest deputation which argued for a lesser cut, especially as it had been reported that the minister had stated that if the police had volunteered a 5% pay cut, the government would have accepted it.[57] Accusations surfaced from within government to the effect that the Police Association was seeking to play 'Communistic go-slow tactics' in warning that police efficiency would decline. Worse was to come. The national Premiers' Plan proposed a 20% cut in government salaries, pensions and allowances in 1931–2. Attempts by some executive members to have this cut apply first to police allowances proved highly divisive when it was shown that nearly half the force was on special allowances. Within the year the Association was served with a log from the public service commissioner seeking a reduction in pay. The Association sought to counter the log by offering to negotiate a further 5% cut on top of the existing 10%, but without success.

The case heard under arbitration was for a further pay cut to bring the total to 20% since June 1930, and in line with that applied to teachers and public servants. The Association engaged experienced senior counsel, Herbert Mayo KC, to argue that police wages since the first determination in 1918 had little relation to the notion of the living wage applied in other sectors. The distinctiveness of police work made it a special case — the difficulty in getting into the police force, police efficiency, the need to bolster policemen's 'moral resistance', their need to be respectable and well dressed at all times, the assaults they suffered, the threats to police in depression time, the limited opportunities for friendship. The initial outcome was favourable — the president of the court rejected the government's first ground for reduction, on the basis that police wages had not previously been set in relation to public service salaries. He left open the possibility of a decision on the basis of fixing police pay in relation to the living wage, given the possibility that deflation had much improved the police position.[58]

A further hearing in May 1932 resulted in a final judgment delivered in June. The president of the court disappointed the government by awarding a lesser reduction than the claim — and worked within industrial arbitration parameters in his justification. Significantly he conceded much of the Association case about the distinctiveness of police employment, while refuting the claim that the depression had made police work more arduous and dangerous. The pay of a constable should put him and his family on a comparable basis to 'the skilled tradesman in regular employment', place him above embarrassment in the community, and enable him to withstand temptation. The president's legalism justified his ignoring evidence of New South Wales and Victorian police witnesses because those states did not have police wages 'fixed by any tribunal operating within the field of industrial jurisprudence'.[59]

In spite of Mayo's stratagem to emphasise the threat posed by the disorder of the times, the outcome of this case was determined more by arbitral formalism. Yet the capacity of the Association to sustain an expensive defence, involving top legal counsel and bringing in police witnesses from other states was telling. Boasting of the achievement in limiting the size of the reduction secretary Fenwick cited the police commissioner Brigadier Leane to the effect that without the Association the cut would have been greater.[60] In spite of the Association's desire to distinguish police from other workers in respect of the standards that should apply in times of hardship, the experience of 1931–2 also drove it towards stronger alliances with the union cause in opposition to the Premiers' Plan and in favour of recouping the losses of the previous years. And Fenwick himself unsuccessfully contested the state election as a Labor candidate the following year, seeking to carry the fight into parliament.[61]

The Depression wage cuts were a major issue in other states. A legislated reduction in the basic wage in Western Australia in 1931 was followed by police union moves to exempt their members on the basis of the special position of the police. That special position had been brought home by controversial policing of unemployed protests in Perth in March 1931, an incident quickly known as the 'Treasury riot'.[62] Further cuts to the government budget including the police department were foreshadowed in the legislation introduced some months later, leading to what was described as the 'largest ever' gathering of police union members. Adopting the language of the labour movement, the union journal claimed the government's bill had only one object, 'to enforce the demands of present day economics compulsorily on those who are unable to defend themselves ...'[63] By February 1932 the *Police News* was warning the government that the gloves were off over the Premiers' Plan impact on police pay and benefits, robbing 'the members of the Force of all they have laboured for years to attain'.[64] Like other wage earners the Western Australian police would nevertheless have to wait for some years for restoration of pre-Depression wage levels. No different was the case of Victoria where the cuts had come earlier and the Association deputised the Labor chief secretary in October 1930 over what was represented as a 'double cut', with allowances being eliminated as well as a percentage wage cut in line with the public service. The Association was not in a position to mount an effective protest however, being in the throes of a dispute with Blamey over its future.[65]

The limits of what a labour union might achieve in the dire conditions of economic depression are best illustrated however through the attempts of the New South Wales Police Association to hold back the tide of wage reductions. Indeed the New South Wales case also affords an opportunity to reflect on the wider political context of police union activity in the inter-war years. The political climate in New South Wales was especially fractious during the depression. At the level of formal politics this was the state with the most combative and radical of Australian governments — at least on economic policy — in the shape of the Lang Labor government. Lang's resistance to the Premiers' Plan, and his rhetorical war against international finance capital prepared for one of the most confrontationist events in Australian constitutional history, when Lang was sacked by the state governor, Sir Phillip Game. Equally contentious was the role of the extra-parliamentary private army known as the New Guard, an outfit that inspired the ire of Police Association members over its attempts to usurp the functions of the police. When the New Guard's Captain de Groot upstaged the official opening of the Harbour Bridge Police Association secretary Charles Cosgrove remarked that in countries he had been in 'if a man attempted to do such a thing he would have probably earned the additional honour of being the first to go over the Bridge'.[66] In these kinds of circumstances it is scarcely surprising to find a complex and difficult relationship over the issue of police pay and its determinants.

Throughout Australia police unions stressed during the depression that police work was different from other work, that police served a central order maintenance function for the state, and therefore they should be exempt from the reductions being applied in other areas. Initially the New South Wales Association had some success in this endeavour. With the assistance of the commissioner they avoided the first 8.33% reduction under the 1930 wages cuts,[67] but only by agreeing to revert to a 48-hour working week. This sign of their commitment to the defence of social order was repeatedly urged on government over the depression years. Police work was held to involve not only more hours, but to be inherently dangerous, and often conducted under poor conditions. At annual conferences and in deputations to the chief secretary, Association officials urged the government to protect police pay, and to carry the argument for police exceptionality into the public arena where necessary. This continued to be the case regardless of the political complexion of government, which changed during the three years 1930–2 from non-Labor to Labor and back again.

The first minister to feel the heat of the Association was the new Nationalist government's chief secretary Captain Chaffey at the 1930 annual conference. Having cautioned the delegates that party politics should not be allowed to creep into the police, he reminded them that they had already been exempted from the first Depression pay cut, at a cost of £20,000. Concerned with the prospect of further cuts to come, the general secretary of the Association in turn reminded the delegates that police are

> absolutely different to other Government servants ... You men must take into consideration what you have done for Government and the manner in which some of you have been working under very serious conditions up on the coalfields, living like blackfellows, doing just what you were told, and often getting no overtime.

He also urged officers not to strike, a proposition which 'a pressman suggested last night to me ... I want you to remember that you are men of good character and are selected from the best in the State and that you are getting a very poor run from the Government'.

The New South Wales Association had already been described by some as a Bolshevik union, and the veiled threats intimated in Fortescue's address as Association secretary were continued by other speakers. One police unionist warned of the consequences for the law of the land if police confidence in the chief secretary was destroyed while another warmed to the theme of political action: 'I say this, when our destinies are shaped politically we must think politically'. Yet another moved that the Association should see the premier, and if not satisfied that police pay and conditions were not going to be cut, then the leader of the opposition might be approached. Emboldened by the rhetoric of the delegates Fortescue provoked the government by going to the press and challenging the minister to go public on the government's intentions regarding possible wage cuts for police. Chaffey confronted Fortescue with his disappointment at this criticism of the government but promised nevertheless to use his influence in cabinet to resist a reduction, while warning that police might have to increase their hours to 48 a week.[68]

Against this background of increasing hostility, it is not surprising to find that on a change of government, the initial deputation of the Association to the new minister in Lang's Labor government, Mark Gosling, could be characterised by the Association as 'the best reception they ever had'. Again politics was to disappoint the union, this time with a vengeance. With the economic situation almost beyond Lang's control the government was concerned to ensure the loyalty of police, and Gosling told an Ex-Officers Dinner in April 1931 that he was 'satisfied ... that Police would loyally serve every Government irrespective of politics', and that he had already done much to stop further reductions in pay. The prominent role of police in controlling political and unemployed protests, and managing evictions, encouraged the development of a 'Police are the buffers' mentality, and continuing insistence by the union on the necessity to guarantee pay levels. Yet, by the end of the year, union threats notwithstanding, the police too had been included in the government's salaries reduction legislation and the *Police News* was left only to berate those who had 'bitterly disappointed' the men and the general sense of public 'ingratitude'.[69]

At the annual conference a few months later, Gosling commiserated on the loss of pay but appealed for police loyalty in trying times.

> No one knows better than the members of the Police Force, the poverty, misery and distress that is in our midst. For that reason I believe and hope that no recommendation of an embarrassing nature will emanate from your Conference to the Government at the present juncture.

There was some compensation in the form of an extra day's pay for the police who had served so well at the opening of the Harbour Bridge, a reiterated commitment to arbitration (the legislation was being held up in the Legislative Council at this time) and an exhortation to stay loyal given the threats around them, with Gosling stressing that 'the Government will not in any circumstances allow anyone to usurp the functions of the Police'.[70] It was a theme, after all the huff and puff over the pay issue, to which the Association might still warm. For as an editorial two months later on 'Police the Buffer' urged:

> As individuals they may be as emphatic in politics or religion as anybody, but when they put on their uniform and undertake a task that so many flinch from because of its personal danger, they cease to be individualistic and become unbiased and non-partisan servants.[71]

We have already seen much evidence that such a view was under challenge by this time. But could the challenge be translated into political action? The answer was yes and by 1930 some had already attempted that translation.

3.4 The developing political role

The consideration of wages struggles during the Great Depression has already suggested some dimensions of police union politics by the early 1930s. But the shape of police union political influence had already been forged in the context of the 1920s aspirations of the unions to institutional reform that would benefit the police. In spite of formal constraints on political activity entailed in the rules of the Associations, the artificiality of these constraints was effectively subverted on numerous occasions by the subtle pressures which police unions could bring to bear on government ministers. As we have seen the unions quickly achieved a legitimacy for their activities, to which the recurrent ministerial attendance at annual conferences bore witness. Nothing is as striking a sign of this as the rhetorical endorsements of the unions that flowed from ministerial lips on such occasions. Of course rhetoric was not always matched by action — and the limited success of the police unions in staving off wage reductions during the Depression has demonstrated for us the burden of this message.

How was political activity understood by the unions during this period and how did they address the formal exclusions that typically operated in their rules of association? The question can be approached through uncovering specific instances in which the rights of political participation were addressed, and through the engagement of the unions in particular kinds of political activities. The former matter was specifically considered by the *New South Wales Police News* in 1926 as it reflected on the political freedoms allowed to the Association. Under a banner headline 'Politics Concern Police, No Discussions Permitted, Be Watchful', the *News* noted that while the rules of the Association prohibited debate in conference or at branch meetings on political subjects,

> the doings of Governments are matters that directly concern every member of the Police Force, in as much as the Police give their allegiance to whatever Government is in power and expect to better their conditions through that allegiance.

This was an extraordinary statement of intent — tying the relation of police and government to an expectation that police would 'better their conditions' through allegiance to a government. The unsaid but barely disguised inference, one that all governments feared during the years in which police unions sought legitimacy, was that the allegiance of a police force was contingent and conditional, not fixed and constitutional. 'We have every right', so the *News* put it, 'to advise our members to study the utterances of members of Parliament'. The context of the comments was that the political situation had become 'acutely interesting' as the government had declared its intention of giving police access to arbitration as well as amending the superannuation act. But it had not fulfilled its promise to increase the number of commissioned officers. Having identified the agenda of issues on which police unionists should note the 'utterances' of politicians, the *News* observed that the Association did not intend to advise members except to say that 'in the hurly-burly of politics they must be ever on the alert to prevent any improvements gained by the Police Association being taken away from them.' In case the message was not getting through, the *News* concluded that when legislation concerning police comes before parliament members should get in touch with local members and establish their position in 'quiet conversations'.[72]

The perspective delivered in this frank account of the politics of police influence is more subtle than might appear. Behind the advice to see what might be achieved through 'quiet conversations' lies an understanding of how policy might be influenced, even by those who still laboured under the feeling that the police were somewhat other than full citizens. What characterised the achievement of the police unions from the 1920s was an incremental process of building legitimacy. Its signs were the positive noises made by police ministers at annual conferences. Its mechanisms were the conversations of police with those of influence in local communities, including not only politicians but all those other leaders of civic life who had occasion to know and appraise police work — the local councillors, small business people, churchmen, school teachers and the like, those who might be found joining the gatherings of tribute to a local long-serving policeman as he moved on from one station to another.[73] Knowing intimately the local community one policed was a mandate given to police officers in their formal instructions. It was also a means by which the desires of police to better their conditions might become known and recognised as desirable. In this respect another sign of the legitimacy of the unions was the success of some of the unions in obtaining for the union journal advertising revenue from local businesses throughout their jurisdictions. In a decentralised state like Queensland this appears to be particularly the case as the volume of small town business advertising in the union journal attests, over many decades.

This is not to say that the police unions had already by the late 1920s achieved a profound and immeasurable influence. Indeed this was far from the case — and as with any form of politics in relatively open states there were counter-balancing forces to contend with, and even tactical mistakes to make. One such was made just a few months after the publication of the article we have just discussed, when the New South Wales Association went over the head of the responsible minister, the chief secretary, Mark Gosling, to approach the premier, Jack Lang, for an increase in pay. At the subsequent annual conference Gosling made no secret of his displeasure at having been by-passed — and tensions between him and the union remained for some time.[74]

It is also clear in the 1920s that while the unions had made considerable gains, things did not always go their way. In South Australia the Police Association was doing more than engage in quiet conversations in the lead-up to at least two state election campaigns. Reports in the press in March 1927 highlighted police agitation over the state of the force, which had been discredited by hearings of a royal commission into allegations of bribery, and was already smarting from what were resented as inadequate pay rises in 1926. A beat-up by *Truth* headlined reports of the grievances with the banner 'Cops' Strike Threat', but the substance of the discontent was also reported more soberly by other Adelaide papers — some police were talking of repeating their mass resignation tactic of 1918 over issues including split-shifts, alternate Sundays off (South

Australia was the only state not to have adopted this) and overbearing supervision by commanding officers. Commissioner Leane commented to the chief secretary that 'similar threats were made just prior to the last Elections'. Strikes were certainly spoken of, but viewed by others as a mistake, as argued by one constable:

> the association had always adhered to constitutional methods. They were on the eve of another election, and would probably again be the "political rags" to be torn to pieces and then get nothing for it. The association had been accused of Bolshevism, but the only Bolshevisim it possessed had been created by the manner in which it had been treated by the authorities.

He wanted a royal commission.[75] The police did not get a commission, but shortly after the Association filed its first plaint with the industrial court, resulting in amendments to leave conditions though not in an increase in pay.[76]

Leane's intimation that union threats needed to be seen in the context of pending parliamentary elections suggests how far the police unions had progressed in thinking strategically about the interplay of industrial conditions and political climate. The contingency of the two had been publicly identified by the New South Wales union some years before. In January 1923, in the wake of a frustrating two years when appeals for better pay, and an appeals board, had come to nothing, the general secretary of the New South Wales Association summed up his mood under the headline 'Police determined triflers will be dealt with'. The 'triflers' were not petty criminals, but the politicians who were failing to fulfil the hopes placed in them. Police were being juggled by politicians 'as pawns in the game of life'. The politicians 'must be taught that they cannot trifle with an important section of the Public Service like the Police, and that if they make promises they must fulfil them'.[77]

Soon after this warning from the union, the chief secretary defensively told the press that the appeals bill had not been abandoned and went into public debate with the Association's general secretary. Keeping up the pressure, the union journal followed with a 'wake up' call for both individual and collective action. Every member of the service was urged to use their 'personal pull with every member of Parliament' to ensure that the Government will 'cease to treat it as the Cinderella of public services'.[78] Regular pressure from the Association appears to have had a significant impact on the government, which steered through parliament the desired appeals bill in early 1924. Described as the 'crowning achievement' of the Association's year, the achievement of establishing the appeals board also represented the most substantial political engagement of the police union to that point in time. In the course of the struggle Association executive members had addressed the ALP state conferences, but were not invited to address the conferences of the conservative parties, which also opposed the government's legislation.[79] Political moderation of the union, or some would say timidity, was at the same time signalled by the executive's refusal to a formal hearing of a Victorian police strike committee member in November 1923 — ostensibly because, as an executive member put it, their immediate concern was that they did not want to 'jeopardise the Appeals Bill'.[80]

In Victoria especially the embittering 1923 strike left an abiding dissatisfaction, the government continuing throughout the 1920s to drag its feet on some of the issues that had unsettled many in the Victorian force earlier. The possibility that the 'quiet conversations' advised by the New South Wales Association in 1926 might develop into other forms of political pressure lurks around reports of Victorian Police Association meetings during the later years of the decade. The ill wind of the economic depression brought other troubles in 1929. Victoria, that most unlikely of Labor states, elected a Labor government in December 1929. It was cheered on its way by a Police Association that had made explicit its wishes for a political solution to the grievances of its members.

The Victorian Association had been alert to the potential of political lobbying as early as 1920, when it enlisted the aid of a parliamentary representative, Mr Carter.[81] During these years in fact the Association demonstrated its independence through continuing success in meeting the minister without the commissioner present. In 1921 the Association sought the aid of police in securing votes for a favoured Nationalist Party politician, Mr Farthing, who was supportive on pensions and whose seat included the Russell Street police depot.[82] The formal legal restrictions on the political activities of police were however substantial. In 1920 the Association sought and obtained from the premier a clarification of police political rights, after the publication in the *Police Gazette* of a memorandum drawing attention to section 4 of the 1906 Constitution Act, which prohibited political activity of police and public servants. The *Gazette*, reported the premier's office, was in fact in error since an amendment of

1916 had altered the position. The formal situation was therefore that public servants (including police) were entitled to take the chair and deliver speeches at any political meeting, ask questions of any candidate for parliamentary election, join any political organisation and generally be entitled to the same privileges as any ordinary citizen. The restrictions were limited to sitting and voting as a member of parliament, criticising the police or any other department, and misusing any official information that should come to a policeman's knowledge.[83]

This advice turned out to be itself a misreading, since it ignored the provisions of the *Police Regulation Act* which, the crown solicitor advised, specified the conditions of police appointment as distinct from public servants. That statute expressly prohibited the police from engaging in political activity. And twice in the 1920s, by governments of non-Labor and Labor persuasion, that limitation of the rights of police was affirmed. Neither were these merely symbolic clauses, especially after Blamey became commissioner. In October 1929 the matter came to a head as the Association contemplated a political campaign in the forthcoming election to oppose promotion changes sought by the commissioner, emphasising merit over seniority. In the November issue of the Association's journal the secretary (not a police officer himself) included material related to an intended campaign to lobby all candidates in the coming Victorian state election. Blamey immediately called in the president and read him a memorandum concerning the illegality of police engaging in political actions. Pre-empting advice from the president that the secretary had been acting independently without the knowledge of the executive, Blamey then quoted the *Masters and Servant Act* to the effect that ignorance of the employer (in this case the Association executive) would not absolve it from responsibility for the secretary's action.

Faced with Blamey's hostility, and following independent legal advice from lawyer Maurice Blackburn, the Association backed down from its proposed election campaign. Yet the degree to which a strong line of political advocacy was already in the late 1920s on the police union agenda was evident in the detailed exposition to members of what had derailed the lobbying campaign:

> Members ... will see by copies of official correspondence produced in this issue that the Association has not the right to do what was originally intended — namely, endeavor to find out definitely, by

> circular letter, just what candidates were prepared to do by way of assisting us if they were elected as members of the Legislative Assembly at the forthcoming election. ... [O]ne is not anxious to jeopardise, departmentally, the interests or careers of individual members of either the Executive or of the Council, and for that reason and that reason only prospective Members of Parliament have not been circularised as intended.[84]

The Association's backdown did not save it from Blamey's ire. In circumstances we will examine in the next chapter, in spite of the subsequent election of a Labor government, the chief commissioner a year later succeeded in dismantling the Police Association and replacing it with a new, more compliant organisation most closely modelled on the Police Federation in England.[85] Even Labor in government in Victoria could not bring itself to alter the constraints on political activity that were considered necessary to guarantee an independent and reliable police force. In spite of strong advocacy from some sympathetic Labor members, the new government's Police Pensions Bill included a provision prohibiting police membership of political organisations, the definition of which was left to the chief secretary.[86]

The Victorian election story was in some ways the epitome of the political rhetoric of the 1920s police union leaders. Throughout the decade police had been advised by their union activists to remember the power of the ballot. Rhetorical as these postures might appear from time to time, their potential could not be so readily dismissed by the politicians before whom they were paraded. Industrial conditions remained the dominant interest of the police unions — but political realities dictated their growing awareness of the possibilities of both 'quiet conversations' and of electoral interventions, where they could be managed. The Victorian Association had stretched the political possibilities beyond caution, and lost, just as the strikers had done a few years before. Even in friendlier political climes in the Labor states unions still had to exercise circumspection in their activities. In the following decades these lessons would have to be re-learned.

Notes

1 *QPJ*, Oct 1917, p15.
2 QSA, A/36820, Circular 1318M (22 Apr 1918). The agreement was published in the Queensland Government Gazette, 17 Apr 1918, no 135.
3 *SAPJ*, Nov 1924, p2; Dec 1924, pp2–7; Jan 1925, pp1–3.
4 *TPJ*, Sep 1951, p13.
5 *Northern Territory Police News (NTPN)*, Dec 1979, p3; and see Bruce Swanton, "Police Association of the Northern Territory" *NTPN*, Sep 1981, pp20–23.
6 Brien, *Serving the Force: 75 Years of the Police Association of New South Wales*, 28, 32.
7 *WAPN*, Oct 1921, p9.
8 *WAPN*, Feb 1926, p17, Mar 1926, pp4–8.
9 *WAPN*, Jun 1919, pp3–4.
10 *WAPN*, Nov 1928.
11 *WAPN*, Jul 1929, p1.
12 *WAPN*, Dec 1943, pp1–3.
13 Tom Sheridan, *Division of labour: industrial relations in the Chifley years, 1945–49* (Melbourne, 1989), 71.
14 *TPJ*, Mar 1937, p4.
15 *TPJ*, Sep 1946, p8; Dec 1941, p5.
16 *VPJ*, Vol 13, No 5, 1 May 1944, p1214; Irene Moyle, "Union History 1915–1957 (3 parts)," (manuscript held by Queensland Police Union of Employees) Pt 3, pp34, 39 citing QPU Minutes, 13 Sep 1955, p3, 7 Mar 1957, p34.
17 Sheridan, *Division of labour: industrial relations in the Chifley years, 1945–49*, 74.
18 Nikola Balnave, "Legislating for compulsory unionism: the New South Wales experience," *Labour History* (1997).
19 Mary Dickenson, *An unsentimental union: The NSW Nurses' Association, 1931-1992*. (Sydney, 1993), 137–138.
20 Queensland Police Union of Employees (QPUE), Executive Minutes, 23 Jul 1917 (held at QPUE).
21 *QPJ*, Jul 1917, p11.
22 E.g. 1941 Police Association of Tasmania (PAT) Conference, see *TPJ*, Aug 1968, p12.
23 E.g. *QPJ*, Jan 1942, p45.
24 *SAPJ*, Dec 1930, pp3–19.
25 *SAPJ*, Nov 1932, pp1–5.
26 *NSWPN*, 7 Jul 1921.
27 *NSWPN*, 7 Mar 1923, p12.
28 *SAPJ*, Oct 1924, p18, reprinting Bavin's comments from the NSW Police News.
29 Dickenson, *An unsentimental union: The NSW Nurses' Association, 1931–1992*, 39–40.
30 *TPJ*, Jun 1935, p1 citing *Launceston Examiner*, 12 Jun 1935.
31 *TPJ*, Aug 1935, p4.
32 *TPJ*, Aug 1968, p12.
33 *TPJ*, Jun 1938, p5.

34 *TPJ*, Mar 1937, p4; Oct 1937, p4. Supt H Hill, then President of the PAT, was appointed Commissioner in May 1944, *TPJ*, Jun 1944, p3.
35 *TPJ*, Feb 1953, pp1–8.
36 *SAPJ*, Jul 1930, pp15–19; Dec 1930, pp3–19.
37 *SAPJ*, Jan 1945, pp1–3.
38 *WAPN*, Aug 1925, pp1–5.
39 *VPJ*, Jan 1946, p1534.
40 *VPJ*, May 1946, p1597.
41 See Noel Loos, *Invasion and Resistance: Aboriginal-European relations on the North Queensland frontier 1861–1897* (Canberra, 1982); Finnane, *Police and government: histories of policing in Australia*, 34–36.
42 *WAPN*, Dec 1929, pp5–8.
43 *WAPN*, Feb 1963.
44 *WAPN*, May 1929, p57; Jul 1929, pp28–33; Sept 1930, p1; Jun 1931, p1.
45 Jenny Fleming, "Power and Persuasion: Police Unionism and Law Reform in Queensland," *Queensland Review* 4 (1997): 63.
46 McCulloch v Eolkin, ex parte Eolkin, *State Reports Queensland*, 1929, 113; *Courier Mail*, 21 Mar 1929, p16.
47 Fleming, "Power and Persuasion: Police Unionism and Law Reform in Queensland," 63, 66, 69.
48 Ibid, pp68–69.
49 *WAPN*, Mar 1928, p3.
50 *NSWPN*, Jan 1925, p16.
51 *NSWPN*, May 1926.
52 *NSWPN*, Jun 1931, p30.
53 *NSWPN*, Dec 1932, p26.
54 *NSWPN*, Jan 1933, p17.
55 *SAPJ*, Jan 1931, pp3–21.
56 *SAPJ*, Feb 1931, p90.
57 *SAPJ*, Mar 1931, pp1–3.
58 *SAPJ*, Apr 1932, pp1–13.
59 *SAPJ*, Oct 1932 pp7–30 (Police Officers Case 1931 no 57).
60 *SAPJ*, Jul 1932, pp1–5.
61 See especially *SAPJ*, Mar 1933, pp21–24.
62 *WAPN*, Mar 1931, pp1–2; see Sandra Wilson, "Police perceptions of protest: the Perth "Treasury Riot" of March 1931," *Labour History* (May, 1987).
63 *WAPN*, Jul 1931, pp1–8.
64 *WAPN*, Feb 1932, p1.
65 *VPJ*, Sep 1931, p7.
66 *NSWPN*, Apr 1932, p15; on the role of police in the incident itself see Keith Amos, *The New Guard movement 1931–1935* (Carlton, 1976), 79–87.
67 *NSWPN*, May 1931, pp11ff for credit claimed by the commissioner.
68 *NSWPN*, Jun 1930, pp6, 9, 24, 28.
69 *NSWPN*, Apr 1931, p28; Jan 1932, p1.
70 *NSWPN*, Apr 1932, pp4ff.
71 *NSWPN*, Jun 1932, p1.
72 *NSWPN*, Dec 1926, p12.

73 E.g. a farewell to a constable after only four years service at Beenleigh station, south of Brisbane, addressed by at least 14 speakers including the local mayor and businessmen, *QPJ*, Jul 1944, pp32–37.
74 *NSWPN*, Sep 1927, p15.
75 *The Advertiser*, 12 Mar 1927, cutting in SASR, GRG 5/2/573/1924.
76 See *SAPJ*, Apr to Dec 1927 for progress of the hearing and its outcome.
77 *NSWPN*, Jan 1923.
78 *NSWPN*, Feb 1923, p21.
79 Brien, *Serving the Force: 75 Years of the Police Association of New South Wales*, 28–29.
80 *NSWPN*, Jan 1924, p20.
81 Brown and Haldane, *Days of Violence: The 1923 police strike in Melbourne.*
82 Sadler, "Sir John Gellibrand and the Victoria Police: a short, unhappy association," 65.
83 *VPJ*, Sep 1920, p15.
84 *VPJ*, Dec 1929, p183 — this suggests, *contra* Haldane, 1986, pp203–204, formal lobbying did not take place.
85 Haldane, *The people's force: a history of the Victoria Police*, 205–208.
86 *VPJ*, Dec 1929, pp189–190.

4: Industrial battlefields

The Labor regime has been marked, too, by the increased boldness of the Victorian Police Association in seeking to interfere with the Chief Commissioner's control of the force. This organisation has not scrupled to attempt to exercise political influence, even to the point of direct disobedience of the law.
The Argus, 16 July 1930

It had been argued earlier that far from epitomising the radicalism of the police union movement, the Victorian police strike was a symptom of its conformism. Rather than the way forward in police industrial relations, the strike was a dead-end. Nothing shows this more conclusively than seeing the Victorian action and its aftermath in international, and national, context. In brief, we have seen that strikes had a powerful effect in mobilising the resistance of police authorities, governments and commissioners, to the role of unions, retarding their influence for some decades in many jurisdictions. Even the constraints on Victorian police seem to emphasise the advances made by Australian police unionists — for across the Tasman, New Zealand police struggled for recognition against both commissioner and government until consent in August 1936 following the election of the Fraser Labour government the year before.[1] In contrast, those Australian unions that were able early to establish their legitimacy in the favourable context of Labor political hegemony were generally stronger and more assertive in their relations with government and more successful in their achievements in the 1920s.

Or so it seemed. The early glow of success was by 1930 more likely than not to be showing signs of tarnish. And the spirit of concession to the legitimate rights of police to unionise was giving way to a grudging and even hostile approach on the part of commissioners to their relations with the unions. In this chapter we examine some critical features of the changing relations between commissioners and the unions during the inter-war years, especially during the 1930s, and the war years. In this period, I suggest, the longer-term effects of the establishment of police unions became evident. Or it might be more accurate to say that what happened during these years shifted the balance in police administration away from the commissioner's quasi-military authority towards a relationship that was based in a greater acknowledgment of the independent status of the police officer as an employee. That constraint was affirmed by legal authority and by political settlement, i.e. by political recognition that police union opinion was worthy of note and should be taken into account by governments in dealing with policing matters, including internal administration.

Two important factors helped shape the events of these years, and the degree of conflict between commissioners and unions. Having lost the battle against recognition of unions, commissioners were prepared initially to make the best of the new world. By the late 1920s however it was becoming clear that police unions were very ready to take their concerns and complaints beyond the formal avenues of dealing with the commissioner or through the arbitration court. Unions in some places obtained the ear of the responsible minister in ways that could undermine the authority of the commissioner, an anxiety that long pre-dated the unions and had been the basis of commissioner antagonism to political influence in matters like transfers.

The problem of divided authority was undoubtedly exacerbated by a second development of momentous importance. The Great Depression shook policing as much as it did the rest of the social order. It did so both in terms of enforced reductions in wages, which we have already examined, and of increased demands for police to act as controllers and even repressors of social and political dissent. The administrative demands on police authorities to manage the wage cut and make do with limited resources in a profoundly disturbed social climate were considerable — and a potent cause of conflict with the unions.

In this chapter we explore the effects of these changes on the relations between commissioners and police unions. In some cases these changes became the conditions under which policing administration would be conducted for many decades after. The conflicts of this period also signal the arrival of a politics of policing that is familiar today.

4.1 The uses of law

Formally, the position of the police commissioner had been quite unaltered by the establishment and recognition of police unions. Australian police forces were administered under legislation that delegated the crown's authority of appointing police officers to the commissioner through the responsible minister, while retaining the power of appointment of senior officers in the hands of the government. As much as the quasi-military character of police was and is spoken about, the fundamental fact was that police were more like public servants, though subject to considerable statutory restraints on their freedoms and entitlements, than they were like soldiers or sailors. That was the formal statutory position. In practice the commissioner wielded very impressive power to appoint, promote, discipline, transfer and dismiss whom he liked. In practice too, of course, these powers were dependent on the advice and recommendations of senior police administrators who reported to the commissioner.

The activities and dispositions of those senior police had been a common cause of complaint by serving police in the decades leading up to and after unionisation. Public attention had been drawn to the arbitrary and oppressive administrative style of inspectors of police in Queensland's 1899 royal commission, attracting critical comment from the commissioners themselves.[2] A provocative element in the decision of probationers to go on strike in Melbourne in 1923 had been the appointment by the commissioner of plain clothes supervising police, the 'spooks', to combat misconduct and corruption.[3] What was seen by a commissioner as a necessary step in maintaining a clean and effective police was increasingly seen by serving policing officers as unwarranted and unfair, even oppressive.

Police unions were key players in the development of procedural fairness within police administration. Resentment at the untrammelled authority in the shape of an inspector's adverse report fuelled much of the early enthusiasm for police unions. The unions empowered the ordinary constable to challenge unfairness in administration whether it proceeded from the top or from the delegated authority of a superior officer. A key means of doing so was legal action. In Australia this meant by the 1930s industrial courts in a number of Australian jurisdictions, and the common law courts in all of them. An exemplary case was fought in 1931–2, its result helping to define what standards might be expected of administrators in their treatment of police employees. At the heart of the High Court judgment in *Gibbons v Duffell* was a formal assertion about the boundaries between the administration of policing, which should be subject to the normal protections to a citizen offered by the law of defamation, and that of the business of state, whose business was privileged. Underlying the judgment was a unanimous affirmation by the High Court of the ordinariness of policing, of its now fundamental difference from military administration. Following from the judgment was an expectation that senior police had better watch what they said and how they behaved in relation to their underlings, especially when the latter had the protection of a police union.

First Constable William Resolute Gibbons was based at a Sydney city police station. He had applied for transfer to another station in circumstances that suggest his desire to escape a situation of great friction with his superior officers. As was expected of him in forwarding the transfer application, one such officer, Inspector Thomas Alfred Duffell, stated his recommendation — in this case not only rejecting the application, but claiming that Gibbons was a 'loafer and a liar of the worst type, a dangerous man and a man not amenable to discipline and a man opposed to law and order'.[4] Gibbons went to his union, the New South Wales Police Association, and won its backing for a libel action against Duffell. The civil suit prompted a key question to be decided by the Supreme Court of New South Wales. Was a report prepared by Duffell in these circumstances to be given the benefit of immunity from court proceedings? Was such a report the subject of absolute privilege, like a communication between ministers of the crown?

Such a court action was a vital test case for the police unions, many of whose members smarted under what they saw as the arbitrary and biased judgments of their superiors. Not without some concern over the precedent it might offer, the union had decided it would support Gibbons. It was equally a vital matter for officers like Duffell, and one in which commissioners and governments might have some considerable interest. In the event, Duffell found himself on his own as the matter proceeded through the Supreme Court and on to the High Court.

The case was costly — the union itself would not pursue the action but provided financial support to Constable Gibbons, in the first instance 100 guineas. The initial outcome was disastrous. After spending 400 pounds in supporting Gibbons, the union was faced in December 1931 with an unambiguous judgment in the New South Wales Supreme Court. Police reports like those of Inspector Duffell were the subject of absolute privilege, and so could not be the subject of Gibbon's libel action. It says something about the depth of feeling on these internal departmental proceedings that the union, at the height of an economic depression, was then prepared to support an appeal by Gibbons to the High Court.

There the matter was viewed very differently. The High Court was unanimous in the view that absolute privilege should be restricted to a limited range of documents, such as court proceedings, those of parliaments, and communications between ministers and between them and the crown. Beyond this the legal authorities had recognised that military reports on armed forces personnel might also be protected. But the notion that police departments should be entitled to operate under the same rules and protections as those of the army and navy, a conclusion adopted in the Supreme Court, was decisively rejected. The main judgment concluded that the analogy drawn between police and the military was 'unsafe ... imperfect and in many respects false. The *Police Regulations Act* and regulations thereunder bear small resemblance to the *Articles of War and the Army Act*'.[5] Justice Evatt reflected dryly on the New South Wales decision:

> The officers of police are seldom engaged in operations of a military character. They are organized to maintain the peace of the King, but that is a right and a duty which the law imposes upon all the King's subjects. The main work of the police force is to prevent and detect the commission of offences against the law of land. They also discharge other functions. To them is committed the control of vehicular and pedestrian traffic, they administer licensing regulations and systems, and they register dogs. No one desires to underestimate the dignity and importance of their principal duty. Perhaps it is sufficient to say that much of their work is not different in kind from what is done by many of the departments of the Executive Government.[6]

Whereas the Supreme Court had described the police as a 'State force organized on a semi-military basis for preservation of the safety of the State from internal enemies, as the Army and Navy are for its preservation from external enemies', Evatt more soberly observed that 'Those who break the law — whether it be contained in the *Crimes Act* or the *Liquor Act* — are punishable by the King's Courts, but they do not become the King's enemies.'[7] For such reasons the High Court concluded that a police inspector's report on another officer could not be regarded as absolutely privileged and that 'There is nothing subversive of Police administration in requiring that he shall act honestly and for the purpose of his duties in making such a report'.[8]

The decision was a vital one for the unions and their members. It helped clarify, at least in the judicial domain, the expectations of due process and fairness in personnel matters. The union journal welcomed the decision, noting that it would not preclude making an adverse report if the claims were true.

> As it appears to us to be simple justice, there need be no fear that it will disturb Police discipline. On the other hand, we believe it will make for better discipline and the triumph of right.[9]

There remains the question whether such decisions in fact helped develop a personnel system in which judgments would be avoided and decisions delayed, in which commissioners and their senior officers would be hamstrung by the fear of legal or industrial action over difficult decisions. Arguably the commissioner's discretion in personnel administration was formally narrowed by this very explicit demarcation of police from military discipline. Later, as we will see, the New South Wales Police Association would seek to consolidate the gains won by a successful move for the repeal of a rule requiring absolute obedience to an officer's superiors.

Whether a decision such as that in *Gibbons v Duffell* would affect administrative practice remained a moot question. The degree to which it did so is questioned by the continuing grievances of rank and file police. In Queensland little seemed to have changed from 1899, if one is to take heed of the campaign of the union in 1937. As the delegates from the Cloncurry branch objected to the attorney-general:

> In the present system of our Administration, an Inspector or Sub-Inspector, may at any time he wishes, forward to the Commissioner of Police, a confidential report detrimental or otherwise concerning a Member of the Force. In the event of the report being of a detrimental nature, frequently no intimation of its existence is received by the Member concerned, and when the matter of promotion is being considered, these reports are referred to and are often the means of impeding a Member's promotion.

The damage caused by 'some irresponsible gossiper' was impossible to contain where principles of natural justice did not obtain, and the suspicions of rank and file about the damage inflicted by rumours and unaccountable slanders made by some against others.[10] The union's grievance fed into the Queensland opposition's attempts at this time to introduce into the police legislation a provision ensuring that senior police did not have the power to exercise discipline or transfer without charges being made in writing.[11]

In spite of the apparent ignorance in some quarters of the effect of the High Court's judgment in *Gibbons v Duffell*, this was not an isolated action in which the unions would support aggrieved junior police to combat the comments of those superior officers. Indeed in an organisation in which rules of natural justice and due procedure were yet to gain a foothold, and in which bureaucratic formalism could rule, and ruin, one's career, it is scarcely surprising that defamation actions remained a common resort of unhappy police — whenever the source of a defamatory statement could be identified.

In such a case, initially a seeming repeat of *Gibbons v Duffell*, Constable Oldfield sued Inspector Keogh over a report reflecting on his competence. In May 1941 the constable achieved satisfaction in the New South Wales Supreme Court. But on appeal to the Full Court the judgment was reversed. The union backed Oldfield's suit — and paid heavily for its support.[12] Most importantly for our purposes here however, the outcome of this case was taken by Commissioner William MacKay as a strong vindication of his senior personnel's probity — that at least was the implication of his fury when he charged in the January 1942 official *Police Gazette* that the Association, having trumpeted Oldfield's victory in the first court, had fallen silent on the findings of the Full Court. MacKay was in fact wrong — the Association had already printed the adverse judgment in a supplement to its *Police News* four months earlier. Yet when the tough-talking Association secretary Charles Cosgrove ridiculed MacKay's mistaken assertion, the Commissioner responded by taking on the union's executive. Cosgrove was a non-police employee of the Association, but the executive were all serving police officers, based in Sydney stations. MacKay resorted to the tactic of punitive transfer — all members of the Association were given temporary transfers to country stations remote from Sydney. The dispute escalated overnight into a *cause celebre* for the New South Wales labour movement. In the following days sympathetic Labor backbenchers lobbied the new state premier who in turn directed MacKay to rescind the transfers. Within a short period of time the new government had not only succeeded in reversing a commissioner directive on the disposal of his police officers, but also negotiated MacKay's temporary removal from his office to a Commonwealth war-time post.[13]

Although the outcome for the commissioner brought him a long way from a legal case involving one of his inspectors, the episode signified the enormous investment of commissioners at that point in time in control of the serving personnel and the security offered by a stable, quasi-military administrative structure. MacKay's woeful misreading of the political contexts of police unionism at this juncture was doubtless in part a personal failing — but it was also a symptom of the shifting position of police commissioners in relation to police unions. His actions turned the legal victory of Inspector Keogh, a reverse of Inspector Duffell's outcome a decade before, into a pyrrhic disaster for himself.

Going to law is notoriously an uncertain business. Union-supported police litigation was no guarantee of the satisfaction of the grievances of junior police who felt they had been wronged by their superiors, as we can see in the contrary outcomes of the two New South Wales cases discussed above. Over and above the particularities of the case outcomes however, we might with justice conclude that the legal domain was becoming by the time of the Second World War one that would regularly shape the modes of administration that prevailed within a police force. Not only did the High Court's judgment in *Gibbons v Duffell* make clear that police administration proceed with some eye to procedural justice. The very fact of litigation as a vehicle by which commissioners and their officer delegates could be made accountable inspired a degree of investment in the outcomes that could spill over into other institutional arenas. The proceedings in early 1942 were extraordinary for their very public canvassing of a government's powers of intervention against a commissioner. But the commissioners were having to get used to the idea that all sorts of appeals might be entertained against their formerly expansive discretionary powers.

Not all the outcomes were against the commissioners, by any means. And defamation actions did not exhaust the legal remedies that might be sought by disappointed police with the assistance of their union. In an extraordinary saga, lasting nearly ten years, the Police Association of South Australia sought from 1933 to mitigate the effects of the commissioner's power in disciplinary proceedings. A 1942 Supreme Court judgment in that case definitively concluded that regardless of the effects of police coverage in an industrial award, the commissioner's powers to demote or dismiss police on disciplinary matters remained unaffected.

The case went back to 1932 when a constable with 10 years service had been reduced in rank. Restored to his previous rank in 1935, he nevertheless sought to recover wages lost in the interim. His confidence in a positive outcome was encouraged initially by earlier success in a magistrate's ruling in 1933 that his lost wages should be paid. An appeal by the public service commissioner on behalf of the crown resulted in further support for Constable Cooper's case. But in 1935 the Supreme Court ruled against Cooper on a technicality, and the commissioner of police restored him to rank. Briefly the Police Association contemplated a High Court appeal, but baulked at the cost and the implications of the government taking the case right to the Privy Council. When nothing came of this, Cooper later joined two other police in similar positions to take out a writ for the lost wages. Ruling in October 1942, Judge Richards concluded that there was no case to sustain Cooper's actions, and hence avoided the implied constraint on a commissioner's powers if the state's industrial award provisions had been allowed to prevail over the effect of a demotion or dismissal.[14]

Similarly the Tasmanian Association was to discover in the 1950s that the courts were of limited use in the face of the large powers reserved to the crown and the commissioner of police. A series of highly publicised police 'bashings' resulted in the dismissal of a detective and demotion of another following a public inquiry in 1955. The dismissal was made by an order of the governor-in-council, seemingly avoiding the disciplinary mechanisms established by the government in the same year. The Association took strong exception to this procedure. Addressing the minister attending the Police Association annual conference a few months later, the union president condemned the use of the governor-in-council order as an 'arbitrary power, fraught with danger of injustice, and not desirable. It has the earmarks of a reversion to a practice common prior to the enactment of the Bill of Rights in 1689'.[15] The Association went to bat for the aggrieved detectives — but found its capacity to help them constrained by its own rules. All the same, with the aid of voluntary contributions the dismissed detective appealed to the Tasmanian Supreme Court, without success, and then to the High Court.

While the High Court in 1932 might have provided some consolation to police aggrieved by unfair administrative process, the court's approach to cases involving governor-in-council decisions consistently affirmed the crown's prerogative to dismiss at will. In 1956 the result was no different, with the High Court ruling in the Tasmanian case that nothing had changed to affect earlier rulings such as *Ryder v Foley* (1906), which had mandated the power of dismissal residing in the crown. The detective and members of the Association were left with major costs out of the action, although the government appears to have conceded some costs. When one of the other disciplined detectives was successful in his appeal the Association agreed to fund 75% of the considerable appeal costs, by calling for voluntary contributions to avoid funds being 'depleted to a dangerous level'.[16]

The results of going to law are always going to be mixed. While examples such as Cooper's in South Australia, and Kaye's in Tasmania were a clear defeat for the Associations and their aggrieved members, they were also another sign of the power of the police to act collectively in ways that might affect police administration. Few individuals had the resources to contemplate legal remedies to address their grievances — but once combined, the police showed their capacity to draw the commissioner and his senior officers into the courts. Whether in the industrial or civil arenas this power of the police unions to take the authorities to the courts was to remain a fundamental weapon in the future shaping of policing in Australia.

4.2 Matters of appeal

There is no argument at all about the institutional effects of some other inter-war changes in the structures affecting the commissioner's authority. These changes were not uniform across the state jurisdictions. But there was a good deal of modelling involved in the process whereby gains in one state would be followed by a short, or long, campaign in other states leading to eventual concession of the right sought by the police union. The changes referred to here are principally those relating to appeals against decisions of the commissioner in regard to promotion, transfer or discipline.

It has been argued, at least in the case of New South Wales, that governments generally only conceded appeal rights to public sector workers when the government/employer was seeking a change in other terms and conditions — such as, for example, instituting merit over seniority in promotions. Reviewing the process of establishment of classification and discipline appeal boards in that state, Thornthwaite sustains her case that union power was of limited significance.[17] Whatever the case for other public sector areas, a review of the Australian experience in policing suggests a good deal of support for such a thesis. Winning appeal rights was a very extended process in some states, but remarkably easy in others. There was some variation in the kinds of arrangements established by government in according police the right to appeal a decision of a commissioner — a variation that also suggests something about the different political climate enjoyed by the various unions.

Before the 1920s, the police regulation statutes bestowed very substantial powers on the commissioners in matters of promotion, transfer and punishment. In Queensland for example, the commissioner was empowered to fine, demote ('disrate') or dismiss any officer after a summary enquiry into a breach of discipline and 'Such investigation may, subject to the Rules, be conducted in any way that the commissioner thinks fit or the Minister directs'.[18] In Victoria there was at least some court of appeal — under nineteenth century legislation sustained through to 1946, a police officer charged with misconduct might seek to have the charge heard and determined by a board of three persons appointed by the governor-in-council.[19] The exercise of the right in practice seems to have been nugatory in effect — it became a constant complaint of the Victorian Police Association for two decades from the 1920s that the police deserved an 'independent' appeal tribunal, presumably one established by statute rather than appointed by the governor-in-council. As with discipline so with promotion and transfer decisions — the nineteenth century statutory heritage left serving police with little resort in the event of decisions going against them.

Such constraints on what police unionists saw as a right to a fair and just hearing of their grievances against the commissioner were steadily reviewed in the years after the formal recognition of the police unions. As with the arbitration of their wages and conditions, the statutory recognition of a right of appeal entailed a further incorporation of police unions into the organisational structures of policing. Unions were becoming agents of the discipline of their own members — and many of the internal battles of police unions in subsequent decades originate in disputes over matters arising from the union's role in these administrative matters. In this sense we can elaborate on Thornthwaite's overview of the history of the regulation of state employment to emphasise not just that concession of a right of appeal flowed usually at the government's, i.e.

the employer's, convenience, but that it entailed a taming of the union, or a marshalling of its considerable potential for containing the frustrations of its members.

The advancement of appeals boards into the administration of policing can thus be seen as having two important implications. First it typically constrained the commissioner's previously untrammelled authority over disposal and conduct of his subordinates. Second, the appeal boards were often structured in ways that gave a voice to the worker, through the unions, but simultaneously legitimised a decision-making apparatus that inevitably would leave some of the customers dissatisfied.

Such lessons may be drawn from the characteristic way in which appeal boards were structured. Queensland led the way. The early favours won by the union included its successful achievement in 1921 of an amendment to the police statutes to establish an appeal board with jurisdiction in matters of discipline and, from 1924, promotion.[20] The board was to include not just an independent magistrate and a nominee of the police commissioner but also a representative of the police union. How far this may be taken as a wholesale victory for the union may be debated — simultaneous demands by the Queensland Teachers' Union for such an appeal board for teachers proposed a single judge, perhaps with a view to ensuring that the union did not get embroiled in such potentially hazardous undertakings.[21] But there was an additional implication of the 1921 establishment of a Queensland Appeal Board for police. Parliamentary debate drew attention to the significant transfer of power represented by this board's statutory powers — its recommendations would go direct to the governor-in-council for approval, thus by-passing the commissioner.[22] In the Queensland context such a change continued a trend of the previous few years, during which the commissioner had become more susceptible to government direction. While not all states would follow suit quickly, the significance of the Queensland Appeal Board for police was evident in the aspirations and struggles of other unions for a similar institution.

In Western Australia for example, an appeal board on the same lines had been sought by both the 1919 and 1920 annual conferences of the Police Association. Raised repeatedly with government in the following years, and even taking shape in a bill that passed the Legislative Assembly in 1927, the demand for a statutory appeals board would not bear fruit until the inclusion of police in a government employees' appeal process in 1945. In the meantime the only relief of Western Australian police was to be found in an internal appeals process established by regulation in 1935, and dealing just with promotions.[23]

More successful was the New South Wales Association campaign which resulted in success in 1923 — with a sympathetic Labor government successfully combating the opposition of the conservative National and Progressive parties. As in Queensland the appeals board in New South Wales was a three-person board — but in this case chaired by a District Court judge, along with two 'assessors' nominated one by the inspector general and one by the police force. This structure became the Australian standard in policing administration. Whether a single appeal board handled both discipline and promotion/transfer matters or not, such boards typically comprised an independent chair, with two other representatives nominated by the commissioner and the police force respectively.

The degree of recognition of the role of the union in the process was symptomatic of the historical moment in which such boards were established in each place. Usually the provisions refer to the election by the police force of a representative to sit on the board — in the case of Tasmania however the 1955 Acts establishing an appeals board on discipline matters entailed specific roles for the Association, including the naming of the secretary of the Association as a possible board member.[24] The process of its adoption is instructive. Tasmanian police had had to wait until 1950 for an independent board to determine classifications and hear appeals, but when it came it allowed for an elected union representative, the first of whom was the president of the union. When the chair of the board suggested that there might be some conflict of interest in the president of the Association being also a member of the board of classification and appeal the attorney-general's department was brought in to rule that there was nothing barring the president from serving as the elected member of the board.[25] The political context was highly favourable, with Labor unchallenged in the state from 1934–1969 — but all the same it had taken many years for the union to get this mechanism in place, nearly 30 years in fact after the first Australian police appeals board was established. Reflecting just four years later on what had happened, the Association president told the 1954 conference that, in response to a government invitation, the Association had prepared its own legislation, drawing on the New South Wales and Victorian classification and appeals boards statutes. Yet when the legislation came forward, the union proposal had been written down:

> notwithstanding that the Hon. the Attorney-General had asked that a sub-committee be formed to make recommendations to him in respect to a Classification and Appeals Board, the proposal were never placed on the Statute Book, but we got legislation we did not want, and were very unhappy about, and that feeling still exists.[26]

The misgivings resided in the narrow range of service conditions covered by the legislation, and the absence of appeals against *disciplinary* decisions (which had for example been included in the 1946 Victorian legislation). As so often, government and commissioner were attentive to union opinion — but slow to act. In this state, the complaints of 1954 were met a year later by the establishment of a Police Discipline Board, again with union representation.[27] In the Queensland case, where it had all started under a Labor government unambiguously favouring unionisation, the appeal board provisions similarly named the union as the means by which employee representation would be secured.[28] From a rank and file perspective the involvement of an employee's representative from the union could be a disappointment. In South Australia, an Association meeting heard in 1933, there had only been one occasion since its establishment in 1925 when the police representative had dissented from the opinion of the appeal board chairman.[29]

What effect did the appeals boards have on the commissioner's statutory powers over his workforce? The question might be answered in terms of both symbolic as well as formal effects. With respect to the latter we have already seen that it was objected by opponents of the Queensland board in 1921 that the commissioner's powers would be written down, in favour of the government through the governor-in-council. So in fact it was, and the model of appeal board transmitting evidence and recommendation to the commissioner who was then required to furnish it to the responsible minister was established.

In the Queensland case however it might be said that there was some formal constraint on the minister's final decision, which had to be made through the governor-in-council. Two years later in New South Wales, and then again in South Australia in 1925, the minister alone was left with the final decision in an appeal matter. In both cases, as in Queensland, appeals were allowed on discipline and promotion decisions to a board chaired by a judge (in New South Wales) or a 'special magistrate (in South Australia), with the recommendation flowing to the minister through the commissioner.[30] Yet South Australian evidence shows the limits of this appeal process in addressing union grievances against commissioner powers.

The South Australian Association was unhappy with the large number of appeal board decisions that were in fact *not* confirmed by the chief secretary, acting instead on the commissioner's recommendation. In 1929 the appeal board recommended that Constable Worrall (a former vice-president of the Association) who had been dismissed for insubordination against his inspector should instead be subject to just a fine — but the commissioner remained set on dismissal and was supported by the chief secretary.[31] The executive of the Association subsequently resolved to lobby the government for an amendment to make the appeal board's decision binding. But after winning political support for this from a new Labor government in 1930, the attempted amendment was blocked by a hostile Legislative Council in 1931.[32] Parliamentarians opposing the changes defended the commissioner's prerogative to administer the force with regard to its overall functioning — and while an appeal board had regard to the particularities of a case, the commissioner would take into account the whole of an officer's service.[33] Following the fall of the Labor government, the South Australian Association tried again, without success — in spite this time of having its expensive senior counsel, Herbert Mayo KC, prepare a submission which noted that the chief secretary's practice was always to stay with the commissioner's recommendation.[34] So unsuccessful were the appeal cases that it was several times mooted in the 1930s that the Association should no longer employ legal counsel for such cases.[35]

Commissioner powers were more directly circumscribed in the Victorian amendments of 1946. There, in cases where an officer contested a charge of misconduct, the commissioner might be avoided by the officer going direct to the misconduct board for a hearing and determination. Victoria however preserved a more judicial approach, distancing government from the business of police discipline — appeals from the commissioner of a board's decision on a charge of misconduct might be made to a county court judge, whose decision was final.[36]

How far such writing down of the commissioner's authority was effective in practice is a matter for more empirical inquiry. Appeal rights of whatever kind, and whether in discipline or promotion matters do not translate automatically into success for the appellant's case, whatever the occupation involved — in Queensland, not a single appeal by teachers on promotion matters was successful from the establishment of the relevant appeal board in 1923 until 1947.[37] The equally unhappy results for police are suggested by the continuity of complaints over the structure and limitations of the appeals process. In 1937 the Queensland Police Union urged amendments to the structure of the appeals board, where it was claimed only one in 50 appeals were successful.[38] In effect, by giving the commissioner a right of comment on the appeal board's decision we see that a *de facto* situation developed whereby the minister's decision typically ratified that of the commissioner.

Consequently the police unions favoured any approach that distanced the commissioner from having anything like a veto power. Hence in New South Wales in 1945, the Association journal greeted a new appeals process with enthusiasm. Under the crown employees' appeal board legislation the board's decision was now final, and the commissioner's intercession avoided. An editorial in the *Police News* trumpeted that New South Wales police history would be made when appellants faced the new board without the threat of what was described as a final 'veto' from the commissioner.[39] Formally there had been no such veto since 1923, and the board's recommendations generally were ratified by commissioner and minister. But the experience of the appeals process from the late 1930s evidently made it seem like there was a veto.[40] Similarly, in spite of Queensland's early gains, the matter of appeals remained as contentious in the early 1950s as it had ever been anywhere else, leading to strong union pressure on government to effect some changes.[41] The commissioner's powers in respect of discipline, promotion and transfer were to remain a bone of contention in future decades, and on many an occasion a reason for police threatening political intervention.

In sum, it appears that within the first three decades of police unionisation, commissioner powers were already being written down, but with limited effect in positive outcomes for those unhappy with commissioner disciplinary and other career decisions. Police unions may not have been good diagnosticians of their members' plight — but they fastened quickly on what were seen as excessive powers of authority vested in the office of commissioner. Legal challenges through the medium of defamation in particular helped to contain that authority, a vital outcome of the High Court decision in *Gibbons v Duffell* in 1932. The gradual intrusion of appeal boards into the routine structures of police administration was another constraint, one given statutory mandate. These important shifts in the legal and statutory fields must also be considered in the light of the changing administrative relations in policing, affected significantly in the inter-war years and after by the activities of the unions.

4.3 Commissioner–union conflict

The growing importance of the police unions can be measured during the inter-war decades by the incidence of political scandals and controversies involving the commissioners of a number of forces in Australia. The frequency of these, and the commonality of tactics employed by some commissioners, suggests a need to address the administrative style of police leaders during this era. The varying success of the unions in combating commissioner policies, or even administrative *dictats* aimed at the union leadership itself, also demands attention. Inevitably these conflicts between commissioner and union spilled over into the public arena, involving in significant measure the responsible minister or even premier of the day. In at least one case, that of New South Wales, the consequences reached down to the 1990s, misremembered however in some significant details.

Just as Melbourne had a memorable police strike so it became home in later years to a bitter battle between would-be police unionists and a recalcitrant chief commissioner. Like some other commissioners of his era, General Thomas Blamey was appointed on the basis of a distinguished military career during the First World War. As we have seen in the previous chapter Blamey's leadership of the police was already in the later 1920s a matter of contention. The substance of disputes around his office related in part to rumours of corruption, allegations of which prove difficult to investigate historically because so many of his administrative files were destroyed, to a degree quite unmatched in the history of the Victorian force according to its historian.[42] But administrative decisions flowing out of Blamey's office helped to sustain an atmosphere of conflict that was embodied in his relations with the Victorian Police Association. Blamey set out to crush it in the late 1920s and was successful to a degree unmatched elsewhere in Australia.

As we have explored in a previous chapter the position of the Association was already in question before its vigorous contestation of the 1929 election — its political involvement was dangerous to its own interests, given its formal status as in effect a company union, whose legal status was tied to its functioning within statutory parameters. In the year after the election however relations between the Association and the commissioner worsened dramatically. The Association had a secretary who was not a serving police officer — such a state of affairs appeared to call into question the legality of police membership in the Association. Indeed an opinion of the crown solicitor on just this point had apparently coincided with a dramatic fall in the Association's membership — from 1,400 to 800, according to *The Argus* at this time.[43] The Association executive however continued its determined assault on new promotion regulations. These implied that even long-serving officers would have again to sit an examination in order to get on the promotion list.

As commissioner in 1930, Blamey faced not only the hostility of a union executive that had played a very public role in resistance to his new promotion regulations. A personal hurdle was that his five-year term had expired — the new Labor government did not renew his appointment but instead left it open to him to apply again, at a salary level reduced in depression conditions by £500 p.a. It was publicly mooted that the government hoped and even expected that he would not apply. In the interim Blamey pursued the Association, and especially its non-police secretary. In the same week that it became known that Blamey would not be automatically re-appointed, *The Age* reported that Blamey had directed an investigation against the Association secretary for 'attempting to spread disaffection amongst members of the force' — a brief had already gone to the crown solicitor who, according to the regulations, could institute proceedings without the approval of the attorney-general.[44] The clarification was significant — for the new attorney-general, William Slater MLA, had been the Association's honorary solicitor for the previous five years.

By this stage the conflict over the position of the commissioner and the future status of the Association had become very public, and the subject of newspaper editorials. Supporting Blamey, the conservative *Argus* was trenchant. Attacks on Blamey were part of a political campaign, of which the recent trade union and Labor criticism of police protection of strike breakers at the wharves, was typical.

> The Labor regime has been marked, too, by the increased boldness of the Victorian Police Association in seeking to interfere with the Chief Commissioner's control of the force. This organisation has not scrupled to attempt to exercise political influence, even to the point of direct disobedience of the law. Its efforts to overawe candidates at the State election in November last on the question of police

> promotion were continued in face of the Chief Commissioner's warning. This was but one episode in the association's sustained campaign to subvert discipline in the force. There has been a determined attempt by the disruptive influences in the police force to dictate a policy of promotion at variance with that desired by the Chief Commissioner, and members of the Labor Ministry have been too ready to lend their aid to these mischievious [sic] activities.[45]

In such a volatile context it may not be surprising that Blamey's reappointment resulted in his bringing Association matters to a head. Not without some supporters within the Association, Blamey aimed to replace the existing executive and restructure the organisation along lines that made it appropriately subordinate. His proceedings were ruthless — but also an exercise in brinkmanship. Acting against the executive he sent one member back to uniform duties, transferring him at the same time from Melbourne to Mildura, and proceeded with the prosecution and eventual conviction of the Association secretary. Blamey followed this with a directive to all Victorian police members of the Association to resign their membership from what was said on the basis of legal advice to be an illegal body. This directive brought him into direct conflict with the government, and, at the Association's request, the chief secretary in turn directed Blamey to withdraw his direction to the force. The political injunction was only temporary, pending court resolution of the legality of the existing Association with its non-police secretary. When one court and then another ruled against the Association the game was up. In the meantime Blamey had organised a group of loyal officers to take over the Association under a new understanding that effectively subordinated the Association to his authority.[46] 'Eventually', concludes Haldane on this episode, 'the new Association returned to its "old" mould and became a genuine union of employees, but that was not for many years, long after the iron-fisted general had left the force'.[47]

Blamey's struggle with the Association makes sense in the light of his military background. While it was claimed by his press supporters, like *The Argus*, that he had been a supporter of the Association, that had only been while it was effectively mute. When a contentious matter like promotion came up, the distance between the Association's conventional affection for seniority as a pre-eminent criterion and Blamey's wish to dispose as he thought best, provoked sustained and very public conflict. Notably his determination to crush the old Association came in the wake of its unashamed entry into the political arena, attempting to achieve its aims through a favourable electoral outcome in 1929. The familiarity of these proceedings to those who have witnessed police union conflicts with government in the last 20 years suggests that this kind of politicisation arises out of, indeed is conditioned by, the institutional conditions of policing rather than the development of some late century crisis in policing and the politics of law and order. That such conflicts could emerge in 1930 is a striking reminder of the longevity of a police union politics embedded in a peculiar institutional strength of the Australian labour movement. That the 'union' seemingly lost out on this occasion may be just the exception that proves the rule. In Western Australia at the same time an equally unhappy commissioner, sought to use the same tactics, of transfer, and the creation of internal division in the ranks of the union — but without the same success. In 1930 Commissioner Connell's transfer tactics were admittedly more muted, but nonetheless noted by the union — and his attempts to establish a separate officers' union came to naught in the face of police union opposition, pressed on the Labor government in 1932.[48]

Blamey's militaristic approach to the Victorian Police Association was in many ways the reaction of an outsider appointed to the police. But not only that — the frequency of similar conflicts between commissioners and unions in the inter-war years suggests also that there were structural and procedural issues at work, including a working through of the new world of policing administration in an age of unionisation. These factors are particularly evident in the history of Blamey's near contemporary in New South Wales. William MacKay came to his post in 1935 from within the ranks of the force. Initially his approach to the police union in that state was congenial — and indeed he had been an early activist, boasting to the Association in 1935 that he had been among those who drew up its rules in 1920.[49] The police union welcomed his appointment — he was after all an insider. The *Police News* 1 April 1935 had spoken of the fears that a 'brass hat' ('retired generals, colonels and others on half-pay pension') would be appointed rather than someone from inside the police force, with an 'intimate knowledge ... [and who] commands the trust and esteem of the men under him'.[50]

The enthusiasm was short-lived. During a turbulent and controversial period of New South Wales police history, MacKay's style of administration leaned towards a conception of the force as more akin to that of a military body. By the conclusion of his term, he had been decisively defeated in an attempt to neuter the union, as we have seen earlier, in the aftermath of the *Oldfield v Keogh* libel case. But his humiliation was not ended by his temporary secondment to an office in the service of the war effort. On his return a year later it appeared that MacKay had lost little of his combative approach to relations with the union — and the union had not forgiven him his tactics of 1942.

Further defeats for MacKay followed in 1943. They are especially pertinent to our themes in this chapter since they arose as matters of central importance to the constitutional and legal, as well as administrative, frameworks of New South Wales policing. In their resolution the Association again triumphed, and demonstrated the importance of a close link with the government of the day.

MacKay's troubles in 1943 originated in an extraordinary saga of the minor courts that brought into play some of the most powerful people in New South Wales. In January 1943 it was reported that two constables had been suspended following the arrest of a man identified initially as Charles McNally, on a charge of obscene exposure. Following the arrest the two constables had been called into the commissioner's office for interview, the files including fingerprints had been removed to police headquarters, and the charge was dropped. Within a few days the police concerned had been suspended and the Police Association executive was involved. On 21 January 1943 the Association called for a royal commission to investigate all the circumstances regarding the dropping of the charges, and the suspension of the constables. The latest actions of Mr MacKay, charged the secretary, were 'a serious threat to all members of the force'.[51] The Association pressed forward against MacKay, writing to all state parliamentarians about its concern that the commissioner was attempting to 'discredit the constables with the object of protecting a man in a highly placed position'.[52]

The Association's pressure was quickly rewarded. The premier, W J McKell, called for a report from MacKay and within a week state cabinet had issued a directive to MacKay to issue a summons to 'McNally'. The Association's request for a royal commission was rejected, but only after a cabinet discussion, which McKell said had taken a 'whole afternoon'. MacKay's initial response threatened to bring him into open conflict with the government, when he indicated instead that the 'Police Act imposes upon me the obligation to protect innocent members of the public against abuse of a policeman's power or any other abuse'. Three days later, after a meeting with the premier, MacKay agreed to issue the summons.[53] In the meantime the Association was building its case against MacKay, claiming on 29 January that a deputation to the premier would list a number of cases to 'support the executive's belief that Mr MacKay, "by reason of his impulsiveness and arrogance, was not fitted temperamentally to control the Police Force"'.[54]

The identity of 'Charles McNally' was soon known. At the summons hearing on 1 February, his barrister, W R Dovey KC, revealed that 'McNally' was in fact Clarence Sydney McNulty, and that he was not a 'clerk, 43 years old' as on the charge sheet, but was editor-in-chief of the *Daily Telegraph*. McNulty subsequently escaped conviction, an unusual outcome in these cases during these years, for it was revealed subsequently that the arresting constables had made some 200 similar charges around the city in the previous year with all resulting in guilty pleas or verdicts. In a sequence of subsequent hearings it became clear that MacKay had dropped the charge after being alerted the same night to what had happened. McNulty had travelled to MacKay's home, together with the newspaper's proprietor, Frank Packer — according to Mackay's evidence in a later libel hearing the commissioner and the paper owner knew each other as 'Frank' and 'Mac'.[55]

In the aftermath of the arrest MacKay had already ordered a departmental inquiry into the policing practices of the two constables concerned. Thereafter for at least two years the Association was dedicated to a political and legal pursuit of the case against MacKay. With friends from the past now in parliament, such as one-time Association solicitor W F Sheahan, the police union was in a strong position to push the case against MacKay. At the Association's annual conference in 1943, alongside a proposal that the Association should affiliate with the New South Wales Trades and Labour Council went a motion called on the government to repeal those laws and regulations that were alleged to give the commissioner dictatorial powers. Sheahan welcomed the motion and 'hoped that before the end of the present parliament the premier would take appropriate action for the repeal of that portion of the Police Regulation Act which dealt with the position'.[56] His confidence that government might do something was not ill-informed. During the McNulty episode government ministers had been reported to be surprised by MacKay's attitude to the directive to issue a summons. One had suggested that 'if

Mr MacKay continued to take no action the Government would have to consider whether the Executive had power to suspend Mr MacKay under the Police Regulation Act'.[57]

Direct approaches to other backbenchers over the statutory powers of the commissioner and aspects of police administration were one means by which the Association pursued MacKay — in court MacKay would later allege that the Association had always been agitating with MPs against him.[58] Another was to fund those legal challenges to MacKay that arose from the McNulty case. The Association was central to the mounting of appeals against the dismissal of Constables Grigg and Carney, following the outcome of the departmental inquiry into their actions leading up the McNulty arrest. Its president was the representative of the rank and file police, on the appeal board, which found in favour of Grigg and Carney by a 2–1 majority, with the commissioner's delegate dissenting. Immediately following this favourable outcome, the Association explored a further legal path to drive home its dissatisfaction with MacKay. In what turned out to be a costly and internally divisive move, the Association executive agreed, but only on the casting vote of the president, to fund a defamation action by Constable Grigg against Commissioner MacKay. Denied success in a jury trial, but still with Association support, Grigg appealed with Association funding, to the Supreme Court, again without success.[59] By this stage the enormous legal costs of such cases were affecting the Association's finances, and became a matter of dissent at the 1945 annual conference, when the secretary was forced to defend the £1,100 already spent in supporting the two police in their appeals and legal challenges.[60] When the bills mounted to £2,000 a disgruntled Association member took the six members of the executive to court — only to fail himself, when Judge Roper found the Association had acted lawfully in supporting Grigg in his legal action over 'the allegedly libellous statement purported to have been made by the chief executive officer and head' of the police force.[61]

Apart from demonstrating the apparently litigious disposition of a good number of New South Wales police in the 1940s, the McNulty case and its aftermath was an exemplary instance of a deteriorating relationship between commissioner and the police union. Beyond the posturing, both parties in this relation were struggling over the control of policing. MacKay's administrative style had become increasingly authoritarian, and politically insensitive, not to say myopic. The Police Association executive had a virtual open line to the ruling Labor party, and the government did not hesitate to make its dissatisfaction with the commissioner publicly known. Viewing Association links of this kind as a challenge to his authority, MacKay here as in 1942 was understandably affronted, but limited in his power to combat the union.

Regardless of the merit of his actions or those of the officers he had tried to dismiss, the entire episode signalled the transitions in commissioner authority since the turn of the century. Not only were appeal rights now firmly established, and effective in overturning departmental and commissioner rulings. Now also a commissioner appeared quite vulnerable to political pressures exerted by the police union, for the good or bad as the case might be. In the McNulty case the game had been played out on territory that almost ensured a significant loss to the commissioner — his associations with a powerful elite could easily lead to suggestions of interventions against the course of justice. His defence of his own case against Grigg and Carney was plausible. Essentially he argued at length in evidence before the Supreme Court in 1944–5 that they had exercised their discretion inappropriately and consistently, in a way prejudicial to justice and perhaps even corruptly, and against the direction of his earlier 1936 circular forbidding entrapment in homosexual cases (as distinct from gambling and sly grog cases where it appeared permissible).[62] The merits or otherwise of these operational matters were of limited appeal however placed beside the strong suggestion of collusion with the powerful. A police union with an independent voice, especially one as loud as that of Cosgrove, was now powerful enough to operate as a significant constraint on the commissioner's freedom to do as he pleased.

4.4 Implications for policing: ministers, commissioners and unions

This chapter has outlined the subtle and uneven progress of a change in policing which was rendering police more like other workers, and the commissioner more like just another employer. A symbolic instance was reported in the *New South Wales Police News* in March 1945. The Association had sought from the Labor government a review of those police rules that fostered what many police saw as oppressive conditions. Following representations to the premier by the Association, the former recommended and cabinet approved the repeal of subsection 7 of section ix of Police Rules. That rule spoke volumes for a past that was no longer a part of policing, requiring as it did that 'Members of the Force will give unquestioning obedience to, and will unhesitatingly carry out, all lawful commands given them by their official superiors'.[63] Such a rule was consistent with the quasi-military character of the police force as some commissioners like MacKay still thought of it — in 1945 he was said to have objected to a proposal to allow secret ballots in union elections on the grounds that 'it was contrary to discipline as he knew it in a semi-military body'. But he was now out of step with the optimistic talk of a democratic policing. The rule was repealed.[64]

The years in which the police unions wound back the power of the commissioners were also years in which unions began to take an active role in decisions about policing matters. For the most part the kinds of changes brought about by the unions that we have spoken about here were those affecting matters of discipline, transfer and promotion of police. These internal administrative concerns were conventionally matters that the commissioner had clear statutory authority to determine. Yet the influence of the unions had by the 1950s clearly impacted on the definition and scope of that authority.

The effect of police unions on matters of policing is a quite distinct area of concern. Policing, what police do, is formally defined by common law and statute — the independence of the constable exercising discretion to arrest and charge was protected by case law, and so constituted a limit on the commissioner's disposal of resources and allocation of priorities.[65] In turn, once a police union was solid enough to represent its members, and the statutory barriers to its freedom of action were modified, the entire arena of policing became police union business. That at least was what was becoming clear by the 1950s. Not only would police unions come to the aid of members finding themselves on the wrong end of a civil suit. Increasingly they would come to involve themselves in decisions about the fundamentals of policing — about decisions to arrest, to investigate, to prosecute, in a word to police. Or else, by virtue of their role in defending their members against charges from whatever direction, they came to promote particular styles of policing. From the 1930s to the 1950s the police unions consolidated their capacity to represent police in matters that bore on the fundamentals of policing. The very legitimacy of the police came to be a matter about which police unions would increasingly concern themselves. The scope of possible actions, and the rationales for them, as well as their implications for policing, are made clear in some episodes discussed below.

A symptom of the police unions' concern for the legitimacy of policing is evident in the growing tendency for the unions to think of themselves as somehow equivalent to the police. The strength of police unionism was a matter of concern to police executives, and doubtless to the permanent, salaried, union secretaries. In turn a perspective developed that would see in the sagging morale of police forces, a threat to the viability of the union. The two were indistinguishable. The perspective is evident in 1938 when the New South Wales Association president reported to conference on the steps which had been taken during the year to boost morale. It had been a bad year for the members — the Association supported the appeals to the High Court of police dismissed in the wake of the SP betting royal commission findings — and lost. Much publicity had surrounded civil writs against other police who had been sued for illegal arrests and trespass. As well the executive had faced the problem of criticism from country branches. Responding to the 'vicious attacks' made by the media, the executive had decided 'that it was necessary in the interests of the force and the Association, to visit as many country towns as possible, and spread useful propaganda, among citizens and Police generally'.

'Useful propaganda' included not only visits by the president and others, but also promotional initiatives to build good relations between the citizenry and the police. At a considerable expense, the Association funded local police to stage dances in aid of charity. In their charitable support activities many Association branches performed the functions of other service and voluntary associations, funding for example the operations of local public ambulances in a number of country centres at this time.[66] The union executive consciously sought to promote a positive image of police. Extending the Association's reach to the public as well as building links with members, the union executive believed that it could thereby do much to 'instill enthusiasm' and avoid the 'danger of apathy affecting the members'.[67] The boundary between police force responsibilities and those of the Association was becoming more than a little bit fuzzy — and it could be argued that a concern to build the public image of the police was of an order with the New South Wales union's moves just a few years later to challenge the commissioner's operational directives. Once the unions moved into a field of significant concern with the legitimacy of the public police then their scope for intervening in a whole range of concerns about the organisation and directions of policing was enhanced.

We can also see such a disposition evident in union interest in criminal justice procedural questions bearing on the police role. In March 1956 the general secretary of the QPU wrote to the commissioner regarding a case in which a magistrate had criticised police officers in the course of dismissing obscene language, assault police and other charges against a Robert Neal Spencer. His letter requested an appeal against the verdict of the magistrate and offered confidential information, 'which completely exonerated the police concerned from any suggestion that the man Spencer was not guilty of the offences with which he was charged'. Reviewing the matter, the executive went further, directing the general secretary to obtain a copy of the depositions for the union's further consideration.[68]

The case is instructive of the union's reach by this time. Its connection with more familiar union involvement in the defence of its members was tangential. Spencer was not himself taking action against the police officers. Rather his charges had arisen in the course of a standard police operation, one that had resulted in some fracas between Spencer and the police themselves. The magistrate concerned had been unimpressed with the police case and dismissed the charges, conveying to the public at large his critical view of police actions in the case. It might be reasonable to assume that at this stage, an operational procedure for the police concerned might be to seek further support from their superiors for an appeal and new hearing. Instead we find by 1956 that an alternative avenue is for the police to approach their duties through invoking the aid of the union, with a direct approach to the commissioner.

Union intercession was of course critical to the maintenance of a loyal member base. Possibly the most contentious and certainly most costly task of the police unions was intercession and support in cases involving civil actions or criminal charges against police for actions arising in the course of their duties. From the 1920s the unions had played some role in providing financial support for legal advice to police in such circumstances. The costs of some actions however were such that a formally established 'Legal Defence Fund' established in Queensland was abandoned in 1928.[69] Legal action was of course expensive, and the executive of any union faced difficult decisions in proceeding to court to defend, or prosecute, an action. Where a matter of precedent might be established the unions had a vital stake — hence the support of the New South Wales Association for Constable Gibbons in his defamation suit against Inspector Duffell in 1931–2.

The legal arena however was not only one where police administrators might be brought to book. It was also a site of ever-present danger to police, whose powers derived from law, and could be limited by law. Against decades of critical analysis of police infringements of civil liberties and abuse of power, it can be easily overlooked that police have been regularly the object of civil suits, and occasionally of criminal charges against them. The most common action faced by police in the public courts appears to have been an action for wrongful arrest. We have noted earlier that Queensland police had faced a number of failed cases in the late 1920s, leading to the union approaching government to cover the costs awarded against police.

The dangers were even greater for police facing civil action where damages might be awarded. These might not be frequent, but they were important markers of the boundaries shaping police freedoms — and police knew it. Few things seem to inspire police agitation like a prosecution or suit against one of their own, and the repercussions of such cases for police union–commissioner and even police–government relations have been considerable. Again New South Wales provides one of the most signal examples in the early decades of the police unions, and one which was closely tied to the shaping of policing policy and the distinguishing, or blurring, of lines of authority.

In a civil action brought by Robert Manners in 1936, three New South Wales police had damages of £300 awarded against them. Manners' suit involved three counts, of wrongful arrest, wrongful imprisonment and assault. The jury hearing the case found against the three police on all three matters, after Chief Justice Sir Frederick Jordan directed it in no uncertain terms:

> A police officer is not entitled to arrest a man until he is prepared to charge him at once. Whether Manners was beaten or kicked, or not, the action of the police was illegal, and amounted to a serious infringement of the rights of Manners as a citizen ... They have no right to seize members of the public for the purpose of detaining them to see whether they could subsequently make out a case against them sufficiently strong to warrant a charge being made.[70]

It was a substantial setback for the police concerned. Other police, 'especially some members of the CIB', were soon reported in the press as claiming that the public would suffer from the Chief Justice's comments 'as few people would take the chance of being sued for interviewing a person whose guilt was strongly suspected'.[71] The sense of police grievance was quickly exacerbated by the government's indication that as usual it would not be covering the legal costs involved in the police defence, let alone the damages claim. Following a subsequent internal inquiry the supervising sergeant was demoted to uniform duties, in the light of his having 'failed to exercise reasonable care' in authorising an arrest, and the other two arresting constables were also disciplined.[72] All matters were aired in the media and the Manners case quickly involved not only senior police administration, but also the state government. In an extraordinary intervention the premier's department called for the case files, before the internal inquiry had been completed. With the police force already under a cloud because of the corruption scandals being revealed in the contemporaneous Markell Royal Commission into SP betting, cabinet maintained an active interest in this case. The government's endorsement of the internal inquiry's disciplinary recommendations was not enough to satisfy the sensational Sydney weekly *Truth* which led one editorial on the case with the banner 'Bashers let loose'.[73]

The union's function in such a case highlighted its capacity by this time to play an active part in public debates about policing. Under its activist secretary Charles Cosgrove, the Association did not shrink from contesting government and media criticism of the police. Its role in the aftermath of the Manners case involved not only the standard ones of advocacy of the interests of the police concerned, particularly in the light of state cabinet's decision that the police should have to pay the crown solicitor's defence costs. In the press, and through legal counsel, the Association sought clarification of police powers.[74] The secretary wanted the crown law department to define exactly what were the powers of police in questioning suspects in relation to reported crimes. In particular Cosgrove suggested it was now the responsibility of crown law to clarify the powers available to police under s36 of the *Police Offences Act* allowing police to stop, search and detain suspects.[75] Beyond this, the Association's criticism of the government's decision on legal defence costs prompted public discussion of the liability of the government for the actions of the police, a subject on which the *Sydney Morning Herald* published a detailed legal opinion dealing with the relations of 'The Crown and the Police'. In the Association's *Police News*, Cosgrove asked whether the intervention of the state cabinet in the disciplinary hearings had breached the spirit of the 1935 statutory changes which had seemingly distanced government from police.[76]

The episode altogether highlighted the potential of a single case in which a civilian had challenged the actions of police to boil over in a wider array of concerns. That it could do so was contingent on the circumstances that were already undermining public confidence in the police — the outcome of the Markell Royal Commission, and the stirrings around Commissioner MacKay, whom government backbenchers were already calling to account, one of them describing MacKay as a potentate with greater powers than the premier.[77] In such a climate the Association might be said to have played an aggravating role, but also one that kept police administration before the eyes of the public. Not surprisingly its activities during such episodes contributed to the gradual erosion of MacKay's endorsement of the union, leading to his badly miscalculated hostility in the 1942 attempt to neuter the union.

It is no accident of history that matters originating in a wrongful arrest could touch off such public conflicts over the styles of policing, and the proper relations of police and government. The arrest power was a critical one for all police, though not one that all police had to exercise frequently.[78] Similarly the interrogation powers of police, the conditions under which they might question a detained suspect, were critical for the conduct of criminal investigation. The police unions displayed in the inter-war years and beyond a regular interest in these matters, and not just in Queensland in 1929 or New South Wales in 1936. The 1936 report into the Victorian police by Scotland Yard's Inspector Duncan disclosed a public distrust of the Russell St-based CIB, a distrust which had grown with complaints over false arrests and abusive questioning, in some cases resulting in damages awards against the police concerned.[79] Such instances stimulated the interest of the Victorian Police Association — its journal editorialised in 1937 on the necessity for a government law reform committee to 'also direct its attack upon the common law where in so many ways the liberties of the subject are affected ... [T]here is a clear necessity for a clarification of the powers of arrest, search, the entry to private premises and seizure of articles, and an application of such powers to uniform circumstances and conditions'.[80] Through such stands the unions, even ones like that of Victoria so limited in participating in political or policy debates, were developing incrementally their role in the politics of policing.

Finally, what are we to make of the implications of this changing role for the third arm of the policing triangle — the minister responsible for police. For it was a phenomenon often repeated that saw unions attempting to get around an obstructionist commissioner by going direct to the responsible minister. And union unhappiness with political leaders was often greatest when ministers stood beside commissioners, refusing to exercise their own discretion on appeal matters for example. Conversely when ministers opened the door part way to a union, the danger was that government relations with the commissioner could be damaged.

It was Blamey once again who had a very determined view with respect to the union's freedom of action. In 1928–9 he repeatedly insisted to the chief secretary that the Association was exceeding its authority by going directly to the minister over complaints that had already been addressed to himself. And in the lead-up to the major conflict over the promotion regulations he was forceful in his views on the proper paths for policy making:

> In my opinion an impossible situation would be created if the recommendations of the Chief Commissioner for the better development of the Force were to be subjected to the revision of a section of the Force before consideration by the Minister.

He was fortunate in having ministerial backing for his views. His conception of the Association was one in which it played a clearly subordinate role in policing — and in any case because the executive was made up of the rank and file it was not qualified to advise government on matters such as promotion policy.[81]

Fortunate Blamey was — because a later Labor government would take a different attitude. The Cain government from 1946 saw fit to receive Association representations directly. The relations between union and government were close, and the commissioner's powers were written down. This was but a temporary respite for the Victorian Association however. The return of conservative government in 1947 saw the pendulum swing again. By late 1948 the Association was facing a new police bill with provisions that were deeply resented. When the Association sought in January 1949 to receive advice from the chief secretary of any future amendments to police legislation or conditions of service, the minister courteously but firmly decline to disclose legislation before presenting it to the parliament.[82] There was talk of extreme measures, though 'short of a general strike', and the Association protested that it had 'always been recognised over the last [sic] three, four, or five years as the properly constituted bargaining authority between the Department, the people and the Government'. Understandably given the recent open relations with the Cain government the executive was aggrieved by the proposed statutory restraint on communications between police and the government, claiming that the police in all other states had direct access to their respective ministers.[83]

In the following years, before the return of the Cain government to power at the end of 1952, we can see the Victorian Association niggling at these boundaries of due process in communication with government. Over operational policy issues such as the arming of police (a major preoccupation before and after the *Firearms Act* of 1953 that sought to tighten gun licensing requirements), the use of sirens on police cars, the obligation to serve civil and distress warrants, and the commissioner's discipline powers, the Association faced a resistant minister and commissioner.[84] When the chief secretary refused to see the union deputation over concerns about the police discipline board, the Association sought out the assistance of Cain, by now the opposition leader. In these years the Association also wrote to all MPs and made the press regularly aware of its dissatisfaction.[85] Not surprisingly, with the return of Cain to power in December 1952 the union hoped for a more receptive hearing on many of these matters as once again there were ministers with a record of sympathy to the union case. There are no certainties in politics however and within a year or so the Association's president was critical of the government's demonstrable apathy in the face of the union's requests.[86]

By 1945, the old order of things was passing. The improvements in the standing of the Victorian Police Association during the subsequent years of the Cain Labor government were symptomatic of a sea change in the position of the unions. Labor at the end of the war was in power in Canberra as well as in all states except South Australia. We will see in the next chapter that in the succeeding years police unions would consider at length what kind of relation they should have to the labour movement, and what they would get out of it. In 1945 it seemed they would get a lot.

Notes

1 McGill, *No Right to Strike The History of the New Zealand Police Service Organizations*, chs4–5.
2 Johnston, *The long blue line: a history of the Queensland Police.*
3 Brown and Haldane, *Days of Violence: The 1923 police strike in Melbourne*, ch2.
4 *NSWPN*, Oct 1930, p38.
5 Gibbons v Duffell, [1932] 47 *Commonwealth Law Reports*, 521–537. (Gavan Duffy CJ, Rich and Dixon JJ).
6 Ibid, (Evatt J).
7 Ibid, (Citing the NSW Supreme Court, Evatt J).
8 Ibid, (Gavan Duffy CJ, Rich and Dixon JJ).
9 *NSWPN*, Sep 1932, p1.
10 QSA, A/3927, Delegates, Cloncurry Branch, QPU, to Attorney General, 30 Jun 1937. I am grateful to Jonathan Richards for this reference.
11 QPD, 22 Sep 1937, pp567–568 (in debate on Police Bill 1937).
12 Oldfield v Keogh [1941] 41 *State Reports (NSW)* 206.
13 This account draws on Brien, *Serving the Force: 75 Years of the Police Association of New South Wales*, 77–83. Also the *Police News* during this time.
14 Australia South, "Cooper, Daly, Juckes v Hunkin," (1942), 162.; *SAPJ*, Apr 1934, pp3–19; May 1934, pp3–5; Sep 1934, pp3–13.
15 *TPJ*, Nov 1955, pp9–10.
16 Kaye v Attorney-General for Tasmania (1956) 94 *Commonwealth Law Reports* 193; *TPJ*, Sept 1955, pp5, 7–8; Mar 1957, pp5–6; Apr 1957, pp7–8. Six years later Kaye was still fighting for reinstatement, seeking Association support (unsuccessfully) for a petition to the Queen, *TPJ*, May 1963, p7.
17 Louise Thornwaite, "Regulating state employment in NSW, 1880–1980," *Labour History* (1995).
18 Queensland, *The Police Act of 1863 Amendment Act of 1891*, 55 Vic no 32, s25.
19 Victoria, *Police Regulation Act 1890*, 54 Vic no 1127, s42.
20 Johnston, *The long blue line: a history of the Queensland Police*, 127.
21 The QTU proposal was unsuccessful and the board included a union representative: Andrew Spaull and Martin Sullivan, *A history of the Queensland Teachers Union* (Sydney, 1989), p175.
22 Fleming, "Shifting the emphasis: the impact of police unionism in Queensland, 1915–1925," 109.
23 *WAPN*, Sep 1920, pp9–10; Jun 1921, pp14–17; Dec 1927, pp13–28; Jan 1935, p1. The Western Australian *Government Employees (Promotions Appeal Board) Act, 1945* covered police but the WAPU sought in 1952 to remove police from its provisions — see *WAPN*, May 1952, pp5–6.
24 Tasmania *Police Regulation Act 1955*, s2.
25 *TPJ*, Apr 1950, pp5, 11.
26 *TPJ*, Nov 1954, p11.
27 Tasmania *Police Regulation Act 1955*, s2.
28 Queensland *Police Act 1937*, s57, following the earlier *Police Acts (Amendment) Act 1921*.
29 *SAPJ*, Oct 1931, pp1–11.

30 NSW *Police Regulation (Appeals) Act 1923*, ss3, 7; South Australia, *Police Act 1936* ss22–32, incorporating the provisions of the 1925 Act, no 1676.
31 *SAPJ*, Apr 1929, pp3–17. See *SAPJ*, Dec 1923, p1 for Worrall's election as Vice-President.
32 *SAPJ*, Aug 1931, pp1–11; Oct 1931, pp3–11.
33 *SAPJ*, Oct 1931, pp11–21.
34 *SAPJ*, May 1934, pp9–15.
35 Eg, *SAPJ*, Jun 1933, pp3–7; Jan 1934, pp1–11.
36 Victoria, *Police Regulation Act 1946*, s22.
37 Spaull and Sullivan, *A history of the Queensland Teachers Union*, 175.
38 *QPJ*, Jul 1937, p61.
39 *NSWPN*, Mar 1945, p8.
40 See the extended discussion of the process following the contentious Manners case, in *NSWPN*, Dec 1936, p10.
41 Johnston, *The long blue line: a history of the Queensland Police*, 228–230.
42 Haldane, *The people's force: a history of the Victoria Police*, 210.
43 *Argus*, 15 Jun 1930, cited in *VPJ*, Aug 1930, pp23–24.
44 *Age*, 11 Jul 1930, cited in *VPJ*, Aug 1930, p22.
45 *Argus*, 16 Jul 1930, cited in *VPJ*, Aug 1930, pp27–29.
46 Based on the correspondence and memos published in the *VPJ*, Jul 1930–Feb 1931. See also Haldane, *The people's force: a history of the Victoria Police*, 204–207.
47 Ibid, 207.
48 *WAPN*, Jul 1930, p3 re transfers, in spite of union understanding with government; *WAPN*, Oct 1930, pp1–3, Aug 1932, p5, May 1933.
49 Brien, *Serving the Force: 75 Years of the Police Association of New South Wales*, 65.
50 *NSWPN*, Apr 1935, p1.
51 *SMH*, 21 Jan 1943, p7.
52 *SMH*, 22 Jan 1943, p7.
53 See reports *SMH*, 28 Jan–1 Feb 1943.
54 *SMH*, 29 Jan 1943, p7.
55 *NSWPN*, Jun 1945, p28 reporting proceedings in Grigg v Consolidated Press, 1945. Brief accounts of this episode are available in other sources, but without drawing on the union journal — see Bridget Griffen-Foley, *The house of Packer: the making of a media empire* (St Leonards NSW, 1999), 115–117. and Christopher Cunneen, *William John McKell Boilermaker, Premier, Governor-General* (Kensington NSW, 2000), 153.
56 *SMH*, 14 Apr 1943, p9.
57 *SMH*, 29 Jan 1943, p7.
58 *NSWPN*, Sep 1945, p34.
59 Grigg v Consolidated Press, [1945] *State Reports NSW*, 45, 247.
60 *NSWPN*, Jun 1945, pp4–5, 11–13.
61 *NSWPN*, Dec 1945, pp27–30. Sgt Stevens appealed this Supreme Court decision to the High Court, where he again lost, with Latham J dissenting — see *NSWPN*, Dec 1946, pp42–48.
62 *NSWPN*, Mar 1945, p31 includes transcript of evidence covering MacKay's Dec 1937 memo against entrapment, following a case involving a prosecution by a constable from the 'Morality Squad'.

63 *NSWPN*, Mar 1945, p19.
64 *NSWPN*, Oct 1945, pp24–25; cf the editorial in the Sydney *Sun*, 31 Jan 1945, on 'Police and Democracy'.
65 For a recent review of the legal regulation of policing see David Dixon, *Law in policing: legal regulation and police practices*, Clarendon studies in criminology (Oxford, 1997).
66 *NSWPN*, Jun 1938, p12.
67 *NSWPN*, Jun 1938, p5.
68 *QPJ*, Mar 1956, p26.
69 Fleming, "Power and Persuasion: Police Unionism and Law Reform in Queensland".
70 *SMH*, 19 Sep 1936, p17.
71 *SMH*, 23 Sep 1936, p15.
72 *SMH*, 14 Nov 1936, p17.
73 As cited in *NSWPN*, Dec 1936, p10.
74 *SMH*, 8 Oct 1936, p12.
75 *NSWPN*, Nov 1936, p8.
76 *SMH*, 19 Nov, p17; *NSWPN*, Dec 1936, p10.
77 *SMH*, 21 Nov 1936, p23.
78 Finnane, *Police and government: histories of policing in Australia*, 98–99.
79 *SMH*, 22 Dec 1936; Finnane, *Police and Government*, pp85–87; Haldane, *The people's force: a history of the Victoria Police*, p216.
80 *VPJ*, Nov 1937, p267.
81 VPRO, VPRS 3992/P Unit 1834 File 9241, Blamey, 4 Sep 1928; id, Unit 1864, File 7332 Blamey, 29 Jun 1929.
82 VPRO, VPRS, 3992/P Unit 2500 File 9744'; id, Unit 2504 File 429, Chief Secretary to Association, 2 Feb 1949.
83 *VPJ*, Feb 1949, pp2165–2167.
84 *VPJ*, May 1952, p404; Jun 1952, p419.
85 *VPJ*, Nov 1949, p2319.
86 *VPJ*, Jan 1954, p643.

5: Alliances and conflicts

History and fact have shown that the working class, as individuals standing alone, cannot improve their own lot, but that with a collective effort much can be done for their common good. That common good is to be found in affiliation with the separate State Labour Councils, and that combination calls for immediate solidarity of action.
New South Wales Police News editorial, December 1947

Surely we are not reaching the stage where police doing their duty are expected to make themselves defenceless punching bags and footballs for criminals and louts who want to take charge of the public streets.
St George and Sutherland Shire Leader, September 1963

The possibility of police union involvement in the world of politics and public policy formation was determined largely by the changes that took place in the two decades following the Second World War. This was an era of contentious politics, internationally and in Australia. The seeming political hegemony of Labor in Australia that characterised the 1940s gave way in the 1950s to a prolonged period of conservative government at the national level — and Labor's hold on government in most states was gradually shaken by the effects of the Split in the labour movement, and the atrophy that accompanies prolonged political success. On the other hand the industrial wing of the labour movement remained strong and built on past achievements. In spite of the bitter divisions over the role of communism in the unions, the latter gained in strength through their legitimate role in wage setting and changing working conditions, including shorter hours and improved leave entitlements — the total number of union members in Australia doubled between the depths of the Great Depression (1932–3) and the last year of the Chifley Labor government in 1949.[1]

These also were vital years for the police unions. Their institutional legitimacy was assured, but they still faced limits on their role compared to that of other unions. In some states, above all Victoria, the disabilities of the unions were aggravations in the 1940s and continued so. In other jurisdictions, the police unions took advantage of their legitimacy to re-think their role and develop as active players in the world of criminal justice policy and administration. As we have seen in earlier evidence, an active role in the politics of criminal justice was contemplated, and a reality, in the 1920s. A number of developments in the post-war decades however accentuated the possibilities of police union involvement in civil and political life. In this chapter we explore some of the ways in which this developed from the 1940s to the early 1970s. First there was the important business of defining the political rights, and aspirations, of the police unions. Second, it was essential that the unions build links with other organisations in civil society, especially the media, and the other labour unions. Constructing alliances however also opens up the possibility of later fracturing them — and the close alliances that were developed by the police union leadership in a number of states with the Australian labour movement were sorely tested in the contending tides of political and industrial strife from the mid-1960s.

5.1 A national union?

The idea of a national body bringing the police unions together went back to the 1920s. It had been the aim of an inter-state conference held in Sydney in 1922, but without significant result. It was another generation before a Federation was to be established in 1947. Since that date it has operated with varying effectiveness, and sometimes without the support of all state bodies. For a time its reach extended beyond Australia to encompass the New Zealand police union. The fluctuations of the Federation movement have also been a mirror to the changing political, economic, even jurisdictional, contexts, of policing in Australia. At times (especially in the 1940s and then during the Hawke-Keating years) the political context aided and abetted the federation idea — at others the differences between the various state bodies fractured those possibilities. Our focus here is less on tracing the detailed history of the Federation (and its successor body established in 1999) than on accounting for its disposition and political/organisational impacts.

The greatest stimulus to the formation of a national police union was provided by the conditions of the Second World War. As recalled by one of the key players, New South Wales Police Association secretary Frank Laut, the state unions from 1941 had corresponded intensively over police wages and conditions. These considerations took place in a national context in which the Commonwealth was enlarging its scope of functions. In war-time conditions it even seemed possible that the future might see a national police — and hence a national union would be necessary. In the upshot there was to be no fundamental re-ordering of Australian policing, which has remained a state function for the most part. But in 1943 the possibility of change was enough to prompt the New South Wales Police Association to seek joint action to obtain best conditions if the Commonwealth government took over public service instrumentalities after the war. This was the thinking behind the inter-state conference of police unions held in Melbourne immediately at war's end in November 1945. For Laut, recalling these events in 1963, the significance of that conference lay in the concession that was wrung out of the Victorian government of the time to allow the Police Association to attend a meeting with other police unions — the Victorian union was thus 'really the first Organisation to gain a reform through Federation activity'.[2]

With the conference agreeing to form a federation of police unions, Laut became secretary of the new organisation in November 1946 and the first biennial conference was held a year later in Sydney. Its agenda was wide-ranging — a strong push for the extension of the 40-hour week to all states, access to full arbitration, and affiliation with state Labour Councils. The possibilities of a more uniform national approach in criminal law and other policing matters were also canvassed. In the following years these matters would be pursued in varying degrees. Alliances with the rest of the labour movement were seen as vital and their permutations will be explored throughout this chapter. The spirit of an activist police union feeling at one with the Australian labour movement in its pursuit of better working conditions permeates the record of these years. It is captured in the Federation's letter to the Australian Council of Trades Unions seeking affiliation in September 1953:

> Affiliation with your organisation will tend to create a better understanding between that great section of the workers which you represent and members of the various Police Forces ... it is necessary for all workers to properly understand the motives of members of the Police Services who are bound by their oaths of office, and who when on duty act purely in the interests of the public.[3]

The Federation was a peak body, but not a registered industrial organisation — and so it was to remain a captive of the shifting dispositions of the state bodies that made it up. The Federation sought from time to time to play a role in moving towards a common standard of workplace conditions and professional objectives throughout the country, but was hampered by the jurisdictional realities of Australian policing.

As we will see below an important weapon in the police union armoury during the post-war period was affiliation with the peak body of the union movement, the ACTU. Just as the general trade union movement tended to favour jurisdiction wide, even Australia-wide settlement of wage claims and a common platform of conditions in employment, so too did the Federation. The ambition to move towards a standard set of wages and conditions was embodied in the development at the end of the 1960s of an 'Industrial Charter'. The Charter was adopted by the 1969 Federation Conference, the occasion being noted as 'the first time that the Federation was near to achieving complete Industrial uniformity'. Uniformity in this case involved a commitment to bringing about a consolidation of ranks similar to that in New South Wales, annual leave of at least six weeks, and various increases in margins and allowances.[4]

Beyond wages and conditions the Federation became a vehicle through which those favouring an enhanced professional image for the police would advance their case. Over the decades the priorities in this respect have changed, but significant among them have been improved training and education. Just as the various state-based unions can be regarded as playing a function in ordering and regulating the world of policing at a more local level, thus being more than the mere expression of rank-and-file opinion or frustration, so the Federation tends to become a catalyst in the promotion of new ideas about police work. Reporting to Queensland members in 1996, the general secretary of the union drew their attention to the significant role played by the Federation in the development of the

> policing profession. National core competencies for Police have been developed and a national common training curriculum is being developed. The objective is to provide all Police in Australia and New Zealand with a universal standard of training and a recognition of Police qualifications.[5]

A third function of the Federation, of particular interest to our developing theme, has been its role in advocacy of a police interest in the political sphere. There has been a formal commitment to develop 'a structure for political lobbying to be coordinated by the Police Federation of Australia and New Zealand'.[6] The co-ordinating function of the Federation in selling to politicians across the country the urgency of attending to police interest and demands has been evident for some decades. We will see evidence in the next chapter of this in relation to matters such as the police response to political dissent in the 1960s and 1970s, or in the campaigns against the Commonwealth government's Crimes Investigation Bill in the early 1980s. The tension involved in such commitments to achieving particular national jurisdictional objectives might be seen as one of the reasons why the international dimension of this Federation was brought to an end in the late 1990s when the body was reconstituted by the departure of the New Zealand Police Association as the Police Federation of Australia.[7] As a facilitator of continuing dialogue between unions, enabling them to compare conditions as well as co-ordinate strategies, the significance of the Federation in all its changing guises cannot be ignored in any of the histories that follow below.

5.2 Political rights

The singular achievements of the post-First World War era had been the establishment of the Australian police unions with a degree of legitimacy unknown in most other comparable jurisdictions. The achievement was uneven. Access to industrial tribunals was not accomplished by all; the definition of civil and political rights was variable. The decades after the Second World War saw a continual assertion by the police unions of the rights of their members to the citizenship rights of civilians.

Expanding the political field to include police was not only a matter of external definition, of setting the boundaries through the gradual elimination of statutory limitations on the rights of those who chose to join the police. There was also in these decades a gradual realignment by the police unions of their own aspirations in the field of politics and law and order. Increasingly police union leaders sought to press on the external world the need to take account of what police thought of the work they did, and the rules they worked under. This meant taking a stand on the state of the criminal law, and on the regimes of bureaucratic regulation as well as government policy and resource constraints. In turning to such matters the unions thus redefined themselves as organisations with an ambit that went beyond wages and conditions of work.

A sign of change of this kind was entailed in the rules of the Queensland Police Union. Already we have seen that the Queensland union was an active player in criminal justice policy in the 1920s, helping for example to shape the substantive reform of a key policing statute in 1930. In the 1950s this aspiration to play a role in shaping the law was formalised when the union declared to the world that one of its objects was the pursuit of all matters pertaining to the rule of law.[8] The phrase could be a mandate for the union's interventions in operational policing matters, though not always to the pleasure of the rank and file. In November 1953 the union's long-serving secretary Talty wrote to the commissioner that 'having regard to the fact that the primary object of the QPU is to deal with all matters appertaining to the advancement of police duties and the Rule of Law', the union requested him to direct Townsville police to suppress the sly grog traffic. Townsville police were incensed at Talty's actions.[9] More commonly the 'primary object' would be used in later years to address police union concerns over law reform, 'law and order', or police strength and resources issues. Police unions in other states had more modest objectives, focused on the welfare of the members, but this did not limit their capacity to address the range of concerns that provoked the Queensland union into action from time to time.

The clarification of a union's political objectives was one thing — but what about the status of unions as institutions and of police officers as citizens? The Queensland union had operated in a more congenial environment than most of its associate bodies in other states. So a perennial issue for the immediate post-war decades was that of the civil and political rights of police. It was an issue on which a significant amount of support flowed to the police unions from other areas of the labour movement, in an alliance that was far from natural and, as we will see later, not infrequently tense. The case for advancing full political rights to police was also supported solidly by sections of the press and certainly by the incipient civil liberties movement.

The flavour of this support is captured in the advocacy of labour historian and civil liberties pioneer, Brian Fitzpatrick, in a 1947 call to governments to address the civil disabilities of police. A New South Wales detective had written to Fitzpatrick outlining the difficulties faced by police seeking to play a role in politics, as they could in Queensland where it was possible for a police officer to stand for election without resigning from the force. In an optimistic post-war world Fitzpatrick developed the argument for full political rights for police. He agreed with the detective that by these exclusions the police were kept apart from the people. The British police tradition, Fitzpatrick affirmed, was that of a 'peace Force'. The alternative tradition was that in Europe where the police was a bureaucracy set apart from the community, with a record of repression and administering of punishment. Hence the role of police in Germany, Spain and Pétain's France. If police had full political rights, Fitzpatrick concluded, it might also make it harder for them to be used in the service of political repression as they had been during the 1930s.[10]

When the unions made a case for political rights for the police in this period they meant in fact a number of things. One was a review of the ban on individual police standing for political office, or being associated with political or industrial organisations. Another was a repeal of sections of police regulation acts that limited the freedoms of police associations. Not all unions were affected equally by these restrictions and the major noise around the issue was generated in the two largest Associations, in New South Wales and Victoria.

Symbolic of the changing mood in Australian government was the outcome of changes sought by the Victorian Association in 1946 to enable it to become a member of the prospective Police Federation. Although the inter-state meeting of the Australian police unions was to be held in Melbourne with a view to forming the Federation, the Victorian Association was embarrassed by the anomaly of its own inability to belong. As we have seen earlier this was an outcome of the 1923 strike — legislation establishing the Police Association had simultaneously prohibited police membership of any industrial or political organisations. The inter-state meeting provided a perfect opportunity for highlighting the issue and the government of John Cain (who had spoken for a reform of the restrictive clauses in 1929) obliged with an amendment to the *Police Regulation Act*. The restrictions largely remained, but a new subsection provided the exception that the 'Police Association may be affiliated with any federation of Police Associations or Police Unions of Australia'.[11]

The attainment, and exercise, of political rights was a matter that would proceed by incremental steps. It was undoubtedly aided by the fluidity of post-war social relations — a country that was facing such a massive growth in immigration and so in the longer run a capacious view of citizenship was not likely to hold out forever on restricting police access to conventional citizen rights. 'Like any other intelligent citizen', so New South Wales Association secretary Frank Laut put it in 1954, 'the Police Officer is interested in the way the community is governed. In other words he is interested in politics'.[12] Already police were ready to claim a wide freedom of action, in spite of putative restrictions. The South Australian president noted at the 1947 inter-state conference that the prohibition on politics 'does not deprive us of our citizen rights', that the Association secretary had once stood for parliament, and 'we are entitled to such a right, if not more than the average individual. We are trained men, and with years of experience, and who has a better right than a Police Officer to have civil rights.'[13] The biennial meetings of the now established Federation were to provide recurrent support for the broadening of the political rights of police.[14]

But in both Victoria and New South Wales the 1950s brought little joy on this front. As police came to see their colleagues in other states, or even public servants in their own, becoming involved in politics, the case was revived again in the 1960s in a determined push by both Associations. Teachers were standing for election in Victoria, and in 1961, 29 year-old Constable Bill Hayden was successful in standing for federal election for the seat of Ipswich, his prelude to a life in national politics. Hayden's election as a Labor candidate was surely a stimulus to more sympathetic consideration of the matter in New South Wales, where a Labor government was being pressed to address the matter of civil and political rights of police.[15] In this instance (as in some others we will examine later in this chapter) Labor in government made a difference. While the non-Labor Victorian government showed occasional interest in the issue, the Association secretary was forced to repeated confessions of disappointment. In 1962 the executive heard his report on approaches to the respective political parties — Labor was supportive, the Liberals were 'considering the matter', and the Country Party said it would reserve its opinion until the introduction of a bill.[16] It was not to be until 1983, when Labor was back in office, that the Victorian police succeeded in having removed the restrictions on their membership of political and industrial organisations, a measure enacted in the *Police Regulation (Amendment) Act* of that year.

The gradual lifting of restrictions on police political and civil rights was part of the process of normalisation of the police occupation. There was another side of course to this process. Over the coming decades, just as police had come to share in the general extension of improved working hours, wages and other conditions and now could also expect to play an active role as individuals in civil and political life, so potentially was it expected that they be subject to the accountabilities that a modern workplace demanded. Special pleading about the unique status of police work would be eroded by the expectation in the future that police be educated, make a career on merit rather than seniority, and even be accountable in some domains to the kinds of scrutiny that other public servants would be brought under. These changes were some way off but their impact would help mould new police union agendas.

5.3 Using the media

The political impact of policing draws much of its impetus from the high media profile of police business. It is possible for police departments and police unions to become active players in the political process quite out of the public eye. And of course they do, as we see throughout this book — and in occasional cases, such as Mundingburra, an attempt might be made to establish a political commitment from a potential governing party to police union policy and operational preferences. Yet the potency of policing and law and order issues depends on the way in which these become known to the public through the various media. And, like all other aspects of this subject, this phenomenon has its history.

That history begins in the long fascination of the modern media with all aspects of criminal justice. In the eighteenth century a popular enthusiasm for stories about crime and criminals was fed by the chapbooks produced around the stories of those who were hanged. As the popular press developed in the nineteenth century as a vital instrument of democratisation, entertainment and political literacy the business of the courts in particular became a staple ingredient of newspapers and popular journals. Nineteenth and early twentieth century press contain a level of detail of lower as well as higher court proceedings that far exceed today's equivalents. But of course the influence first of radio and then especially television has in turn provided new sources of media focus on the worlds of law and policing.

We should not think of the production of news, of images of policing and crime, as a process in which the agents of criminal justice are simply the objects of attention. The formalities of the trial court have certainly meant that such a perspective would be merited to a greater degree for the role of judges, and to a lesser extent magistrates. These officials of the court structure their commentary on the phenomena before them but the formalities of their office mean their role as actors in the resulting news reports is limited. The contrast with the position of police officers or prisons staff is striking. There the degree of control exercised over the flow of information is large, indeed verging on the monopolistic. In consequence routines developed over time to manage such a flow. The role of police roundsman as a regular journalistic occupation is familiar — somebody who would know the work of the lower courts in particular and through regular contact with working police become a medium of information flow between police and public.

Having control over information is not however enough to guarantee that the appropriate message will be conveyed through a press report, or a photo. Journalistic conventions and the technical capacities of the medium have been vital ingredients in shaping the way in which police information will become represented to the public. It is not surprising that in this uncertain world of public opinion formation, the police unions have become involved in the business of managing the flow of information. In this they have been assisted, sometimes indirectly, by the way in which these matters have been approached by police departments themselves.

The hunger of the news media for stories about policing has increasingly been the focus of more formal management by police departments, and of course by ministerial staffers. The political contexts in which police stories could be used to shape media attacks on the reputation of governments were explicitly addressed by the president of the Australian Journalists Association addressing a police dinner in 1957 — journalists, he suggested, could be and had been asked by their employers to write exposés of police administration to justify an attack on a government.[17] From about 1960 it became common for the departments to establish their own public relations and media offices. Commissioners would henceforth include some consummate performers in the world of news. Others would struggle to keep control of the flow of bad stories that afflicted their departments, and even the reputation of their own offices — and there were many commissioners before who had fallen foul of the press, Blamey in Victoria being among the best known of the casualties.[18] How could police departments present the activities of police in the best light, satisfying the sceptical journalist, eager to discover cracks in the façade that would help sell a story to a public keen to read about the failures as well as successes of policing? Well before the creation of press officers the relations between police departments and the press had been a matter of policy attention and regulation.

In 1939 for example police roundsmen and senior police in Victoria held a conference to consider the protocols governing press access to police information. The outcome was of interest to police unions as much as to journalists. The latter had their own interest to protect in such negotiations — as 'Roundsman' put it in the *Australian Journalist* 'a wrong action by one Pressman usually brings a string of reprisals, and the innocent find themselves treated as suspect'. The conference agreed to a set of guidelines on press access to police information, and penalties for 'the careless reporter', who would be reported to his editor and debarred from 'facilities for collecting news at Russell Street [police headquarters]'. An information section was based at Russell Street to which press could have access. As well there were various other categories of police who were entitled to pass on information about accidents, crimes committed and other matters. Witness statements obtained by journalists were expected to be submitted to police for approval, and newspapers were expected not to publish statements that the police thought might be harmful to an investigation.[19] The guidelines were an important statement of the interdependence of police and the media. But they were not adequate to the task, so often sought by the members of police unions, of keeping bad news out of the public eye.

Bad news for police usually flowed from reports of police misconduct of one kind or another. A civil case against police for damages arising from an alleged assault or other action was good copy for the press, as we have seen in the Manners case in the 1930s. The 1939 Victorian guidelines were oriented primarily to the reporting of crime, and could not touch the freedom of the press, especially papers like *Truth*, to pursue any scandal or adverse story regarding police. Even where police might seek to control access of journalists to inside information, there were always the courts to provide salacious or just critical stories. In 1950 the Victorian Association fielded complaints about continuing bad publicity flowing from a regular item on 'Stories from the Courts' in the *Sun News-Pictorial*. Every story it was said was one in which the 'policeman is made to look like a dumb cop', a 'doddering fool who should never have been in the job'. The Press Liaison Office in police headquarters, it was said, should do something to get reciprocation for the information they passed on to reporters. Those who knew the police–press beat however recognised there was little that could be done in this particular case. The reporter concerned was not a police roundsman, was not provided with copy by the Press Liaison Office, nor by the police in court. In sum there was no *quid pro quo* and the hope of one member that the 'Press Liaison, by a little ordinary common sense or even blackmail, might be able to even the column out a bit', came to nothing — the *Sun* journalist, as the Association president put it, 'doesn't come this side of the road, and he is not under the jurisdiction of the Press Liaison'.[20]

The cosy accommodation between press and police suggested by this story could thus be breached by those in the media working to different agendas. For the most part we can also see the strong identity of interest between department and union in seeking to secure good news stories in the popular press. When the press did not keep its side of the good news bargain there were options — libel law being one. It was an option well known to police since they made such regular use of it in attempting to obtain satisfaction against their superiors, or others within the force. Taking on the media was more challenging, given the resources available to the latter, and the danger of the action rebounding. All the same there were some who sought satisfaction and won, even against legal advice. When *Truth* published an article in 1966 on the prison escapees Ryan and Walker under the headline 'Walker's Brother is a Cop', the said detective sought Association assistance in obtaining legal advice. Although the legal opinion was negative the case was pursued and Detective Walker settled out of court, with the newspaper paying substantial damages.[21]

The 1939 Victorian 'agreement' discussed above points to a constraint on the press that journalists of particular persuasions inevitably sought to get around. The very attempt by the police hierarchies to manage the flow of information became a condition under which the media turned to the unions as a vital source of opinion and information on police matters. By regulating media access to work-a-day cops the department opened up a great opportunity to the police union as a relatively autonomous body, with privileged access to matters of policing. The scope of the department's management of the media can be seen from the fact that by the 1960s the Russell Street headquarters of the Victoria Police had a news gathering centre that was reportedly hosting 17 press workers a day, from all the Melbourne newspapers and TV and radio stations. Abysmal working conditions in this centre, a converted toilet block, could not hide the substantial importance placed by the police on the management of media stories.[22]

We can see some other passages in the development of the new world of media attention to police affairs through the police unions in the history of Commissioner Norman Allan's office in New South Wales during the 1960s. Allan started with good relations with the media. Yet as his time in the office extended he was faced by increasing controversy. As we will see later his failure to advance a strong case for more police during the last years of the Labor government rendered him the loser on an issue fought long and hard by the union. His disastrous handling of the Wally Mellish house siege in 1967 was a further blow to an already crumbling reputation.[23] His response by this stage was to control the media as far as possible. Initially this strategy developed as an initiative to build better relations between the media and police. In 1965 the executive of the Australian Journalists Association visited Allan to discuss the relationship between police and the press. In August the union journal reported that senior police attended a four-hour meeting with about 80 journalists at the Journalists Club where Allan spoke for about an hour before the meeting broke into discussion groups with the various senior police present, the heads of licensing, traffic, CIB and so on. Allan followed up with a letter of appreciation on matters to be addressed, including the issuing of new press passes to facilitate reporters passing through police lines.[24]

On the other hand this same openness appears to have gone hand in hand with a determined attempt to control the access of ordinary police to journalists. Allan is reported to have banned all but departmental heads from speaking to the press. According to the contemporary study of Chappell and Wilson a result was that journalists received only 'an official and often colourless report of activities in the criminal field'.[25] Given the continuing subsequent critical press coverage of his force's activities, Allan's attempts to control the quality of news reporting may be seen as futile. Their larger significance for our concerns is that they were precisely the kinds of measures that opened the way for developing journalistic access to the police unions. If police departments were going to make themselves inaccessible then the media might seek out more keenly those other vehicles for conveying police opinion — the police unions.

Formal evidence for such a development occurring around this time is not easily gathered. But what makes it plausible is a background of union concerns over the nature of press coverage going back many decades, as well as the emergence of police union officials willing to take an advocacy role in television spots from the 1960s. As we have already noted, police unions had long been concerned about the effect of media reporting. In Tasmania for example, the Police Association president gave voice to the ambivalence of police organisations, both departments and unions, when he addressed the 1954 annual conference. Tasmanian police and press relations had 'always been good', more so than in other states:

> The press is a great adjunct to the Police in that it assists in the suppression and elucidation of crime, and on many occasions a criminal has been driven into the hands of law by means of Police-Press co-operation.

This standing consensus did not prevent occasional unwanted disruptions to the cosy relationship — for that very day the president had read the headline news in the *Hobart Mercury* 'that a detective forced a confession from a man by thrusting a loaded rifle down his throat'.[26] Over the following year the police union had many concerns over the press focus on alleged 'police bashings', some of which led to at least one officer being dismissed following official inquiry — and in August 1955 the Association appealed to the Federation of Police Associations for advice on handling the press criticism.[27]

That was also the response of the South Australian union in facing what it termed the 'violent criticism' flowing from the controversy over the Stuart case in 1959, when police interrogation practices were put under the microscope. The responsibilities of the press were clear, according to PASA:

> The Press and Radio have a duty to the public to expose anything that is against the public interest, but they should be doubly sure that any attack is based on sound premises.[28]

Just as a police union offered collective support and resources to individual police in defending themselves against what was seen as harsh or oppressive treatment by their superiors, so it might sustain them in their defence against public criticism. The freedom of individual police to engage in public comment on policing issues was formally very limited. In 1958 continuing public political attacks on the New South Wales police were the occasion of widespread condemnation by the police. The Liverpool union branch saw the matter as tied to the continuing political and civil disabilities of police: if they had full rights then police could defend themselves against press criticism, while at present they couldn't even write to the newspapers. The branch was not isolated in its response —the union executive at this time had received over 30 motions from around the state in response to the call by a member of parliament, Mrs Melville MLC, for an official inquiry into the police. Some police wanted mass meetings to protest against these continuing attacks in the press and parliament. All the same the executive appears to have counselled caution, being reluctant to hold general meetings of police 'with their inherent dangers', and advising that little could be done about press criticism, unless it verged on libel in which case individuals were entitled to take action.[29] The volatile state of policing in New South Wales in fact seemed to guarantee continuing press criticism — and repeated calls from the branches for the union to pursue legal or other actions.[30]

Not all criticism was unanswered. The annual conferences of the unions were occasions on which politicians would be likely to mount a strong defence of the police against whatever press criticism was being waged. In May 1954 New South Wales Labor Premier Cahill opened the annual conference of the Police Association with a 'stirring speech' condemning the then current press criticism which was undermining the people's confidence in 'the Force of law and order'. Such occasions were also moments for intoning the mantra of politicians and police commissioners — Cahill reminded the assembled delegates that Commissioner Scott had returned from an overseas study tour to tell the newspapers that the 'New South Wales Police Force is equally good, if not better, than any other Police Force in the world'.[31]

Not all the press was critical. And the union journals were ready to wave the flag when support came on side: as did the *St George and Sutherland Shire Leader*, in September 1963 defending police against recent press allegations of bashings. The *Leader* pointed to the good and necessary work of police dealing with violent gangs: 'surely we are not reaching the stage where police doing their duty are expected to make themselves defenceless punching bags and footballs for criminals and louts who want to take charge of the public streets'. In what was to become a familiar trope the police were said to be hampered by restrictions in dealing with events such as the disgraceful scenes of gang battles at Cronulla the previous summer: 'These are the bashers and thugs who need to be dealt with and the police are hampered enough now. They can't even charge a juvenile without authority from the officer-in-charge of the area'.[32]

Policing gang violence was only one of the many public order issues provoking public controversy during the 1960s. The political dissent that would increase dramatically as Australia deepened its involvement in the Vietnam War occasioned heated debates around the role of police. This became a concern for the police unions once again and stimulated their intervention in operational matters. In the increasingly fractious protest climate of 1968, the New South Wales Police Association met with the Australian Journalists Association (AJA). A demonstration in Martin Place had been marked by a high degree of conflict between students, police and journalists. The AJA and police union executive agreed on the need to maintain good relations — but some on the police side were subsequently to question whether there should be a review of the conditions governing the issue of police press passes.[33]

Union officials by the 1960s were becoming used to the expectation that they would need to cultivate friendly relations with the press — and use the opportunity it provided for advocacy of the police case, whether on industrial or law and order issues. By this time it was not uncommon to see police union secretaries appearing on TV programmes dealing with relations between police and the public, including of course the press itself.[34] The media had its dangers — but they were best avoided by fostering good relations and being ready to speak publicly for the police cause. There were always those who felt that a negative press would be best countered by limiting media access — but when such a case was made those who were of longer experience counselled otherwise. As Victorian Association vice-president McConville advised in 1947, a new member of the executive who had proposed limited access to the media 'probably did not realise the assistance the Press had given in the struggle for better conditions'.[35] The more in fact that police departments and police commissioners sought to 'manage' press relations, the greater opportunity developed over the decades for police unions to fill the gaps left open for a media hungry for good copy.

5.4 Are police workers?

If fostering good relations with the media was one part of the unions' tactical armoury in the post-war era, another was the consolidation of links with the rest of the labour movement. We have seen already that in the special conditions of Western Australia, the police union there had even gone to the extent of affiliating with the Labor Party in 1943. Although such an outcome seemed unlikely in other jurisdictions, a much more common step was affiliation with the labour movement through the industrial arm. Support for such a commitment was widespread in the police union leadership in most states from the 1940s to the 1960s. Interest subsided as conflict between police and various groups of dissidents accelerated in the late 1960s, but was also a casualty of a changing political climate in which the Labor party was gradually falling out of favour. The history of the police unions' links with the Australian labour movement tells us much about the possibilities of police unionisation — and its limits.

Fear of being tainted with a red brush had been behind much police union resistance to closer links with the industrial union movement in the inter-war years. Typical enough was the opposition of the writer in the *New South Wales Police News* in 1931 who characterised those advocates of affiliation with the Trades and Labour Council as 'hot heads' — but in its attention to an article in the *Canadian Police Bulletin* dealing with the question of such linkages the writer also highlighted unwittingly the perennial potential of this issue.[36] The same conditions that had fostered caution in 1919 about links with 'reds' and radicals also persisted in the years of the Great Depression — the mood of other unionists towards police who were often involved in conflict with striking workers and the unemployed was scarcely such as to encourage the police unions in the direction of affiliation.

By the war years the mood was quite different. Consensus around the war effort combined with union determination to assert claims for wage improvements to alter rank and file police attitudes as well. As Sheridan argues in his account of industrial relations during the Chifley years, there was a rare popular support at the end of the war for unions and labour rights, and an improvement in conditions of employment.[37]

The degree to which this mood affected the police labour movement can be seen at its extreme in Western Australia in 1943–4, but is evident in other states. For example in South Australia too the labour movement found strong advocates in the Police Association when members voted 503–121 in favour of affiliation with the local Trades and Labour Council.[38] In spite of the strong vote in support, the rumblings of those opposed to such links continued to warrant occasional defensive positions by the Association leaders. Long-serving Association secretary Sergeant L B Fenwick (he had been there since 1923) felt compelled in April 1945 to defend the South Australian affiliation with the labour movement in the face of Victorian criticism. Like other union advocates of links with labour he stressed what police had in common with other workers. To those who said that 'other unions are too red' he replied that police involvement would give a 'little more balance' to the labour movement. The old perennial of what police would do in case of a general strike demanded attention, Fenwick responding that 'The police will never be asked to join in a strike unless it is their own, and let's hope that this will never happen'. When policing strikes, police were neither pro-masters nor pro-workers, but rather there to 'protect life and property'.[39]

The mood at the end of the war was generally up-beat and Labor's political hegemony seemed assured. So some of the support for links with the labour movement came from a genuine ideological commitment to the spirit of collectivism and social reconstruction, a commitment that one finds in labour movement materials reproduced in the union journals in 1945. Such was evident in the enthusiasm of those who saw unionism encapsulating the principles of democracy, 'the right of free men to organise, to associate with their fellow-men in action for the common good, to speak freely and without fear, and to act according to their conscience.' The post-war era offered the opportunity to those who believed in unionism to 'prove that free men co-operating can out-produce slave labor, that voluntary committees can accomplish more than the whip of the Gestapo, and that free men living together decently can do more than slaves working under sub-standard conditions.'[40] Police were even encouraged by some of the mainstream press to see their future as identical with the new order, as suggested in a Sydney *Sun* editorial of 31 January 1945 on 'Police and democracy'.[41] The clarity of choices made possible in the conditions of war would not long survive its end. Renewed social and industrial conflict in the years after the war, and the onset of the international Cold War — both would demand that police unions look at links with the labour movement in a more pragmatic light.

In this context it was more likely that affiliation with the trade union movement would be sold on the basis of what it was likely to achieve in simple terms of improved wages and conditions. The aggressive pursuit of higher wages and a shorter working week by Australian labour unions in the post-war period would involve police at two levels — as the front-line of social defence and managers of order, and as beneficiaries of accumulating benefits. To gain the latter however meant being part of the new order. Industrial strength for the police in the decade after the end of the Pacific War flowed from industrial linkages of two kinds.

In the first place the 'Federation' movement now came to the fore. The enthusiasm of the early 1920s had evaporated in the face of more immediate struggles at a state level. The renewed support for a federation of police unions came at a time when the political landscape in Australia seemed to promise more support for political and industrial standardisation at a national level. The Commonwealth government had won substantial increases in central powers over the states, especially in financial but also social policies, after 1942 — and the Curtin and then Chifley Labor governments were pursuing an extension of these achievements into the post-war world, an era of 'reconstruction'. Police union advocates of federation found that their day had dawned. Federation gave a particular edge to arguments for closer links with labour — and it facilitated such links through the almost inevitable association between national leaders of industrial organisations with such resources behind them.

Increasingly from the 1940s there is evidence of networking between police union leaders and their confreres in other labour organisations. When the president of the New South Wales Teacher's Federation appeared at the annual Police Association conference in 1945 he did so as a gesture of solidarity with police pursuit of their rights as 'Australian citizens'. Nor did he lose the opportunity to press the advantages of closer links between police and the labour movement, informal results of which had been evident when the state Labour Council supported the police union during its joust with Commissioner MacKay in 1942.[42]

In spite of strong support at union leadership level, there were many among the lower ranks of Police Association delegates who were sceptical about too close a linkage with the rest of the labour movement at this time. Opponents of affiliation with the Labour Council argued at the 1945 New South Wales Police Association conference that affiliation would inevitably make the union political, or that the potential of such links would be compromised by the difficulty that police could not go on strike, an otherwise essential weapon in the industrial battlefield.[43] A more 'leftist' stance was evident in the New South Wales Association at this time, with the 1945 conference proceeding only cautiously down the arbitration path since, as some delegates put it, arbitration was no longer serving union interests, with employers and governments backing it.[44] This was not a position easily sustained since other experience seemed to promise better outcomes from arbitration — the Queensland police were ranked as the best paid in Australia by September 1945, and the *Police News* noted that they had rights of arbitration.[45]

In contrast then to the Western Australian and South Australian positions, New South Wales was slower to come on board the union train. What made a difference in the end was the double effect of police union federation and union leadership networks. The sceptics of 1945 were confronted again in 1947 by the advocates of labour solidarity. Union secretary and solid Labor man, Frank Laut, was the likely author of the December 1947 editorial that brought the merits of police federation and union solidarity together. The renewed federation had not yet resulted in hoped for federal arbitration, but unity of police across the nation was vital, especially on the matter of political and civil rights of police, on which New South Wales still had much to do. The editorial stressed the importance of standing with the trade union movement:

> History and fact have shown that the working class, as individuals standing alone, cannot improve their own lot, but that with a collective effort much can be done for their common good. That common good is to be found in affiliation with the separate State Labour Councils, and that combination calls for immediate solidarity of action.[46]

The editorial flowed from a recent visit to an executive meeting by the general secretary of the Western Australian Police Union. He had already urged the benefits of affiliation at the Interstate Federation conference. In Western Australia he said, the police union had had trouble getting itself heard until it affiliated with the Labor Party. Since then it had found that it had the backing of the party organisation, and of strong unions, in pressing its case for improved conditions such as the 40-hour week. The link had been vital because, the secretary noted, 'you will find Labor Governments have a conservative feeling with regard to a Police Force — that it is not a good tradition to allow the Police to get too many improvements'.[47]

The Federation conference had called on all states to seek affiliation with their local trades hall bodies. Some state bodies faced minimal opposition to such moves — the Tasmanian Commissioner told the local Association in 1949 that he didn't object to discussion of affiliation with the state Trades and Labour Council.[48] Yet there was resistance still within the ranks of the police to the idea of too close affiliation with the labour movement. In 1956 the Association was still debating affiliation with the state Council. The executive made a strong case for affiliation, and downplaying in a familiar fashion the worries of some about being unwillingly involved in strikes and levies for other unions. An influential former president of the union put a fundamentally constitutional case against this. While the High Court in 1932 had dismissed analogies between the position of the army and police, it is clear from Berryman's attack on affiliation that the analogy was still one held dearly by some police. The police force he described as a 'civil army' before going on to ask how it would be possible for the Australian Army to affiliate with Trades Hall:

> If the Police Association gain affiliation to the Trades Hall Council they will be morally supporting [strike action] ... The nature of our employment and the oath we subscribe to make it impossible.[49]

The Victorian Association, still burdened by the provisions of the *Police Regulation Act*, faced extreme difficulties in meeting the call. In 1944 the Trades Hall Council secretary had invited the Association to affiliate, and in 1947 Association members voted for affiliation but could not put it into effect.[50] The disjunction between political rights of police in different states was highlighted by the subsequent chequered history of the Victorian Police Association's links to both the Police Federation, and the labour movement. When the Federation eventually affiliated with the Australian Council of Trades Unions (ACTU) in 1954[51] the Victorian Association was placed in an ambiguous position. Although strong supporters of the union cause, Association leaders were unable to represent the Federation at ACTU meetings, because of the statutory exclusions of the *Police Regulation Act* — legal advice from Slater & Gordon confirmed this in 1954, while suggesting some flexibility by way of proxies.[52] By 1967 when tensions with other labour unions and the affiliation costs prompted the Federation to disaffiliate from the ACTU, the Victorian Association had become so dissatisfied with the Federation's limited achievements that it determined to cease its links with that body. At the same time the Association was impressed with the ACTU's star industrial advocate Bob Hawke. An executive motion sought an amendment to the Articles of the Association in order to make donations directly to the ACTU so that 'we could hold our heads high and help to pay the cost of wage claims and Mr Hawke's wages'.[53]

The importance of local political networks was evident in the story of the Victorian Association's high regard for Hawke's opinion. The ACTU headquarters were based in Melbourne, facilitating the link. Throughout the years 1969–71 the Victorian Police Association debated the issue of re-affiliation with the Federation, in view of the latter's links with the well-regarded ACTU. In spite of the minister's view that the Association could not affiliate to a body that was linked to an external, non-police organisation, other legal advice cleared the way for it to explore the possibilities. At an executive meeting in December 1970 the secretary indicated that he would be speaking to Bob Hawke about affiliation with the ACTU. Subsequently Hawke attended the executive meeting in 1971 and predictably urged the benefits of solidarity:

> ... any Association or Union of workers or salary earners should be part of the overall organisation from which they derived a considerable amount of their basic benefits and advantages and in the Australian situation there was no doubt that the basic benefits in regard to wages and conditions emerged from the action of the overall confederation of trade unions, which was the A.C.T.U. If the only way in which Victoria could participate in the wider organisation was by way of membership of the Australian Police Federation, then Mr Hawke felt it appropriate that we should belong to the Federation. Mr Hawke said he found section 126 of the Police Regulation Act repugnant and something which the Association should take action to have repealed.

Responding to Hawke's advocacy the secretary suggested informing the other police unions in the Federation that Victoria was giving 'very favourable consideration to re-joining the Federation'. However, this would depend on 'whether we could expect them to re-affiliate with the A.C.T.U. as they were prior to 1967'.[54]

The curious history of the Victorian Association's flirtation with the ACTU — placing the former at odds with the other police unions in the Police Federation — reflects the contentious history of its institutional status. In spite of its continuous history of industrial disputation, accelerating through the 1970s and down to the end of the century it was not until the last years of the Kennett government that the Association finally did something that had been debated for decades — affiliated with the local Trades Hall.[55] This was a final signal that Victorian police had thrown over the heritage of its inter-war experiences, battered in the police strike and their union dismantled by Blamey.

That history was very different from the freedoms enjoyed by other police unions. Nevertheless the cosy conditions fostered by Labor ascendancy in states like Queensland and Western Australia did not always ensure a comfortable linkage of the local police union to the rest of the industrial movement. How far police could be just like other workers was always a debating point. In Western Australia the police minister urged the Police Union conference in 1956 to get more involved in the labour movement in both its political and industrial wings[56] — his speech reflected the distance that was still evident between police and the rest of the labour movement in that state, in spite of the closest institutional affiliations.

Even when a union was prepared to get into effective alliances with others, the danger was that it could become too closely identified with the wrong side. In Queensland about this same time the labour movement was fractured and police union affiliation was perhaps predictably linked to the more conservative wing of the industrial movement. The more radical Trades and Labour Council stood on one side, including many blue collar urban unions — it had a long history of conflict with the Australian Workers Union (AWU)-dominated Labor Party which ruled Queensland to 1957. Collaboration with other unions was nevertheless seen as vital in the management of the arbitration process, particularly on broad wages and conditions issues, such as the basic wage and leave arrangements. By the early 1960s the Queensland Police Union was involved with an AWU-led Combined Industrial Unions' initiative — this brought together Queensland's major industrial union, with a strong representation in the bush, and a range of mainly clerical and white collar unions, including the State Services Union, the Federated Clerks, the Queensland Teachers Union and the Royal Australian Nurses Federation. An address by the AWU's Edgar Williams was largely attended in 1962, giving a chance to the QPU to receive endorsement on its directions and priorities from one of the state's most influential labour movement figures, head of a union with 72,000 members. Asked about the contentious matter of union dues, Williams insisted that the QPU members got good value from their £6 p.a. (compared to £3 p.a. for the AWU) since the police union dues also supported their mortality and legal defence funds.[57] Unwittingly perhaps, Williams was also drawing attention to the respects in which police were something other than workers — legal liability was not a risk in most other occupations in the way that it persistently was in the case of police.

The processes of union formation, union identity and labour movement affiliations were some of the ways in which police occupational status was affirmed as akin to that of other workers in the Australian context. There were yet other ways in which the question whether police were workers would be raised — in the legal environment testing their status as 'servants' or employees, in the industrial arbitration context where the unions would seek recognition at a national level for their combined industrial agitation for better wages and conditions. A further dimension is cultural, and gendered. In an occupation that was almost an emblem of masculine identity, police unions reflected to a good degree the ambivalent, if not hostile, disposition towards women's changing role in the workforce in the twentieth century. In this they were almost at one with police departments, which for many decades perceived the role of women police as one that was almost wholly confined within a domesticated definition of the role.[58] While women were evidently entitled to membership in some police unions (e.g. South Australia and Victoria), they were explicitly excluded in New South Wales in the early decades.[59]

If anything, police unions however were somewhat ahead of departments, at least until the 1970s when equal opportunity and discrimination became important political and workforce issues. In earlier decades the police unions saw unequal wages as a potential threat to their members' interests. Consequently the South Australian Association was strongly opposed in 1952 to the attempts of the police commissioner to reduce the wages of the few women police to 75% of male rates, a reversal of equal pay that had held in South Australian policing from the year of its advocacy by the Association at the 1918 arbitration of police wages. The Association's support for the even more vigorous resistance campaign waged by the women police themselves resulted in the government withdrawing the proposal to cut women's pay rates, by exempting them from a wage rise awarded to male police. One result was that most of the women police joined the Association, which they had shunned since the 1930s, because it was said they 'considered it improper for women to belong to the police force's "union"'.[60] Similarly in 1956 the Queensland Police Union argued in the industrial court for equal pay for women police, who had only been admitted as full members of the union the year before. The case was opposed by the police department, which successfully removed women police (who were not even fully sworn officers at this stage) from the general police award and established pay rates at 80% of the male rate.[61]

These indications of a liberal disposition of union leaders on pay issues were not always replicated at rank and file level. The long-standing view that women could only be engaged in a restricted set of policing duties, a view repeatedly sustained in the police union journals in the early decades, was re-awakened as policy and practice started to affect police recruiting from the 1960s. Not only were women now instated as regular, fully sworn police — but also they were gradually recruited in greater numbers. Union forums, whether conferences or journals, allowed some recalcitrant male police to give vent to their antagonism — perhaps speaking for a larger number in querying the embrace being given by union leaders to the principle of equal opportunity. At the 1975 New South Wales Association conference one speaker who was later to become president of the union questioned whether women could really do the man's work of policing.[62] In the same year two women police nominated for election to the Victorian Police Association executive — in this International Women's Year, the *Victorian Police Journal* suggested, 'it would be fitting to see one or both ladies [sic] who have nominated so far, elected to the Executive'. Neither was successful, but shortly after the first woman delegate was elected, becoming a strong and public critic of discrimination against women police.[63] In spite of the gestures of some police union leaders in support of equal opportunity at this time, these years were ones in which changes to work and gender roles could also provoke resistance at the top of the unions — evident especially in Queensland, where Commissioner Whitrod's recruitment of women into the police provoked opposition from the police union.[64]

In the post-war decades police unions for the most part were content to identify with the broader objectives of the labour movement — until the political identity of governments began to change in the 1960s, and political conflict spilled out onto the streets, affecting public estimations of the police and encouraging in turn a tendency for the police to retreat into their own bunkers. Were police workers? Was policing a male business? Should police unions be part of the labour movement? The answers given to such question were not pre-determined but rather shaped by the contexts in which those questions would be asked.

5.5 Fractured relations

Something like a consensus had emerged during the Second World War around the rights and justice of the labour movement cause. We have seen that this was the context for a drift of the police unions towards affiliation with the peak institutions of the industrial labour movement, the trades halls in each state and even with the ACTU. The identity of police unions with the aims and objectives of other parts of the labour movement was nevertheless shaky. There was of course a great range of political dispositions in that movement, epitomised in the rapid deterioration of industrial relations in the post-war years, and in the eventual split within the Labor Party in 1957. But by the late 1960s there was a new order of political dissent that challenged the very role that police played in the management of social order. From the perspective of some police unionists it was one thing to parley with the unions in the euphoria of the end of the Pacific War, another to embrace them at a time when so many labour unions and unionists were participating in repeated attacks on the police themselves.

Some measure of the scale of change during these years might be indicated by the divisions within the police union movement over the question of communism. Surprising as it might seem now, it was by no means self-evident to police union leaders that police should take a stand against the influence of communism in Australian politics. The question was addressed at successive Police Federation conferences from the late 1940s. Victorian delegates were to the forefront of those who wanted the Federation to press the Commonwealth government to legislate against communism. In 1947 their attempt was ruled out of order because the matter was deemed 'political'. The item was again brought to the 1949 conference by the same Victorian delegates, calling for 'united action from the conference to force the Commonwealth Government to take some steps to combat this canker in our midst'. Again the motion was lost, by a large majority.[65] The fight against communism was seen by some Victorian members as especially pertinent in view of allegations that had been made in the press and at a royal commission regarding communist cells in some police forces — but even in the Victorian Police Association there were those who considered the police unions should stay out of the debate as it was 'political'.[66]

On such matters police unions reflected to a degree the divisions of opinion in the community, and the defeat of the Victorian delegates' attempts to get the Federation to take a stand were a portent of the Australian electorate's later reluctance to back the Menzies government's attempt to ban the Communist Party. The response of police unionists to political dissent of other kinds remained varied. The tasks of police in public order policing were an operational matter to be determined by the commissioner and senior officers — but politicians from both sides of the political fence could be found proffering advice, or even demanding changes in policing priorities in response to the challenge of mass demonstrations. Within the unions could be found those who counselled caution and discretion. A Queensland Police Special Branch officer, Don Lane, could be found in 1969 advising police of the hazards they faced in the new era of public disorder, hazards they could avoid by 'exercising self discipline, behaving as professionals and always acting within the law'. Lane's excursion into social analysis identified some of the new factors at work which police found challenging — especially the presence of many whose avowed aim was to challenge the law itself, to invite arrest and to provoke police officers under the eye of TV cameras. What Lane identified as 'the seemingly unlimited legal aid available to the protest movement' placed the protestors 'in a position of considerable strength — a position probably never shared before by any section of the community'. Hence some police had found themselves the object of civil actions by those individuals they were expected to police.[67]

In an often repeated phrase, police found themselves the meat in the sandwich in the divided society of the late 1960s. What initially appeared to the *Victoria Police Journal* as a lack of public support for the anti-war demonstrators in 1966 was transformed by later events into a much more combative protesting public. By 1969 the Victorian Police Association was receiving letters on the one hand from trades unions condemning police heavy-handedness, while other citizens wrote in supporting the police. In the widespread public debate over the developing disorder in public demonstrations the Association's secretary ventured out to the universities to put the police perspective. The police disposition was not helped by changing expectations of government — the early tolerance of public protest was being challenged in cabinet and without and by September 1970 the Association was reporting that the chief secretary had hardened his stance against demonstrators. Not only Vietnam protests were involved — the 1969 protests over government anti-union legislation brought additional challenges, and tested yet again the tenuous linkages between the Association and Victorian Trades Hall.[68]

The police unions could be easily affronted by the criticism of other unions. There is little doubt that the depth of conflict over policing of public order in the late 1960s fuelled an unprecedented degree of conflict between the police unions and others. As an affiliate of the Trades and Labour Council and of the ALP in Western Australia, the Police Union was especially sensitive to attacks on the actions of police, such as those inspired by the policing of a major industrial dispute at Port Hedland in early 1969. Calls for disaffiliation from the ALP began to come in to the Perth office of the union. In the following year the union disaffiliated from the Trades and Labour Council.[69] It was a notable turnaround for a union that had sustained strong links with the political and industrial arms of the labour movement from the 1920s, and as recently as 1967 had opposed the Police Federation's disaffiliation from the ACTU.[70]

Handling dissent drew police unions and administration together more than it drove them apart. In Western Australia where the police commissioner was in any case a member of the union this may not have been such a new outcome. But the effect of political dissent was to increase the risks that police would become embroiled in political controversy, as they had on occasions before when political tempers in the country had flared — in the 1930s in New South Wales, leading to legislation protecting the position of the police commissioner, and in the 1910s in Queensland around the controversial Commissioner Cahill. Instead by the late 1960s it was more likely that police unions might be called on to become the spokespersons for the whole of policing. The Victorian Association executive agreed in July 1969 that the secretary might meet a trades hall delegation for talks on police attitudes to demonstrations but would be required to draw their attention to the fact that the interview should really be with the chief commissioner.[71] In Queensland such distinctions were tending to be forgotten. After student radical Brian Laver appeared on the TV programme 'Meet the press' in February 1968 criticising police 'thuggery' in recent demonstrations, the programme dedicated its following week to an extended discussion over the state of Queensland policing, not with the police commissioner, but with the police union general secretary, Merv Callaghan.[72] Callaghan's defence was wide-ranging, and successfully evasive — but its significance lies most of all in his readiness to speak on behalf of Queensland police generally, not as unionists, but in their capacity as police officers and across the whole range of their duties. That state of readiness was becoming characteristic of police union officials. It was useful of course to a media hungry for comment, and not always able to get it from official sources.

As Don Lane's article in the *Queensland Police Journal* had noted, the policing of dissent generated another kind of problem for police — that of civil actions against police. The temper of the times inspired action and counter action. In Queensland the union levied members $4 to enable police to defend the many writs taken out by students arrested in demonstrations in 1968.[73] The Victorian Association instructed solicitors to pursue the possibility of counter actions against those complaining of police assaults. After three police were assaulted at Preston in 1969, the union decided to support a civil action by the police officers concerned, the executive agreeing that it would be useful 'get the publicity to show it was dangerous to assault a policeman'.[74] The Association had been encouraged by its recent use of this tactic, with a number of successes leading to a perceived decline in civil actions in the previous year.[75]

Not all police union response was hostile to the demonstrators. Indeed, just as police operational commanders in some places moved in the longer term to a less confrontational approach in the policing of public order, there were those in the police union movement who recognised that there were alternatives to the frequent clashes that might lessen the danger of police being injured or incurring the dangers of civil damages suits against them. The risk of police facing civil actions was only one of a number of adverse outcomes of too heavy-handed an approach to demonstrators. The union journals include advice on the importance of restraint, with members being advised of the importance of self-control. It was important, advised the South Australian *Police Journal*, not to be 'thin-skinned', to use powers of arrest minimally, and only when demonstrators were breaking the law. American cases of use of excessive force during the Newark race riots were examples to be avoided.[76] Hence the 1969 Police Federation conference considered a motion from the Tasmanian Association that the Federation develop a policy 'that will give protection to Police Officers against false accusations and civil claims arising out of demonstrations', while a South Australian motion urged conference to 'discuss the various methods used to handle demonstrators in the various States'. In discussion a further motion was put, to the effect that the police commissioners consider 'establishing liaison between the Police and students and other bodies likely to demonstrate'.[77]

In any case police unions had long experience of feeling embattled and trampled on. This perception justified the seemingly tasteless approach of the Police Association of South Australia in 1972 to the Council for Civil Liberties for assistance to pay the legal expenses of officers involved in the Duncan inquiry. Dr Duncan had died in suspicious circumstances near a homosexual beat, following his interception by police. The Council asked, as well it might, for 'an indication as to the way in which it is thought civil liberties are involved'. The case was to linger long in the state's political memory and police reputations did not fare well when it was finally subject to sustained inquiry in the 1990s. The Police Association's extraordinary request for legal assistance in these circumstances was a symptom of a mentality that felt police were always being judged by a double standard. That perception was evident enough when the Association received a request the following year from the Aboriginal Legal Rights Movement for donations towards the establishment of a bail fund for Aborigines charged with offences. The secretary could have been content with the reply that there was no power within the Rules of the Association to make such a donation, but added that there was not such a fund 'available to our own members'.[78]

The sense of grievance over the effects of political dissent in producing what the police unions saw as a declining respect for police in society was evident in the 1971 Federation conference. There a motion was passed requiring the Federation's general secretary to write to every federal and state politician in the country concerning the increased violence and demonstrations faced by police. Conference, in the words of the motion, expressed

> alarm at the growing tendency of certain sections of the community who resort to actions of organised violence and lawlessness at demonstrations in the streets and other places throughout Australia.

The subsequent letter to politicians detailed police unhappiness with a lack of support from politicians and government to maintain effective policing at a time of increased 'lawlessness'. The controversy over policing of demonstrations at the Vietnam Moratoriums and Springbok tour protests was seen by the police as contributing to a poor climate for recruitment and retention of police officers. Politicians were being asked then to 'support a campaign designed to provide better police services and to assist the police in achieving their objective of making the community free and safe for all persons'.[79]

No more than those in power against whom political dissent was specifically targeted, the police unions found it difficult through the 1960s and 1970s to deal equably with the challenge of social disorder. Their members were necessarily the meat in the sandwich, formally by virtue of their duties to maintain the peace. But as the embodiment of authority police were proxies for an otherwise invisible state. Their industrial arm almost inevitably got swept into a combative stance that compromised yet further the independence of police. In such a context the optimistic talk of the 1940s about solidarity with 'the working class' and the progressive development of Australian society was no longer to be seen. After the political climate softened in the wake of Australia's withdrawal from Vietnam and the election of a federal Labor government, different kinds of challenge would put ideas of such solidarity to rest. Police unions would from the 1970s become embattled institutions, constantly struggling for improved conditions but also grappling with new demands on the nature and accountability of police work.

Notes

1 *Australian Historical Statistics*, 1987, pp162–163; Sheridan, *Division of labour: industrial relations in the Chifley years, 1945–49.*
2 This account draws especially on Laut's recall of the early history, in *NSWPN*, Sep 1963, p13.
3 Idem.
4 *TPJ*, Jan–Feb 1970, p2.
5 *QPJ*, Dec 1996, p7.
6 *QPJ*, Dec 1996, p7.
7 *TPJ*, Dec 1998, pp23–26.
8 Fleming, "By fair means or foul? The impact of police unionism in Queensland, 1915–1932", 50.
9 QSA, A/44887, Talty to Commissioner of Police, 16 Nov 1953.
10 *NSWPN*, Mar 1947, p6 a reprint of Fitzpatrick's Weekly Letter in the popular *Smith's Weekly*, 1 Feb 1947.
11 Victoria, *Police Regulation Act*, 1946, s23 1 (d).

12 *NSWPN*, Aug 1954, p3.
13 *SAPJ*, May 1947, pp9–23.
14 See *VPJ*, Oct 1951, p306; Aug 1952, p438; Jul 1954, p729; Jul 1955, p958.
15 *VPJ*, Jul 1961, p122; *NSWPN*, Jun 1962, p10.
16 *VPJ*, Sep 1962, p154.
17 G F Godfrey, "The police and the press," *Australian Police Journal* 11 (1957).
18 Haldane, *The people's force: a history of the Victoria Police*, 210–214.
19 *NSWPN*, Oct 1939, p44, originally in *Australian Journalist* (unknown date).
20 *VPJ*, Jun 1950, p100; Jul 1950, p115.
21 *VPJ*, Feb 1966, p177; Mar 1966, p195; Oct 1969, p132.
22 Jim Scott, "Police Press Facilities Under Fire", *The Journalist*, Dec 1966, p1.
23 Stuart Gardiner, *The Commissioner Allan Story*, Dee Why West: Tempo, 1973, pp44, 84.
24 *NSWPN*, Aug 1965, p15.
25 Duncan Chappell and Paul R Wilson, *The Police and the Public in Australia and New Zealand* (St Lucia, 1969), 131.
26 *TPJ*, Nov 1954, p15.
27 *TPJ*, Sep 1955, p7. See Finnane, *Police and Government*, p83.
28 *SAPJ*, Jan 1960, p6. *VPJ*, Dec 1959, pp210–215 for 1959 Federation Conference minutes, which do not report discussion of press issues.
29 *NSWPN*, Jan 1959, p7.
30 *NSWPN*, Nov 1963 for such a call from the CIB following Daily Telegraph attacks on police integrity, 21 Aug 1963.
31 *NSWPN*, May 1954, p6.
32 The report was reprinted in *NSWPN*, Oct 1963, p1.
33 *NSWPN*, Oct 1968, p3.
34 *VPJ*, Aug 1965, p59.
35 *VPJ*, Oct 1947, p1884.
36 *NSWPN*, Feb 1931.
37 Sheridan, *Division of labour: industrial relations in the Chifley years, 1945-49*, p317.
38 *SAPJ*, Jan 1944.
39 *SAPJ*, Apr 1945, p1.
40 *SAPJ*, Vol. XXVI, no 5, Feb 1945, p19. This was an article from the Sydney labour paper, *The Standard Weekly*, and had already been published in the *NSWPN*, 1 Jan 1945, p8.
41 Warmly acknowledged by the No 1 Branch of the NSW Police Association, *NSWPN*, 1 Apr 1945, p22.
42 *NSWPN*, May 1945, p3, Jun 1945, pp15–17.
43 *NSWPN*, Jun 1945, pp15–17.
44 Idem, pp19–21.
45 *NSWPN*, Sep 1945, p4.
46 *NSWPN*, Dec 1947, p8.
47 *NSWPN*, Dec 1947, p10.
48 *TPJ*, Jun 1949, pp3–4.
49 *TPJ*, Nov 1956, pp5–7.
50 *VPJ*, Feb 1945, p1358; Feb 1954, p660.

51 *VPJ*, Jan 1954, p647 — the decision was taken at the 1953 conference of the Police Federation in Hobart.
52 *VPJ*, Nov 1954, p793.
53 *VPJ*, Nov 1967, p127.
54 *VPJ*, Jan 1971, p225; *VPJ*, Mar 1971, p279.
55 *VPJ*, May, 1976, p13; Feb 1991, p41; on the context and significance of the affiliation and its ramifications see David Baker, "The evolving paradox of police unionism: employees or officers?," in *Unions 2000: Retrospect and Prospect*, ed G Griffin (Melbourne, 2000), 22–43.
56 *WAPN*, May 1956, pp3–10.
57 *QPJ*, Sep 1962, pp13–14.
58 Tim Prenzler, "Women in Australian policing: an historical overview," *Journal of Australian Studies* (Sep 1994).
59 *NSWPN*, Aug 1930, p30; Dec 1932, p4.
60 Higgs and Betters, *To walk a fair beat: a history of the South Australian Women Police, 1915–1987*, 127–131. *SAPJ*, Jul 1940, p2; Sep 1952.
61 Moyle, "Union History 1915–1957 (3 parts)," Pt 3, pp9, 34–6, citing *Qld Industrial Gazette*, 30 Jun 1957, pp454–456.
62 Brien, *Serving the Force: 75 Years of the Police Association of New South Wales*, 141–142.
63 *VPJ*, Jun 1975, p5.
64 Jill Bolen, *Reform in policing: lessons from the Whitrod era*, The Institute of Criminology Monograph Series (Sydney, 1997), 86.
65 *VPJ*, Jan 1950, p12.
66 *VPJ*, Sep 1949, p2279, 2290–2291; Feb 1948, p1959.
67 *QPJ*, Jul 1969, pp40–41.
68 *VPJ*, Aug 1969, p73.
69 *WAPN*, Apr 1969, p8; Apr 1970, p4; Nov 1971, p2.
70 *WAPN*, Mar 1969, p16.
71 *VPJ*, Aug 1969, p73.
72 See transcript of the program, *QPJ*, Mar 1968, pp35–51.
73 *SAPJ*, May 1968, p5.
74 *VPJ*, Dec 1969, p181.
75 *VPJ*, Aug 1969, p76.
76 *SAPJ*, Mar 1968, p13.
77 *QPJ*, Oct 1969, pp54–55.
78 *SAPJ*, Nov 1973, p2.
79 *TPJ*, Apr 1972, p2.

6: Political interventions

Whatever Government is in power should realise that the loyalty of the Police Force on whom they depend should be recognised and the same consideration should be given to the items which our Association submits as to those other organisations which use their Unions to place pressure on the Government.
Tasmanian Police Journal, March 1958

Our mates from up the country
Joined the Policemen from the town
And made a mighty meeting
That near brought the building down

We damned the Beach Inquiry
That blundered five hundred days
And challenged their sense of Justice
And their Theme of "Crime now Pays"
'Unity', by L J Blogg, *Victorian Police Journal*, Nov 1976

The only royal commission that should be held is one dealing with the unwarranted persecution of Police officers.
Tony Day, President NSW Police Association, 1994

The 1965 New South Wales state election ended 24 years of Labor Party rule. It represented also the emergence of a new focus on policing, one in which the police union played a significant role. This was a 'law and order' election, resulting in the victory of the Liberal-Country Party coalition, led by Robin Askin, over a tired Labor government. The subsequent history of policing during the ten years of Askin's rule was arguably a turning point in New South Wales policing — but in exactly what ways remains a difficult question. Was it the beginning of an unparalleled period of corruption in the New South Wales police force, wedded as it had become to a government that promised so much? Or does its significance lie more in the consolidation of policing issues as a matter of electoral importance in Australian politics? A third view might be put. Far from representing a point of origin for law and order politics, the detailed history of the previous 40 years of police union history in Australia suggest that

Askin's election was the culmination of an incremental politicisation of policing, one in which police unions had played a vital part. If it was such a culmination, it remains nevertheless a starting point for numerous elections afterwards that focused on police numbers as the core of what was wrong with the management of law and order.

Over the next three decades the policing context in Australia was rarely out of the public eye. It is not so much that policing had been a matter of indifference in the earlier decades — indeed we have seen many examples in this book in which police unions had been deeply involved in police–government and police–citizen conflicts to a degree that is little different to the most intense confrontations of more recent years. It is arguable, however, that the intensity, duration and governmental effects of the public conflicts over policing have been greater in these more recent decades, and warrant detailed scrutiny for those reasons. That is in good part a consequence of the multiplication of agencies and interests with an articulate commitment to the question of how policing should be organised and conducted. There was undoubtedly a politicisation of policing in these decades, but one that is more complicated than frequently connotated by that phrase. Whereas vocal critics charged in the 1980s and after that policing was being politicised by governments seeking to control its outcomes, or by police seeking to increase their advantages and powers in the workplace and on the streets, it can be seen in retrospect that policing was politicised in a much more general sense. In brief, policing, its functions and its modes, became a practice in whose outcomes a wide variety of forces became interested. The focus of this chapter is on the multiplication of forces and interests affecting policing since the 1960s and the police unions' attempts to respond to these. The police unions became more adept politically — but they did so in a context in which inevitably they could not hope to guarantee the outcome.

What were some of the characteristics of police–government and police–citizen relations that have shaped the context of police union activity in the years since 1965? We can identify a number of key developments from the mid-1960s that will organise the treatment of police union politics in the remainder of this chapter. First, the period was characterised by a deep and persistent political protest movement, or rather plurality of movements, that frequently identified the police role as one of its targets. While the policing impact of this was a matter for commissioners and senior officers, as well as their political masters, it was inevitable that police unions would be affected by the nature of the seemingly perennial clashes with demonstrators and protestors. While the Vietnam war protests were the highlight of this conflict, the occasions for conflict were many and various and persisted well after the end of Australia's military participation in 1972. They included the Springbok tours of 1970, the peace movement campaigns against the sale of Australian uranium, and protest in support of Aboriginal land rights from the time of the establishment of the Aboriginal tent embassy in 1972. We have examined the police union response to this phenomenon in the previous chapter.

Second, from the 1960s there was an Australian development of what was a more widespread international phenomenon. Increasingly it appeared that the old institutions of government were incapable alone of providing guarantees of accountability and conformity to standards of justice and good governance. It is worth noting just how much has changed in the administration of government business since the 1960s. Where previously there had only been the courts of justice as a remedy for dissatisfied citizens, or the ballot box and political office for those organising to change the law, from the late 1960s there was an increasing demand for new institutions of accountability and policy advice. Politically the demand for these new institutions in Australia was fruitful from about the time of the election of the Whitlam Labor government at federal level (1972). The changes had already begun in the states, where most policing was organised. From the early 1970s we see the beginnings of new institutions of policy review and advice such as the Australian Law Reform Commission (ALRC) and its various state counterparts, of research advice such as the Bureau of Crime Statistics and Research in New South Wales, and of administrative accountability, such as the Ombudsman's Office in a number of jurisdictions. Significantly the last of these usually was without power to review police actions — and a constant demand of civil liberties groups through the 1970s and 1980s was for police operations to be made amenable to such bodies, or else for the establishment of specific bodies such as a police complaints tribunal. The plethora of new institutions added to the noise around policing — and was much noticed by the police unions. In addition there were not infrequent inquiries by the established mode of a royal commission or other official inquiry. Law reform recommendations and other intrusions on the policing domain met with often vigorous response from the police unions, as we will see later in this chapter.

A third factor shaping the policing environment from the 1960s, and increasingly so from the early 1980s was the managerial revolution in the workplace. We have seen that police unions had helped shape the work conditions of police in the four decades after their establishment, especially in the areas of promotion and discipline, but without fundamentally altering the hierarchical presumptions of police administration with its top-down command structure. From the late 1970s however there were increasing pressures for a change in police administration. These were only to reach substance a decade later, but their impact was almost immediately to threaten the security of policing as an occupation. Accountability for performance, a consolidation of merit over seniority, an expectation of advanced education and training, a move to contract employment, policing by objectives rather than simply reactive to offending — all these were the kinds of interventions discussed in major reviews of policing like those of Lusher in New South Wales (1980) or Neesham in Victoria (1986). As the collective voice of serving police, the unions were well placed to take an active role in facilitating or resisting the incursions of managerial change. The vigorous interventions of police unions in public debates about major policing issues need to be seen in many cases against a background of the internal changes taking place in policing during these decades — not surprisingly the police unions and their supporters often enough represented themselves as engaged in a war of defence against enemies from without and within.

Police unionists themselves of course were conscious of some of these changes, and articulated the new opportunities and threats that arose out of them. In 1981 for example Tom Rippon, a long-serving Victorian Police Association secretary and then also president of the Police Federation, recounted the rise of what he described as 'police militancy' in recent times. He attributed the rise to two factors — the effects of civil liberties and law reform activism, which had resulted in a feeling of police being under seige; and a marked generational change in police ranks, with 54% of all police in Victoria for example being under the age of 30 years. The latter was of such significance that he warned of the challenge ahead for police managers in dealing with the generation gap in police ranks.[1] His sense of a time of crisis and change replicated the factors we have suggested above as influential throughout this period. It will be evident that the decades being examined here, roughly the 20 years from 1968–88, are congested with change in institutions, discourse about policing, and actions of police unions and other players in policing. The argument here does not seek to judge the rightness or otherwise of police union activities during this period, but rather to appreciate the development of police union perspectives and consequent actions during this turbulent time.

6.1 A thousand more police, or two

In the previous chapter we focused on the ways in which the police unions sought to establish and consolidate political alliances in the post-war decades, as a means of advancing their members' claims. This focus should not be allowed to obscure the fundamental objectives of the period — as before and after, the unions were above all concerned with the elementary but vital issues of wages and conditions of employment. These were the basics — and evidence of government indifference could readily inspire political threats whose rhetoric goes back to the 1920s and flows through to the end of the century. An instance from Tasmania in the late 1950s could be replicated through the conferences of many police unions. This Association, protested its president in 1958, 'does not resort to pressure tactics'.

> Whatever Government is in power should realise that the loyalty of the Police Force on whom they depend should be recognised and the same consideration should be given to the items which our Association submits as to those other organisations which use their Unions to place pressure on the Government … [In spite of the Association's strong support for measures to] bring about better public relations, more efficiency and discipline … we feel they have overlooked one of the main principles of good relationship between the police and the public, and that is … a happy and contented police force.[2]

Over the next decades the unions would discover that 'pressure tactics' were indeed necessary if they were to achieve desired objectives. Those pressure tactics were increasingly likely to involve dealing with both sides of politics, as Labor hegemony in successive states began to collapse.

With the collapse of Labor power at state level (see table below) the rationale for the alliances of the post-war period began to founder. The importance of this fundamental alteration in the political landscape should not be underestimated in accounting for the emergence of a much more focused use of the political bargaining chip by the police unions.

Political party in government, Australian states, end of year						
	NSW	VIC	QLD	SA	WA	TAS
1945	Labor	Labor	Labor	Non-Labor	Labor	Labor
1960	Labor	Non-Labor	Non-Labor	Non-Labor	Non-Labor	Labor
1970	Non-Labor	Non-Labor	Non-Labor	Labor	Non-Labor	Non-Labor

The bargaining chip of preference from 1965 was the issue of police numbers. While a good deal can be said about the advantage of this way of highlighting police union interests, it is important to recognise that the issue had a workplace context. Much difficulty flowed for police forces from the increasing conformity of police employment with some fundamentals of Australian working conditions in the post-war period, especially the adoption of the 40-hour week. Simple mathematics showed that this implied an increase in required personnel to cover the expected shortfall in policing the beat, which still in the 1940s was the dominant mode of street policing. Indeed such was the impact of the 40-hour week on staffing requirements that the Victorian Association undertook to run its own police recruiting campaign in 1948 to address the pending shortage — the immediate impact of the shorter week was evident in a reported shortfall in 1948 of some five to six hundred men. The reality of shortages delayed the introduction of the 40-hour week in other states like Queensland and South Australia.[3]

Police numbers were to become a preoccupation of the unions by the 1960s — and as such to influence the development of the most explicit political divisions over policing that had yet been manifest. While press criticism of the New South Wales police had been aggravated during the 1950s and 1960s the media was also a friendly agent in the campaign waged by the Police Association from about 1962 to 1965. The primary object of the union campaign was an increase in numbers of police. The matter was the subject of numerous conference and executive resolutions, approaches to government, appeals through the media, and take-up by politicians. From 1961, Association conference resolutions to approach the government for an extra 1,000 police developed as the basis of a campaign that won media support, in spite of the often critical treatment of police business in the Sydney papers. By March 1963 both the major Sydney dailies were running reports and editorials very sympathetic to the police case and criticising the Labor government for its failure to attend to the need.

'One thousand' is a good round number — the New South Wales union was not unique in its affection for this figure, which the Victorian Police Association also embraced at this time, in a sustained campaign that replicated some features of the New South Wales case. In the Victorian context however the demonstrable shortage of recruits to enable the force to make up its already approved strength was used by the commissioner and government to mute the Association demands for an increase in police numbers.[4] One reason the New South Wales government was not attending to the union case was that the police commissioner was publicly sceptical of the need for more police. The union case was built on a claimed increase in workload in the different police divisions. There had been increases in the strength of some areas — in traffic for example by 160% since 1947, and in the CIB with a 54% increase. The numbers of general duties police were said to have increased by only 19%. These claims by the president of the Association at the 1963 annual conference quickly made their way into the press, with the *Sydney Morning Herald* supporting the union case in an editorial a few days later. Commissioner Allan's response appeared complacent:

> never before in the history of the Commonwealth has the Police Force been better organised in basic aspects of police duties. It compares more than favourably with every other force in the Commonwealth and, indeed, on a population basis, with the world.

He and the government stood their ground on the fact that the police to population ratio in the early 1960s was the same as it had been in 1947, when the 40-hour week decision had come down.[5] The transparent weakness of Allan's claim flowed from this last fact — if average working hours of police had been reduced then the maintenance of a similar police/population ratio implied that there had been effectively a reduction in the availability of police per capita.

Allan's stance against the union case continued through the following year. It was strikingly demonstrated when the Labor Premier Heffron opened the 1964 annual conference with a strong defence of the integrity of the police, rejecting the then common calls for a royal commission. The government was in the process of recognising the political rights of police, an act of faith that Heffron hoped the police would respect. In contrast to the premier's conciliatory mood, the commissioner chastised the delegates for the mode of the campaign for more police. The Association had recently sent a letter to every municipal council and shire in New South Wales, asking whether they were satisfied with local police, whether there were sufficient numbers and, if the answer was 'NO', how many extra were needed. The commissioner objected that such a questionnaire could not produce persuasive evidence because the councils did not have access to the required evidence such as the number of offences in their areas. To the union claims that municipal councils were employing their own security officers Allan countered that they had in any case employed rangers and special constables for many years. Further such a practice was desirable since '[i]t is not the part of the Police Force to give specialised attention to any particular individual or organisation'.[6]

In embarking on such a direct address to local councils throughout the state the Association had entered new territory. A 'Strength Committee' had been appointed to manage the campaign, receiving complaints from the branches and attending to the ongoing publicity demands in support of the case.[7] As the year wore on there was increasing interest by the leader of the Liberal Party, R W Askin, in the political potential of the issue. By late 1964 Askin was attacking the government for being soft on crime and criminals, and in turn affirming the Police Association case for extra police to combat what he described as the 'present vicious crime wave'.[8]

A number of shocking crimes in 1964 served to bolster the case for more police — and in January 1965 two teenage girls were sexually assaulted and murdered at Wanda Beach south of Sydney. Almost immediately the leaders of the opposition Liberal and Country Parties issued a joint statement urging a major increase in police strength, which would 'prevent many outrages of the type being currently committed'. The statement drew a lesson about government neglect: 'for years the Opposition parties have pressed the Government to enlarge the Police Force to ensure the proper preservation of law and order and to guard the safety of the people, particularly women and children'.[9] The press supported the statement with commentary that linked the Wanda Beach murders to the lack of police. By this point the original target of 1,000 extra police had escalated to a Police Association call for 2,000 more, as it sought to apply a ratio of 1:530, a benchmark figure drawn from a recent United Kingdom Royal Commission into the Police, and endorsed at their 1964 biennial conference by the Australian Federation of Police Associations as a national standard.[10]

Allan however persisted with his limited response, playing the issue by the book. He had earlier directed senior officers to prepare a report on the needed strength, a report that took two years to bear fruit. In March 1965, with a state election only weeks away, the Labor premier, Jack Renshaw, announced that the government would appoint an extra 500 police over the next two years. The announcement was a gift to Askin — the Police Association condemned it as totally inadequate since it was now calling for 2,000 more police. As much as the Association might be judged to have played with arbitrary figures of needed strength, little authority could attach to the commissioner's own statistical sleight of hand, arguing that the population base should exclude the young and the old as they were not the targets of police attention![11] The Association's desired 1:530 ratio by this stage was also becoming a media benchmark by which the media judged the government's response. In April the *Police News* applauded the *Newcastle Morning Herald*, which had run the headline, 'Where are the cops/ Answer blows in political winds' over an article highlighting police population ratios as high as 1:6,500 at nearby Toronto.[12]

Neither Allan nor the government had handled the police strength campaign effectively. Writing in *The Bulletin*, criminologist Gordon Hawkins addressed 'the police manpower situation' in terms that affirmed the union case. He regarded the 1:530 ratio as 'comparatively modest' since the USA and West European ratios were already better than that — and New South Wales at 1:718 had the worst ratio in Australia. One consequence seemed to be a rapid growth in private security organisations. Without addressing Allan's claims about police efficiency directly, Hawkins questioned the reliability of the New South Wales crime clear-up figures which at something like 80% of serious crimes cleared was 'exceedingly high not only by Australian but also by world standards' (e.g. compared to 45% in Victoria and 26% in the USA).[13]

The stage was set for an election campaign in which the opposition would triumph, with Askin promising at least 1,000 extra police, a promise he publicised in a circular directed to police. The *Sun Herald* urged the new government to 'lose no time in adopting and implementing the Police Association recommendation' — and questioned Commissioner Allan's post-election claims that 'comparisons with England's higher ratio of police to population are misleading because our policing methods are more effective'.[14] The *Police News* saw the strength campaign as vindicated. The former premier had listened too much to Commissioner Allan and not enough to the Association.

> That the Association was able to assist the then leader of the Opposition to more properly assess Police strength requirements is clear proof of the value of organised representation and public outcry about this important aspect of the Police Force.

Within a few months Askin had approved the addition of 1,000 extra police over three years. The Association was heartened but not satisfied — since the ratio of 1:530 continued to justify a further 1,000 police 'to make the strength position adequate'.[15]

The New South Wales 'law and order' election of 1965 deserves our attention as it demonstrates exactly what the Police Association was able now to see as a precedent — the potential for a political opposition to ride into government on the back of a promise to deliver extra police and so more protection to the community. As an autonomous body with access to privileged information about the state of the police stations the police union was in an especially powerful position to shape the debate about police numbers. In this particular case it was unwittingly aided by a commissioner who seemed more intent on maintaining a united front with the government ('our Minister and our Government', as he was inclined to say) than on establishing a *credible* defence of existing resources. The development in 1964–5 of an especially well focused campaign that addressed not only the media, but local government (a strategy of both the New South Wales and Victorian Associations at this time), does seem to mark a transition towards a more advanced capacity of the police unions to engage in the electoral process. As such it represents an important moment in the story we have been tracing. After 1965 police unions had behind them a successful campaign, in which political alliances had been built and made effective.

One can gauge how instrumental the New South Wales election was by at least reminding the reader of some later instances. The commonality is the selection of a readily marketable figure as the number of police required to secure the public safety. The figure is always higher than the present number of police — a requirement that we have seen is at least based historically in the reduced number of working hours won by police in the course of the twentieth century. The figure must also be capable of being easily remembered. No police union will go into a 'police strength' campaign, as they have become known, with an argument that what the local police force needs is 273 extra police, or 3,129. The preference is for a good round figure — 1,000 will be a starting point for the larger forces, but this can almost imperceptibly leap to 2,000, or in one case 4,000. Predictably enough opposition parties, following Askin's lead, and regardless of party identity, have found themselves all too willing to endorse the need for meeting a police union's demand for more police. In some cases it has become useful, if not necessarily effective, for the police union to be able to appeal to cross-border political party commitments as a means of prodding the issue along.

Some of these patterns can be seen in the early and mid-80s 'Police strength campaign' run by the New South Wales Police Association. Again the New South Wales union might be regarded as having led the other police forces in the style and imagination of this campaign. The campaign came at a time of high pressure for the union. Relations between the Wran Labor government and the police — department and Association — had been difficult for some years. This was in spite of Wran's determination from the outset of his government to keep communication open with the Police Association. Indeed on the very matter of police strength, Wran had responded in the first year of his government, by establishing a working party to review relevant guidelines and make recommendations on strength, against the background of a policy commitment to increase the personnel of the force. The Association indeed was represented on this working party by its president — but the recommendations, which mixed a commitment to an increase with a needs-based and staff allocation review, did not conform to Association policy which had long favoured a population ratio system of determining police numbers.[16] As much as Wran's subsequent commitment of a minimum increase of 600 over three years kept faith with the policy, the Association was again restless on police numbers within a short period.

By 1982, the recently completed Lusher Inquiry into Police Administration, described in the *Police News* as a 'secret' inquiry, promised an unsettling future of administrative reform in policing. Persistent rumblings about police corruption were added to other signs of government dissatisfaction with the prevailing modes of New South Wales policing, evident in the repeal of the *Summary Offences Act* in 1979 and its replacement by the *Offences in Public Places Act*, in intervention by the government to force the return of a painting seized by the vice squad, as well as ongoing contention over police complaints and the role of the Ombudsman. Developing an effective police strength campaign — whose potential is almost guaranteed by the seemingly irrefutable claim that governments don't provide enough police — could be seen in retrospect as having played an important role for an industrial organisation whose members were under so much pressure in their workplaces, and in the political environment in which their work was to be carried out.

The 1980s New South Wales campaign was signalled by the president of the Association, Tony Lauer at the 1981 annual conference. The priority of more police numbers was established by him on the basis of needs flowing from the improved working conditions won in the recent industrial award, such as changes in the rostering system. Lauer built on his case — applying a recent study of Victorian police strength needs by the Police Service Board to the equivalent New South Wales population was said to justify a need for an additional figure of 4,176 police in the state. A recent study by the New South Wales Bureau of Crime Statistics on popular perceptions of major issues was used to suggest that anxieties about crime were second only to inflation and were especially felt among those in lower income brackets. 'A government of the political complexion of the Government of this State surely cannot reject the concern of those people', concluded Lauer, portentously.[17] Conference endorsed the call, but by way of noting that the continuing expectation to improve working conditions should not be forestalled by insufficient numbers of police. As it was put in the record of the conference:

> In some Divisions the shortage of Police is leading to a situation where it is difficult for members to obtain their rest days and the accumulation of these matters is having adverse effects upon members' personal health, in their working environment, socially and domestically.

After noting that the Arbitration Committee of the Association had a charter to improve the working conditions of members, the conference affirmed that

> The Committee will, therefore, continue its programme of improving conditions of service in the industrial area, but notes in this

> report for the record, the urgent necessity for an increase in the strength of the Police Force to use the terms of the Industrial Agreement to be observed and applied in accordance with the intentions of the parties, the Police Association and the Public Service Board.[18]

Noteworthy in this record of the issue is the absence of substantive law and order concerns. Police strength was a matter of facilitating an improvement in the working conditions of police, arguably (some would say demonstrably) only indirectly related to crime control and detection. The subtleties of crime statistics and the effectiveness of policing do not however make good bedfellows with the demands of a political campaign for more police.

The result was that once the 'Police Strength Campaign' reached launch date it was already transformed from an industrial issue into a law and order matter. The 4,176 police of Lauer's calculation were rounded out to 4,000 'under strength' — with a pragmatic concession to reality in the demand for '2,000 right now'. Veiled threats of strike action were intimated by a rhetorical rejection of it as a tactic that had never been pursued by the New South Wales police. Industry representatives had blamed the shortage of police for high road fatalities and increasing numbers of bank robberies. The message was primarily one of the lack of police protection.[19]

The Association prosecuted its $30,000 campaign under the slogan 'make the police force a real force again'. It was, it might have been thought, advantageous timing, with a new police minister, Peter Anderson, still finding his feet in the job — although his previous career as a police officer and also a member of the Association prepared him better than many in that office. The campaign was pursued by deputations to the minister, simultaneously with a vigorous advertising campaign. A widely published advertisement showed a bank robbery, under the banner 'Withdrawals have never been easier'. 1981, it was said, had been a bumper year for hold-ups. The police were about 4,000 under strength, and needed 2,000 more right now. The 'trouble is Mr Wran doesn't agree', the readers were advised — to help 'Make the Police a **Real Force** again' they should call the Premier's Department.[20]

The media played its role faithfully, with some newspapers allegedly running the Association ads for free. Like the 1964–5 campaign this was a state-wide effort — and the global demand for an extra 2,000 police was backed up at local level by newsworthy stories of understaffing fed to the media by local Association representatives. The campaign received a useful boost from across the border, where the Victorian Labor opposition had announced its police policy in December — with a key element being a promise to increase police recruits from 650 to 1,000 per year, for a force that was already ahead of the New South Wales staffing levels.[21] Suburban and country town newspapers generated their own stories of local crises, with increasing crime and the road toll being said to be symptoms of the local shortage of police.

With the government resisting the campaign the Association went into the May 1982 conference under the same slogan. Addressing the conference, police minister Anderson said nothing about police strength, focusing instead on measures to deal with corrupt police, and the administrative restructuring following Lusher. Conference replied by upping the ante — it now wanted 4,000 extra police and threatened industrial action if they were not forthcoming.[22] By July there was an indication from Anderson that his budget submission would include a case for extra police — but he was non-committal about the numbers.[23] The budget outcome was mixed — some recognition of the Association's claim of understaffing as the government approved an increase of 400 (not 4,000), but off-set by other measures of financial attrition whose effects would be felt over the coming months in a squeeze on overtime, combined with a direction from the commissioner for an increase in general duties policing. The Association prepared itself for another major media campaign, only to find an early 1983 federal election stand in the way. The mood was epitomised in the consideration by the executive of the need to re-consider the 'non-political status' of the Association.[24] Accordingly the 1983 conference approved an amendment to the rules to the effect that the 'Association shall be non party-political and non-sectarian'.[25] The change was subtle — from non-political to non-party-political. It summed up the transition since the 1960s and confirmed the degree to which the police unions now saw their role as independent of any particular political interest.

The 1983 conference also saw a small retreat from the focus on a particular strength increase. Perhaps partly in response to a strongly-worded defence of the government's record, including its increased police budget and additional 400 police commitment, the conference resolved simply that there should be an annual increase on a needs basis and for future planning and development. The magic figure of 2,000 needed now had been established in public discourse — addressing the conference the new state opposition leader, Nick Greiner, committed the Liberal Party to that increase 'over the life of the next parliament'. It was a figure he thought justified whether by statistics, or just 'the intuitive gut feeling, which is the basis of most political decisions I have come to see'.[26] The success of the Association's campaign might be seen in the longer term by the readiness with which 'gut feeling', massaged by occasional press publicity and media advertising, would rule the commitments of future governments, in New South Wales and elsewhere.

One could take almost any other jurisdiction to see similar forces at play in these decades. The New South Wales Association made much in its 1982–3 campaign of the countervailing commitment of the Labor opposition leader in Victoria to an extra 1,000 police. It was a promise that would haunt the Labor premier, John Cain (son of the former Labor premier and sponsor of police union advancement in the 1940s), once in government. A decade later the mistrust of police union leaders for election promises was embedded –- anticipating a police strength auction in the forthcoming state election Victorian Association president Danny Walsh in July 1992 warned the parties that if there was a promise of 1,000 or 2,000 extra police this time around, 'we expect it in a time frame'.[27] Across the Tasman, the New Zealand Association, which had quite literally taken some lessons from its Australian colleagues, ran its own '1,000 more' police campaign in the late 80s, resulting in a promise by the Muldoon-led National Party of an extra 900.[28] In 1991 Prime Minister Muldoon delivered a 'horror budget' in New Zealand, but Australian police unionists noticed that it could still include an extra 300 police, of the 900 promised.[29] Back in Queensland, in spite of the scandals of the Fitzgerald inquiry, the incoming Goss Labor government was saddled with a law and order policy that promised an extra 1,200 police — an increase mandated by the Fitzgerald report which had concluded that the local police, in spite of the rhetoric of the National Party government, had long been under strength, and was certainly the most understaffed in Australia.[30]

The criminological evidence for the proposition that more police means less crime, or less risk of victimisation, is negligible. The political appeal of a campaign on police numbers however was immense for the three decades following the successful Askin election. Such appeal was aided and abetted by the lack of public scrutiny of 'how police resources should be organised and deployed'.[31] The dispersed nature of the police workforce and its tasks makes policing issues potentially a lively matter in every electorate — and the comprehensive unionisation of the police services enables a campaign to develop its jurisdiction wide potential. There is little reason to doubt the reality of the administrative pressures that have given rise to the demand for more police — a product in part of the historical improvement in working conditions that limited the working week and enhanced the leave entitlements of police like other workers. The linking of the demand for more police to the threat of rising crime rates has been more contentious — but, in the right circumstances, effective in pushing the police case on to the front pages. How productive such campaigns are in producing desired outcomes may be doubted, a reason for the increasing frustration and depth of cynicism one finds in the police union journals throughout the 1980s and 1990s. That mood however was also the product of the many other pressures police found themselves under during this time.

6.2 Damage control — commissions and inquiries

Public inquiries have played a significant role in the history of Australian policing — though sometimes with only limited direct effect. The temptation to deal with crises or scandals in policing through appointment of a royal commission or a parliamentary select committee hearing has been great, for both government and opposition. For governments a royal commission may be a means of saving the day against rising parliamentary or media criticism. An official inquiry may avert criticism, bury it, or through excessive length wear out the problem. For political oppositions the winning of an official inquiry may promise some further disclosure to embarrass a government, or hobble a minister. When it comes to policing matters, the police unions historically have been suspicious of inquiries, but on occasion have in turn sought them as a means of clearing the air of what are seen as groundless or unfair rumours and scandal-mongering.

An important function of the unions from the 1930s was the capacity to deliver legal services to the aid of their members. Through a commitment to litigation as one of the weapons in either defence or advocacy of police officers, the unions developed over time a considerable expertise as players in the world of formal inquiries. Able to marshal the financial resources of their large memberships, the unions could often employ the best silks. Industrial courts, appeal boards and the civil courts were familiar territory, and sometimes fertile. The tradition of litigation as a response to difficulty helps to explain the approach taken by some police unions in the recent past to the mounting of official inquiries. Others have played a more constructive and collaborative role, seeing in the development of an official inquiry a means of addressing widespread discontent with particular aspects of police administration or police-work. Both approaches deserve attention if we are to understand the public disposition of police unions in the handling of official inquiries. In the following pages I deal only with special purpose inquiries, leaving to later the unions' response to civilian oversight bodies of a more permanent form.

The police unions have not always opposed the establishment of public inquiries. As other political interests look to a royal commission as a political tactic so too the unions could regard such an inquiry as serving the purpose of clearing the decks, combating scuttlebutt and rumour. Recurrent public rumblings of alleged corruption and maladministration in war-time Queensland were addressed by the police union in 1942 through a referendum to determine whether 'it was desirable to hold a Royal Commission into certain allegations which reflect adversely upon the good name of the Force'. The vote reported by secretary Talty to the minister was 949–168 in favour of an inquiry. Cabinet rejected the need for an inquiry, declaring its 'complete confidence in the honesty and integrity of the police force'.[32] Consistently through the years 1949–53 the Queensland Police Union publicised allegations of political protection of illegal betting and sly-grog shops, leading to a royal commission on betting in 1951–2, but with minimal outcomes. In an extraordinary demonstration of the conflicts over the policing of these areas, officers of the union executive debated in 1953 whether they should themselves make a raid on a sly-grog shop in Brisbane, which had been the subject of complaints by police union members: the motion was defeated only on the casting vote of the president. Then in 1957 union disputes with department and government over the suspension of two police during inquiries and charges over the death of a civilian at Mt Isa led to further executive calls for an official inquiry into the administration of the force.[33]

Rarely in fact do we find that union and government coincide in their agreement on the need for an inquiry. The case of the Queensland Police Union's pursuit of such public inquiry in the 1940s and 1950s is also unusual. The story we have to tell about unions and public inquiries in the following pages is largely one of resistance, and damage control, once the inevitable reveals itself.

A signal of the kinds of challenges to police authority in the coming decades was provided by the South Australian Stuart Royal Commission in 1959. Rupert Max Stuart, an Aboriginal man, had been arrested, tried, convicted and sentenced to death following the sexual assault and murder of a young girl in 1958. Widespread concern over the circumstances of the arrest and conviction of Stuart resulted in numerous appeals for clemency in relation to the death sentence, and eventually the appointment of a royal commission. The public dissent was continually countered by the Police Association, and in circumstances that called into question the protocols governing the role of police in public discourse, and more generally the role of the union and its members in such inquiries. An executive meeting in August 1959 unanimously resolved

> That this Association pass a vote of the fullest confidence in the integrity of all the officers concerned in the Stuart case, and that the Association stand squarely behind them, giving them complete backing.

The motion had been put by a member who spoke of the 'unjustified adverse publicity being given to the police in the Stuart case'.[34] This was disingenuous. The furore over police involvement had been aggravated a month earlier by an extraordinary public intervention by both the president and secretary of the Association. In this case the president happened to be the detective who had interrogated Stuart and signed a contentious record of interview. Both Association members had revealed to the papers what they alleged to be details of Stuart's criminal history and other matters that had not been raised during his trial.[35]

The Association's intervention prompted widespread concern. The president of the Law Society of South Australia said he was 'appalled' by the statement and regarded it as surpassing 'the bounds of ordinary decency, to say nothing of the question of contempt of court'.[36] In spite of his self-confessed conflict of interest, the president of the Association went on to make further statements in defence of the police involved in the case, including himself. The Association did not stop there. A radio broadcast by Don Dunstan, Labor MP, member of the Howard League, penal reform advocate and later premier of South Australia, had criticised the police. The Association instructed the secretary to write to the leader of the opposition to inquire whether Dunstan's views were those of the Labor Party. And finally the Association wanted the next Police Federation conference to consider what might be done to counter 'unjustified attacks by the press on the honesty of the Police from time to time and consider ways of combatting same'.[37]

The establishment of a royal commission to inquire into Stuart's conviction was welcomed by the Association. It pursued the Dunstan radio broadcast, to the point of frustration when the Australian Broadcasting Authority reported that it was not empowered to require a transcript of matter from a radio broadcast. When the report of the commission was handed down (already superseded with respect to Stuart's fate by the commutation of his sentence to life imprisonment), the Association welcomed it as exonerating the police concerned. While affirming the integrity of the police, the report was much less complimentary of police methods. But the Association was less concerned with such matters, focusing throughout on the matter of police innocence of wrong-doing.[38] Outside the ranks of the local police union, those who were concerned about the conduct of criminal justice included the historian of the Stuart case, who concluded at the time:

> Even if the president had not been the officer in charge of the investigation, and even if further judicial proceedings had not been possible, this [the Association statements to the press] would have been the kind of action which could imperil public confidence in the police force as a fair and dispassionate instrument of the law.[39]

In the Stuart case, the South Australian Association had welcomed public inquiry. Thirty years later another police union, this time in Western Australia, proved less disposed to public inquiry into police conduct with respect to Aboriginal people.

In 1988 the Western Australian Police Union went to the courts in an attempt to foreclose an official inquiry into the conduct of policing of Aborigines whose deaths had become the subject of inquiry. The Royal Commission into Aboriginal Deaths in Custody was established by the Commonwealth and state governments with terms requiring the commissioners to investigate both individual deaths and 'underlying causes'. The Police Union was sufficiently exercised by the development of the Royal Commission's brief to launch a number of legal challenges attempting to limit its scrutiny. Funded by the state government, which itself had established the terms of reference of the Royal Commission in co-operation with the other Australian governments, the union sought injunctions on a number of occasions to stop the Royal Commission proceeding with its inquiry into particular deaths.

The attitude of the Western Australian Police Union was not a matter of surprise to those who had observed its public disposition on Aboriginal criminal justice issues over the previous decade. After the death of an Aboriginal teenager, John Pat, following his arrest by police in Roebourne in 1983, a coronial inquiry had found sufficient evidence to justify a prosecution against five Roebourne police for manslaughter. Subsequently the police were tried and acquitted. The union's response to this sequence of events was to call on state and federal governments 'to implement a full-scale inquiry into the Roborne [sic] Coronial Enquiry and the consequential matters that arose therefrom'. In particular the union was exercised by the fact that pressure for scrutiny of police actions in relation to policing of Aborigines was coming from government-funded bodies. Hence its simultaneous call for the inquiry to cover 'the financial contributions of the Federal Government and the State Government to Aboriginal advancement and welfare, throughout Australia including the funding of the National Aboriginal Conference and all Aboriginal Agencies'. The union was supported in its demand by the Police Federation.[40]

The Royal Commission of 1987–91 was thus predictably viewed by the Western Australian Police Union with hostility and suspicion. The commission's final report described the union's attitude as 'bitterly opposed'. The union retained counsel, funded by the state government, for the commission hearings. Not only did it mount legal challenges to jurisdiction of the commission. In submissions on policing and Aboriginal people it disclosed a depth of antagonism to reflecting on the history and position of Aboriginal people in Australia and the role of police in that history. Racist postulates about the purity or otherwise of blood lines were combined with relentless attacks on special assistance to Aboriginal people or organisations. In considering some issues that were being canvassed by the commission, and already in practice in other jurisdictions, the union continued to question the notion of a right of access of Aboriginal detainees to lawyers from what it described as a 'racially titled service group':

> the creation of the Aboriginal Legal Service ... has induced an expectancy of acquittal into Aboriginal offenders. This has led to

> insolence for authority mainly in the younger people, which is now visible in the development of hatred for those vested with the task of law enforcement.[41]

For the Commission, the union's view of the 'Aboriginal offender' suggested 'a belief that Aboriginal detainees are "offenders" and are necessarily guilty and there is an assumption that the assertion by an Aboriginal person of his/her rights vis a vis police is "insolence"'.

Like its position on police complaints (which we examine later) the position of the Police Union was one characterised by extremes of defensiveness, informed by prejudice and a triumphalist assertion of police rights over those of the citizens it policed. The union submission proclaimed the commitment of police to equal treatment of all, but its language and ethos spoke otherwise. The final report of the commission concluded:

> In the light of the Police Union's submission, my Commission cannot, with any confidence, accept that there are not police who negatively stereotype Aboriginal people and therefore they do not exercise their very wide discretionary powers in a discriminatory fashion; that they do not use insulting words; that they do not use excessive force in arrest and detention of Aboriginal people. It is a shame that such officers are the ones that create the image and perception amongst Aborigines that all police must be the same. Further it is a misguided sense of loyalty and solidarity that enables such deficient officers to remain within the Police Force. Nothing will improve as long as solidarity overrides the need for truth and an ability to stand up to one's mates at times. The measuring stick for both Aborigines and police should be (i) whether they would like to be treated the way they treat others; (ii) why persist in actions and activities that do more to dehumanise oneself than another.[42]

The negative disposition of the Western Australian Police Union in the course of the commission was nevertheless not reflected in other police union response to the commission. In spite of the Police Federation's attitude over the previous decade on issues like legal aid to Aborigines,[43] a submission from the Police Federation to the royal commission was more reflective and less defensive. The commission's report went out of its way to welcome the positive stance of the Federation. Noting the history of government policy and police practice in implementing it for example, the Federation submission stood in stark contrast to the Western Australian union's sharp denial of the inequalities of policing:

> There have been sustainable allegations of differential and discriminatory use of the criminal justice system against Aboriginals. The statistical reports speak clearly under this heading. At the dictate of Government heavy policing has permeated Aboriginal life, producing through incarceration destructive effects on individual and communal lives.

In the commissioners' summary view, the Federation submission

> acknowledged that Australia's history of colonisation had dominant features of dispossession, expropriation, repressive control, dependence, de-culturation and near genocide of Aboriginal people. The Federation supports Aboriginal self-determination.[44]

It was telling, argued the commissioners, that it could scarcely have been expected at the outset of the inquiry in 1987 that the police unions might produce such a strong statement, reviewing the history of policing in Australia with a greater sense of realism about its actual effects on a disadvantaged population.

The Federation's positive engagement with the issues addressed by the royal commission was perhaps to be expected from the peak body, with its distance from the individual interests driving the local unions. While the commission's report noted for example the good relations with the Police Association of South Australia, other unions besides that in Western Australia provided a challenge to the commission. The shooting of David Gundy in Sydney during a police raid in April 1989 was eventually brought into the commission's jurisdiction after a coroner's jury inquiry had resulted in an accidental death finding. The initial declaration of the commission's intention to pursue an inquiry was accepted without comment from the New South Wales Police Association. But a deputation of the police involved, from the Special Weapons Operations Squad (or SWOS, a paramilitary police unit), resulted in the Association executive agreeing to fund a challenge to the commission. To the union president the prospect of the police (this 'Squad With Out Support) being 'dragged before' the commission was abhorrent. A single judge of the Federal Court upheld the union's challenge on whether the commission had jurisdiction, but the commission won an appeal to the full bench and the inquiry proceeded.[45]

The unions' reactions to these two major inquiries involving the policing of indigenous people in Australia, events separated by 30 years, appear in the main to be characterised by a profoundly defensive approach. This is not of course surprising since in the end a union has only two roles — advocacy of its members' interests, and defence of its members against external attack. The position taken by the Police Federation in the case of the royal commission was more in line with a stance that flows from a positive view of the union as an organisation of professionals, with a capacity to play something other than a purely reactive part in response to public inquiry. A succession of other very public inquiries during these same decades suggests that the disposition of the unions in the cases of inquiry into indigenous people was above all determined by the structural role of the unions, i.e. by their need to fulfil their objective of defending their members. Two episodes stand out in this respect — the Beach Inquiry in Victoria and the fate of its recommendations; and the Fitzgerald Inquiry in Queensland, which for the first time addressed the difficult question of the police unions' scope and role in the criminal justice system.

The Beach Inquiry into allegations of police corruption in criminal investigation made by abortionist and law reform campaigner Dr Bertram Wainer in 1974 was held during the years 1975–6. Even before the official release of his report the recommendations, including prosecution of 55 police, were leaked to the media and became the subject of a widespread and extensive political campaign by the Victorian Police Association. Two-thirds of the Association's 6,400 members attended a rally in Melbourne's Festival Hall in October 1976. Two concerns were central to the mood of the mass meeting — the prosecution of the police officers and the changes in police investigative procedure recommended by Beach. In both respects the magnitude of the police protests led to the government retreating from implementation of the Beach recommendations. The difficulties faced by the government from the outset were evident in one vital symbolic action — the appearance on the platform at the protest meeting of the chief commissioner. Although Commissioner Jackson urged restraint, he spoke as a past executive member of the Association and the mood of his speech is captured in the response of this mass protest meeting — applause and an enthusiastic vote of confidence. The unity evident in this reciprocal affirmation of loyalties was undoubtedly a critical element in the outcome. On the particular matter of a review of police procedures, the Association formulated as one of its work-to-rule objectives that 'any change in police procedure be the result of conference between the

Government, the Police Department, the Police Association and not based on Mr Beach's recommendations'. Within a month the secretary of the Association was able to tell the executive that the government had promised that no procedure would be changed without this consultation with the Association.[46]

The Association's work-to-rule approved at such a massive protest meeting was a warning to government of the weight of police opinion. The events were also an encouragement to ultra-defensive posturing by the Association. The Christmas message of the president, L J Blogg, said it all:

> The past year has not been kind to our Police Service. Our morale, confidence and public image have been unjustifiably damaged by the Beach Enquiry and Report and for those of our members who are the victims of a conspiracy, my sympathy goes out to them ... I am confident that our membership will survive this onslaught and repel the suggested future restrictions that will prevent our effective police operations. ... Remember we are facing formidable foes of power and influence in this community which only police unity will overcome.[47]

The 'conspiracy' imagined by the police unionists was a large one — involving the top end of Bourke St, i.e. the government which was seen as having betrayed the police, the 'learned gentlemen' of the bar, 'some with the initials of Q.C. after their name', and the 'scum' of the streets, the criminals whose allegations about police practices had been led as evidence at the Beach hearings. In the overheated atmosphere of a Festival Hall meeting of 4,000 police, the October protest had been told that this was all part of an attack on 'law and order':

> History has shown us that if subversive elements are able to undermine law and order which is one of the primary pillars of democracy, it is the preliminary step to bringing down the Government. In the past when crises occurred within the community the police have been able to produce leaders who have been able to steer the people through the wilderness until peace and tranquility have been restored. We are now on the threshold of the most critical peacetime crisis for more than 50 years.[48]

The reference was to the police strike of 1923. While police unionists sometimes spoke in 1976 about strike action, they heeded the advice of their chief commissioner and resolved instead on the work-to-rule campaign. The evidence of government back down, no convictions from the reduced number of prosecutions anyway, and the very public display of police opposition to the adverse results of a public inquiry into their methods support Haldane's conclusion that the success of the Association's campaign 'was almost absolute'.[49]

The story of another corruption inquiry was less of a triumph for the police unions involved. The Fitzgerald Commission of Inquiry in Queensland between 1987 and 1989 extended beyond the investigation of allegations of police misconduct to scrutinise the nexus between police corruption and the political system in the state. The credibility of all too predictable denials of impropriety or corruption by senior police at the start of the inquiry were gradually undermined by police confessions in the course of the public hearings. More so than was usually the case in such inquiries the scope of the investigation came to encompass the whole contemporary history of a police–government compact in which the police unions themselves (in Queensland, there was a separate, generally lower profile, union of Officers, as well as the main one of 'Employees') had become implicated.

The Fitzgerald Inquiry was so concerned by the evidence of widespread political interventions of the police unions going back to the beginning of the 1970s that the issue of the proper role of a police union became the subject of recommendation. Reflecting a concern that, as we have seen, goes back to the beginning of police unions, the Fitzgerald Report questioned the appropriateness of union intervention in discipline matters. The Police Union, it was recommended, should 'revise its Rules to preclude any concern with police disciplinary matters other than as relevant to industrial relations'.[50] While noting the interest and support of the union in the matter of the current reform initiatives, the past role of the union, especially as it had been detailed in relation to the erosion of Commissioner Whitrod's early 1970s reform programme, came in for special attention. It was 'singularly inappropriate for the Union to demand the right to influence the selection of the Police Commissioner or Minister'.[51] This direct criticism of a long-cherished interest of the Australian police unions in the appointment of police commissioners was not welcome in Queensland any more than it would have been in other states — its spirit was to be flouted within a few years by the specific demands of the Queensland Police Union in the Mundingburra by-election.

The background to the Fitzgerald Report recommendations was evidence of the role of the union during the Whitrod reform period of the 1970s. Whitrod had offended a police ethos at the outset by his very appointment — the first appointment of a commissioner from outside the service since the 1930s, and the first ever appointment of a person from outside the state (or even colony, going back to the 1860s). While various writers have characterised this something of a Queensland phenomenon[52] it is more likely that resistance to the appointment of outsiders is part of the ethos of an employees' organisation. Queensland in fact provides a very rare instance of a union at one time demanding the appointment of an outsider — during a period of sustained conflict between the union and the government and police department, the executive unanimously moved in November 1953 for just such an appointment.[53] This was exceptional. Promotion through the ranks was a core interest of the police unions in all jurisdictions and those who had proved themselves as stayers were also those who could expect some consent from the ranks. As the *New South Wales Police News* had noted at MacKay's appointment in 1935: 'The Force feels safe with him as he has risen by sheer ability from the lowest rung of the ladder of promotion'.[54] For similar reasons police unions in other states had frequently sought to put pressure on government to appoint a commissioner or other senior officers from within the ranks. Astonishingly, even in the wake of the Fitzgerald Inquiry's purging criticism of police corruption and police mismanagement during the Lewis years as commissioner in Queensland (1976–87), the Labor Party in opposition in 1989 was still happy to curry favour through the old preference for an insider by telling the police union of its support for the appointment of a new police commissioner 'drawn from the ranks of the Queensland Police Force'.[55]

Whitrod's problems with the unions went well beyond his personal disadvantage in coming from outside the Queensland police. His reform program was already mandated by ministerial support for his appointment in the shadow of a long period of incompetent police leadership in the state. Whitrod wanted not only to clean up the force, but also to modernise it — hence his advocacy of police education and training, his policies of promotion on merit rather than seniority, and his commitment to improving the recruitment of women police. Added to these seemingly modest police reforms was an insistence on due process and restraint in public order policing.

In these circumstances the response of the police union in Queensland was to seek political intervention. On the one hand, the campaign against Whitrod was pursued through standard union tactics of votes of no confidence. On the other, and more insidiously, since less accountably, the union went directly to the premier with its complaints about the commissioner, who was being strongly supported by his minister. The saga of deteriorating relations was described in detail in the Fitzgerald Report. This was the context in which a police union had unprecedented access to the leadership of government, dealing directly with the premier of the day, Joh Bjelke-Petersen, when the commissioner or the minister pursued polices or made decisions that displeased the union leadership.[56] This culture of access was lost once Bjelke-Petersen was forced out of office. Fitzgerald's compelling disclosure of the evidence of political intervention by the Queensland police unions over a long period of time was background for the nevertheless somewhat inconclusive prescriptions for the curtailing of police union power. This was scarcely surprising — the status of police unions as independent industrial organisations of employees with legal capacity to advance and defend their member's interests was now long established. Whether or not a union had political influence and used it was a matter of its own disposition, and the responsiveness of the government of the day. The results were seen in Queensland almost immediately after the conclusion of the Fitzgerald Inquiry. On the one hand, there were campaigns to undermine the standing of the new 'reform' commissioner, Noel Newnham, appointed, like Whitrod, from outside the force, on the other, increasing frustration with a government that would not prove as responsive as Bjelke-Petersen had been, especially through its insistence on a program of administrative reform and in pursuing prosecution of corrupt police.[57] The longer term outcome of that frustration was the tactics pursued by the union, under a new leadership, going into the Mundingburra by-election.

The critical differences between the outcome for the unions in the quite separate experiences of the Beach and Fitzgerald inquiries tell us much about the limits as well as possibilities of police union power. Like the later Wood Royal Commission in New South Wales (1994–6), the Fitzgerald Report was able to develop a comprehensive set of recommendations in a political context that was transformed by the very process of the inquiry. Even in advance of the outcomes, the public hearings of Fitzgerald and Wood managed to set an agenda of public expectation about change that pre-empted union opposition. That possibility was in turn shaped by the scale and substance of the corruption — widespread as it was, it was nevertheless possible to see such practices as deviant, and therefore legitimately the target of attack. In contrast the Beach Inquiry was intruding into the ambiguous world of criminal investigation, very much at the core of public perceptions of police business, and even more so with respect to police self-image. Police in general felt attacked by Beach, as they generally do when their domain of discretion in crime control and investigation is under question.

Above all however the unity of police department and police union in the Beach episode must have presented the Victorian government with a much more formidable opposition to reform. In contrast, police authority from the commissioner down through senior management was shaken apart by the Fitzgerald and Wood inquiries — in the former case the commissioner ended up in gaol, in the latter the commissioner (a former police union leader) was forced to retire in ignominy after his public denials of corruption came to be seen as the result of ignorance or incompetence in management. Such conditions make a reform of institutions possible, and the resistance of police unions at least more difficult — in such conditions unions can be brought on side for change.

6.3 Law reform — the unions for and against

Law is not the only structure governing police work, but it is nevertheless an important one.[58] Why else would police unions since the 1920s have engaged in their own occasional policy advice, and pressure, to see that appropriate law reform would be pursued? As a test of police union activism, engagement in law reform is among the more useful. Without evidence that police unions have engaged in debate or actions around law reform issues, we might conclude that their preoccupations were narrowly industrial, i.e. primarily about wages and conditions of service, leave and pension provisions. The history of police union engagement with law reform also suggests that law reform concerns may be a vicarious satisfaction of industrial objectives. More subtly, to the extent that a union may be concerned not just with pay and conditions, but with the substance of its members' work, then law reform has at the minimum a symbolic dimension. Indeed it is the symbolic dimension of statutory law reform that seems most prominent in many of the examples that have surfaced in recent years. If police union statements on statutory reform are so often reactive that is because so often law reform is seen as part of a climate of hostility to the prerogatives of police.

In a number of campaigns in Australian jurisdictions police unions have been active opponents, or protagonists, of law reform in recent decades. We have seen earlier in this book the concerns of police unions already in the 1920s over law reform in areas such as vagrancy and police offences acts, and firearms legislation. Both these areas of legal regulation in fact emerged again in the 1970s and 1980s as the focus of police union action. In New South Wales the highly organised protests of the police union over the repeal of summary offences legislation has been well documented — the actions of police included apparent selective enforcement of the law in the electorate of the Labor attorney-general, who had initiated the reform legislation, as well as more conventional protest action.[59] The campaign was characterised by a great deal of rancour between the government and the Police Association, especially after the appearance of a full-page newspaper advertisement, under the heading 'You can still walk on the streets of New South Wales, but we can no longer guarantee your safety from harassment'.[60] Police unions could also be pro-active in supporting law reform — once again firearms regulation was the focus of union lobbying during the 1980s and 1990s, especially while governments vacillated over the issue in spite of a number of highly publicised multiple gun killings.[61] From 1991 the revised Police Federation policy on gun control included a demand for uniform legislation and other measures that were not to get the consent of all governments until after the Port Arthur massacre in 1997.

These examples of activity in law reform highlight the importance of recognising the longevity of police union involvement in quite specific domains of regulation affecting the powers of police in carrying out their duties of peace-keeping and crime prevention. What these examples have in common is a predictable desire of police to enhance their capacity to control space and activity — in some cases this must be pursued through resisting regulatory reform, in others through pursuing it. The police union however is only one player on a highly-contested territory, complicated in recent decades by the multiplication of parties with an active and informed interest in law-making and its implementation.

The temptation to see law reform as part of a wider agenda aimed at writing down the powers of police, even of demeaning them in the eyes of the community, was enhanced from the 1970s by the association of law reform with the new agencies created for that purpose. The dilemma of what position police unions would take in participating in review of legislation affecting police powers was already foreshadowed in the mid-1960s when the Victorian government initiated a review of police practice in interviewing suspects. The annual meeting of the Police Association debated whether to make a submission to the review, conducted by the state's solicitor-general. Some members were concerned that such activity might legitimise recommendations that were not in the police interest. One member even took a highly formalist approach to police powers, pointing out that 'our duty as Policemen was to enforce the law, not make the law, and he felt we should keep out of it'.[62] In the end the Association voted to make a submission and drew comfort from a report that was 'far more favourable to the police (and the community)' than had been expected.[63]

Law reform became a matter of continuing review from the time of establishment of the various state law reform commissions and finally a federal body, all within a decade of this review in Victoria. The inquiry and report of the Australian Law Reform Commission into Criminal Investigation[64] was a signal to the unions of threats to old ways of doing policing. The prospect that an enhancement of suspect rights, and a closer regulation of questioning in custody, would flow from the federal jurisdiction into the states was greeted with hostility. But the opposition took place over a number of years and in relation to different types of initiative flowing from the ALRC report.

The police unions early opposed law reform protecting the rights of Aborigines under police questioning. In what was to become a familiar stance against proposed reforms of criminal investigation, the first target of the unions was an attempt by Queensland Senator Neville Bonner, the country's first Aboriginal parliamentarian, to legislate for the protection of Aborigines and Islanders in police custody. Bonner's private bill, introduced in 1976 (and again in 1978 and 1981), sought to limit the admissibility of confessions obtained by police from Aborigines, Torres Strait Islanders and Pacific Islanders, along lines recommended by the Australian Law Reform Commission in respect of confessions generally, and later also in conformity with the recommendations of the Lucas Report into police investigations in Queensland. The Queensland government strongly opposed the bill — and its lengthy statement of opposition was forwarded to the President of the Queensland Police Union by Queensland parliamentarian and ex-police officer Don Lane. It was published in the *Queensland Police Journal* under the heading 'The Notorious Private Bill Introduced by Senator Bonner'.[65]

Claiming that there should be 'justice for all', the Queensland union was complacent in its response to Bonner's strong attack on the high levels of imprisonment of Aboriginal people. Writing to Prime Minister Malcolm Fraser, the union urged the government to ensure that Bonner's bill did not become law.

> Over a long period of time the Queensland Police Union has had considerable dealings with the coloured community of this State and we have always found that the Law as it is presently framed particularly with respect to the 'Aborigine questioning' leaves nothing to be desired in guaranteeing the community of Queensland a proper and complete law enforcement program.[66]

The union's motion opposing Bonner's bill was agreed by the biennial conference of the Police Federation in March 1977.[67] The message was taken up by others. In July the *New South Wales Police News* asked the question, 'Why Handcuff the Police?', when listing Bonner's bill among a number of legislative initiatives indicating

> an apparently suicidal desire by Governments to severely curtail the ability of one group within the community upon whom the same Governments rely so heavily to combat the tidal wave of crime which is steadily building up in this country — the Police Force.[68]

The opposition struck home. The Federation's 1977 resolution had been conveyed to the federal government and the next biennial conference in September 1979 heard that the bill would not be proceeding.[69] Police opposition to any special rights for Aborigines was to become an anthem in the course of the next decade and more as Aboriginal–police relations continued to attract headlines. The concern over possible statutory protection of Aboriginal rights in police custody was only part of a wider syndrome of attitudes in which the activities of Aboriginal legal services were equally liable to be attacked — the evidence that some departments (e.g. South Australia) were developing pro-active initiatives in the improvement of police–Aboriginal liaison was overshadowed at union conferences by the generally negative disposition of delegates.[70]

The subtleties of the issues entailed in the regulation of criminal investigation continued to be lost in the simplicity of police opposition to concurrent and continuing attempts to reform the law. Simultaneous with Bonner's bill dealing with Aborigines, the federal government was initiating legislation to address the ALRC recommendations. At the prompting of the Victorian Association, the police unions (and departments) took up the cudgels against what was seen as an anti-police bill, with a widely published poster summing up the union case.[71] The Criminal Investigation Bill 1977 was said to 'protect the rights of individuals' — against a foregrounded photo of an armed hold-up in a bank, the poster asked 'whose rights are being protected here?' Law-abiding citizens' rights were being 'slid under the counter like these terrified hostages'.[72] The analysis of the bill in more extended commentary in the police journals stressed its impractical codification of all aspects of police/suspect interaction, its lack of respect for the integrity or professionalism of police, and even its possible threat to the roles and functions of public police. The bill was taken as yet another sign that

> the police community is just another victim, another scapegoat of an increasingly selfish, hedonistic society whose principal motivation is expediency .... If the vocal minority has its way the quest for law and order will become subordinate to the quest for procedural perfectability, and the rights of the law-abiding will be discarded in favour of the rights of the anti-social.[73]

Opposition from police was thus vocal, and effective — the bill failed to advance any further in 1977. Four years later a revision was attempted. Again the unions were opposed. Writing in the *Victorian Police Journal*, Association secretary Tom Rippon attacked it as a mess that would ensure that the 'front line Police' continued to lose ground 'to the upsurge of crime in the community'.[74] In Tasmania too the Police Association was alarmed by Labor proposals for law reform on matters affecting police interrogation and taping, seeing in them evidence of an 'absolute lack of confidence in the integrity of police officers'.[75]

'A lack of confidence in the integrity of police' — this was a comment that captured the climate in which police unions throughout the 1970s and 1980s embraced a new activism. The campaigns for more police were complemented by the need to defend police against the forces marshalled against them, as the police unions saw it anyway. The campaigns of the Victorian Association over the Beach Inquiry prosecutions and of the New South Wales Association over the repeal of the *Summary Offences Act* uncovered a police union assertion of police rights — defensive seen from the outside, but affirmative and necessary seen from the viewpoint of union activists. In this context the old guard of Labor-sympathetic union officials could be depicted as having failed the cause of police. The new style police unionism would be more determined to take on governments and the public in pursuit of police objectives. The transition was not un-noticed. In South Australia for example 1981 brought a new executive and interviews with the press that promised a 'fresh force behind police'. Past secretary and a former vice-president of the South Australian Trades and Labour Council Ralph Tremethick was immediately concerned by the tone of some comments, warning: 'let us not be too loud in our protests about false reports against police'. The depiction of the past leadership of the union as having been too soft on issues of concern to police was misleading since 'for many years past the Association has been outspoken about such things as lenient sentences and early parole'. Tremethick insisted however that when the Association spoke about such things it did so in the capacity of a citizen. There was a boundary to be drawn between speaking as a citizen and acting as a criminal justice officer. 'Police should be careful', he argued, 'not to assume a role which may make them appear to be stepping into the shoes of Judge and Jury'.[76]

Such views, with their careful distinctions between the roles of police unions and those of police officers, would not disappear from internal debates in police unions. But the range of union actions and interventions we have been considering in this chapter makes it clear that Tremethick's was the kind of considered positioning that could easily be lost in the reactive politics of police unions. By the 1980s the unions often felt themselves and their members embattled. That posture informed responses both to the establishment of civilian oversight mechanisms and of managerial change that was spreading into police departments. In the resulting struggles police unions (sometimes in collusion with their respective police departments) showed in some jurisdictions that reform would not proceed without their consent.

6.4 The politics of victimhood

There has been perhaps no more striking instance of the capacity of police unions to exert political power in a matter involving the public interest than in the stances taken on civilian oversight of police actions. Prior to the 1970s there were only two important mechanisms of accountability that might address civilian complaints about police — the law and the parliament. We should not gainsay either of these — individuals did take legal action against police who had assaulted or otherwise harmed them; and police commissioners were sensitive to the range of complaints that might come through the minister's office, or by representation from politicians, though we yet lack a substantial study of the effectiveness of either of these mechanisms. Reforming governments from the 1970s on however asserted the right of the public to have more effective and accessible agencies that might address their complaints about police behaviour. The contests between these agencies and the police against whom their inquiries and recommendations may be targeted were among the most troubling of conflicts in the regulation of policing during these years. In these conflicts police unions played an important, indeed vital role — but they did not stand alone. This was an arena where unions and commissioners often played on the same side, a combination that only the most determined of governments in the most favourable of political contexts could combat. By provoking debate over the autonomy of police these contests around civilian oversight of police and civilian redress against abuse of power also fostered the right conditions for police to generate 'law and order' campaigns.

The recurrently defensive posture of police confronted by new agencies of oversight or accountability has been addressed in numerous studies in recent years.[77] The particular roles of police unions tend to be obscured in the reality that both unions and departments have shared this defensiveness. The degree to which they do so is of course variable by jurisdiction and over time. Police managers charged with the responsibility of taking police forward in the wake of the negative results of corruption inquiries are less likely to share the sentiments of the union executive. But a commonly articulated vision in union rhetoric is of a united police confronting government swayed by sectional interest in advantaging the criminal against the community. As the president of the Victorian Police Association captured the moment in 1988, a year in which the union was busily generating a law and order campaign around gun laws, police powers and police equipment and in the wake of a successful defeat of a civilian oversight authority:

> We, the Police, are still confined within a system which curiously continues to endow an offender with undue advantage, at the expense of the victim, and the community.

In this world view police are always being misunderstood and frustrated, their interests frustrated by sectional interests.

> We, the Executive, you, the members, together with the Police Department, have all experienced and continue to experience tardiness, procrastination, false promises, obstruction and groundless assumptions by Governments over the years, relating to areas of law and order.

The police unions facing the challenges of the modern era claim to speak for police as a whole and, implicitly or explicitly, for the community generally.

In truth of course the play of politics was one in which the unions were as adept as any other sectional interest. The result throughout the decades after Askin's 1965 election victory in New South Wales was that the unions were accutely conscious of their power to affect political outcomes. Far from being victims of trickery and obstruction, the field of police politics commonly allowed unions to play a significant role in the establishment of legislative and institutional mechanisms for dealing with civilian complaints. In some cases, such as South Australia and Western Australia in the early 1980s, this involved decisions by governments to consult the unions in the course of legislative drafting, producing mechanisms that watered down the original expansive capacity of complaints procedures. In others, notably the notorious case of Victoria, a sustained campaign against an already established civilian oversight body, the Police Complaints Authority, resulted in the dismantling of the organisation.[78] One of the principal studies of the politics of these events concludes, however, that in more recent years the police unions in many jurisdictions, not only in Australia, accommodated themselves to the reality of independent complaints authorities, usually after obtaining important concessions from government.[79]

Like the police strength campaigns, or the resistance to major corruption inquiries, union resistance to the incursions made by law reformers and civil complaints activists must be read in political and organisational contexts. The defensiveness of the unions did reflect a reality — the reality of police being too frequently placed in the role of defendants in actions brought against them by their superiors or by civilians. In this role police could assume the status of victims — victims of a system that expected of them a fine level of discrimination and self-control in often difficult situations and in the event of them failing the test, that subjected them to trial without the protections of a 'right to silence' and that punished them with significant loss of earnings during investigations into their behaviour. The struggles of recent decades over police accountability and police autonomy can translate at the police worker level into a system that is seen to make police into victims. The demands of organisational change appeared in the 1980s and 1990s to do little but aggravate such a mentality, as we see in the next chapter.

Notes

1 *WAPN*, Jul–Aug 1981, pp16–17. For a contemporary commentary on police industrial militancy see Swanton and Page, "Police industrial dispute resolution processes and their implications for militancy".
2 *TPJ*, Mar 1958, pp3–9.
3 *VPJ*, Nov 1948, p2111; Sep 1949, p2279; Jan 1950, p12; Aug 1951, p285. Cf Haldane, *The people's force: a history of the Victoria Police*, 234–235.
4 See eg *VPJ*, Apr 1962, p53; Feb 1963, p17; Jun 1964, pp1–2.
5 *SMH*, 26 Mar 1963, p8; *NSWPN*, Apr 1963, p23.
6 *NSWPN*, Apr 1964, p21. Similar approaches to local government appear to have been pursued by the Victorian Police Association in 1965 — see *VPJ*, Mar 1965, p223 and May 1965, p245.
7 *NSWPN*, Nov 1964, p4 for CIB Branch motion on the need for more police to compensate for the loss of hours flowing from a recent increase of one week in annual leave, a motion referred to the 'Strength Committee'.
8 *NSWPN*, Dec 1964, p11.
9 *SMH*, 15 Jan 1965, p1; *Daily Mirror*, 17 Jan 1965.
10 *NSWPN*, Feb 1965, p11. See *NSWPN*, May 1965, p19 on the origins of the 1:530 ratio; *VPJ*, May 1965, p249.
11 See *NSWPN*, May 1965, p19 for comment on this.
12 *NSWPN*, Apr 1965, p15.
13 Gordon Hawkins, 'Investigating the police: More B.A.'s needed" in *The Bulletin*, 16 Jan 1965, pp19–20. The article was reprinted in *VPJ*, May 1965, pp249–253.
14 *Sun-Herald*, 9 May 1965, p38.
15 *NSWPN*, Aug 1965, pp3, 12–13.
16 *NSWPN*, Sep 1977, pp307–308.

17 *NSWPN*, Jun 1981, pp32–33.
18 *NSWPN*, Jul 1981, pp34–35.
19 *NSWPN*, Feb 1982, p4.
20 *SMH*, 10 Feb 1982, p15; 11 Feb 1982, pp2, 6.
21 *NSWPN*, Mar 1982, pp2–3; cf *VPJ*, Mar 1982, p35.
22 *NSWPN*, Jul 1982, pp8–9, 15.
23 *NSWPN*, Sep 1982, p16.
24 *NSWPN*, Dec 1982, p19; Mar 1983, pp21–23.
25 *NSWPN*, Jun 1983, p19.
26 *NSWPN*, Jun 1983, p15.
27 *VPJ*, Mar 1982, pp33, 35; Feb 1984, p87; Jul 1992, p3.
28 *SAPJ*, Oct 1990, p10; McGill, *No Right to Strike The History of the New Zealand Police Service Organizations*, 175.
29 *SAPJ*, Sep 1991, p6.
30 *QPJ*, Sep 1994, p55. See G E Fitzgerald, "Report of a Commission of Inquiry into Possible Illegal Activities and Associated Misconduct," (Brisbane, 1989).
31 Russell Hogg and David Brown, *Rethinking law and order* (Annandale, NSW, 1998), 35.
32 QSA, A/4708, Talty to E M Hanlon, 24 Aug 1942 and Cabinet minute 31 Aug 1942.
33 Moyle, "Union History 1915–1957 (3 parts)," Pt 3, pp23, 41 citing QPU Minutes, 17 Mar 1953, p4 and 15 Nov 1957, p178.
34 *SAPJ*, Aug 1959, p1.
35 K S Inglis, *The Stuart Case* (Parkville, 1961), 58–61.
36 Ibid, 60.
37 *SAPJ*, Aug 1959, p6; Oct 1959, p2.
38 *SAPJ*, Dec 1959, p1; Jan 1960, p1. See also Finnane, *Police and Government*, pp49–50, 88–89; Inglis, *The Stuart Case*, 292, 315.
39 Ibid, 315.
40 *VPJ*, Feb 1985, p45.
41 Police Union Submission, (1990), 8.
42 Royal Commission into Aboriginal Deaths in Custody, *Report* (hereafter RCIADIC, *Report*): Western Australia, Regional Report — 5.12.11.8 "Police view of complaints process", citing Police union Submisson, p8.
43 *NSWPN*, Sep 1979; Dec 1986, p9.
44 RCIADIC, *Report*: National Report, 29.1.9; see also 29.6.8 on the Police Federation's acknowledgement of the reality of racism as a problem with some police.
45 RCIADIC, *Report*: National Report, 3.5.5 (PASA); Vol 5, Appendix B (re Gundy). *NSWPN*, May 1990, p3 for the 'Squad with out Support'.
46 *VPJ*, Nov 1976, pp9, 11, 31; Dec 1976, p51.
47 *VPJ*, Dec 1976, p7.
48 *VPJ*, Nov 1976, p39.
49 Haldane, *The people's force: a history of the Victoria Police*, 292.
50 Fitzgerald, "Report of a Commission of Inquiry into Possible Illegal Activities and Associated Misconduct".
51 Ibid. See also Bolen, *Reform in policing: lessons from the Whitrod era*, 80–85 for a discussion of the role of the unions during the Whitrod years.
52 Bolen, *Reform in policing: lessons from the Whitrod era.*

53 Moyle, "Union History 1915–1957 (3 parts)," Pt 3, p26, citing QPU Minutes, 10 Mar 1953, p5.
54 *NSWPN*, Apr 1935, p1. For other police unions seeking appointment of an insider, *VPJ*, Jun 1946, pp1615–1616; Mar 1953, p564; *SAPJ*, Feb 1956; *SAPJ*, Jun 1971.
55 Bolen, *Reform in policing: lessons from the Whitrod era*, 107.
56 Fitzgerald, "Report of a Commission of Inquiry into Possible Illegal Activities and Associated Misconduct".
57 Bolen, *Reform in policing: lessons from the Whitrod era*, 104–112, Lewis, *Complaints against police: the politics of reform*, chs8–9.
58 See especially Dixon, *Law in policing: legal regulation and police practices.*
59 Sandra Egger and Mark Findlay, "The politics of police discretion," in *Understanding Crime and Criminal Justice*, ed Mark Findlay and Russell Hogg (Sydney, 1988).
60 *NSWPN*, Sep 1979, p307.
61 *NSWPN*, Sep 1979, p331; *SAPJ*, Nov 1987, p16; *NSWPN*, Oct 1991, p15; *SAPJ*, Jun 1992, p7.
62 *VPJ*, Oct 1965, p100.
63 *VPJ*, Nov. 1965, p1.
64 Australian Law Reform Commission, "Criminal Investigation," (Canberra, 1975).
65 *QPJ*, May 1977, pp11–17.
66 Commonwealth of Australia, Senate, *Proceedings*, 26 Oct 1978, p1660 (cited by Senator Bonner).
67 *NSWPN*, May 1977, p161.
68 *NSWPN*, Jul 1977, p226.
69 *NSWPN*, Sep 1979, p331; *VPJ*, Sep 1979, pp21, 29.
70 *NSWPN*, May 1977, p161 reporting discussion on 'Police and Aboriginals' at the 1977 Police Federation Conference.
71 *VPJ*, Aug 1977, p43, Oct 1977, p21.
72 *TPJ*, Oct 1977, p2.
73 *TPJ*, Oct 1977, pp5–11 (an article originally published in the ACT Police Association journal).
74 *VPJ*, Feb 1982, p9; *QPJ*, Jun 1982, p21.
75 *TPJ*, Nov 1978, pp2–5.
76 *SAPJ*, Feb 1981, p6.
77 See especially Lewis, *Complaints against police: the politics of reform* Ian Freckelton, "Sensation and Symbiosis," in *Police in our society*, ed Ian Freckelton and Hugh Selby (Sydney, 1988), Andrew Goldsmith, ed, *Complaints against the police: the trend to external review* (Oxford, 1991).
78 Freckelton, "Sensation and Symbiosis."
79 Lewis, *Complaints against police: the politics of reform*, 54–56.

7: The politics of change

We have seen Rationalisation, Regionalisation, Integration, Civilianisation and in some instances Bastardisation — our hope now is for Stabilisation.
Tony Day, President NSW Police Association, May 1990[1]

The previous chapters have highlighted the changing contexts of policing during the 1970s and 1980s. These were times in which a contest for control over policing — its budgets, its accountability, its powers — had become the stuff of everyday politics in Australia. In some of these matters police unions played a pro-active and initiating role — especially of course in relation to the police strength issue, but also in relation to law reform. In others, they were on the back foot — defending the interests of members against the prying eyes of an increasing number of public inquiries and standing oversight bodies. Our analysis has sought to demonstrate the mixed success of the unions in their pro-active and defensive postures in the public arena.

These were also decades in which police organisations were changing, and in ways that powerfully affected the domain on which the unions had long traditions of engagement. Consistent with the changes taking place in workplaces throughout the last three decades police departments began to adopt initiatives in management of personnel and resources that departed from the conventions long established in the public sector.[2] Parallel with this went new priorities in focus that were more specific to policing — a change in discourse for example from force to service, from citizen to customer, from criminal to community. At times the reaction of the police unions to these changes seemed to range only from the sardonic to the hostile. But unions themselves were changing, and there have been some implications of the managerial revolution and customer focus that have been consistent with the more forward looking objectives of the peak body, the Police Federation.

Another kind of change was embodied in the burgeoning expectation of civilian oversight of policing. The acceleration of moves towards civilian oversight of police from the 1970s have been among the greatest challenges to police self-image and the dispositions of the unions. They also helped to fracture the post-war consensus in which unions would focus on wages and conditions issues in a framework that brought government, police department and union together. As the terms of that agreement changed so also within unions did pressures build up for a more aggressive response to any hint of external control, to a new order in policing that would involve other parties.

This chapter then will provide an opportunity to review the role of the unions during a period of substantial change in the organisational conditions of policing.

7.1 New agendas and old responses

In what might in other circumstances be taken as a caricature of the clash between old and new agendas in policing, New South Wales detectives reacted sharply to the police administration in 1987 over the shaping of the new objectives in community policing. For the new police commissioner, John Avery, author a few years earlier of a provocative study, *Police: Force or Service?*, the future belonged to 'Community Based Policing', a task in which police would be valued as professionals, and police would see their work as a 'vocation — an occupation of immense worth to the community'.[3]

In New South Wales community-based policing became the policing rationale for a fundamental reorganisation of the force. That reorganisation was to take the shape of a division of the police into regions, in contrast to the old centralised structure with its primary divisions on the basis of function. The long-standing functional divide between detectives and general duty police, epitomised in New South Wales by the century-old Criminal Investigation Branch, was to be diminished by regionalisation. The inevitable tensions involved in such a reshaping of a large organisation were aggravated in 1987 by the release of a series of papers on the new concept of community-based policing. Embedded in one paper was a provocative analysis of the division between detectives and patrol officers. Reprinted in the union journal, *New South Wales Police News*, the analysis sought to identify the basis of the likely anatagonism and resistance of detectives to the implementation of community-based policing. The concept was seen as one which clashed with the privileges and culture of the detective branch, whose higher status within the police was attributed above all to 'their strong cohesion as a group, with its expected effect of reinforcing shared values — the most easily discernible and highly tangible of these values being the need to solve unsolved crime'. Disbanding the detective branch was essential to establishing community-based policing, with all police, detectives and patrol officers being part of a team. The challenges faced by the police department in dealing with the detectives were summarised bluntly:

> The detectives' perception of their job will remain "my job is to solve crime" until they are removed from the grouping which reinforces it. Their goals will remain the same until their professional territory is redefined. Their professional territory, if they are to adopt and understand the ideals of community policing, needs to be a defined segment of the community shared with a team. Such considerations will depend to an extent, on the constraints imposed by union power; resistance to redistribution of detective personnel, especially if it goes along with a demystification of their role, will be huge.

The final insult was left to the end — a reference to the findings of research on policing, one of the central messages being 'most crime is solved by citizens witnessing the offence, not by criminal investigators'.[4]

This somewhat brutal attack on the detective culture, one of those parts benefiting most by 'the perpetuation of the old traditional culture', was predictably taken up by the detectives. The Association president attacked the community policing paper for its attempted 'isolation of the detectives'. The slight was seen by the detectives themselves as a symptom of the state of affairs in government more generally. Governments, and police departments with them, had insufficient care for the fundamentals of police work, being distracted by the play of special interests. The attribution of crime solving to citizens rather than police was especially hurtful. Such a statement could only come from

> a person living in a fantasy world, a world which ignores the realism [sic] of crime and those who, believe it or not, are not going to change their criminals ways no matter how many times they're slapped on the wrist.

The commissioner was seen as an enemy of the detectives, one who did not trust the CIB, 'would be happy to see the Branch divided and eventually fall apart ... we will all eventually go back to Uniform and become "investigators" in name only'.[5]

The divide between the old and the new — between the street-educated and crime-fighting detective cop and the new, 'academic' staff officers was captured a month later in the *Police News* as it farewelled the CIB, the 'most notable casualty of the march towards Regionalisation'. A hard hitting attack by a former CIB Superintendent, Ray Blissett, provided also a frank assessment of some practices of the detective branch over the years, including an analysis of the infamous 'Paddy's Book' era, during which the police had cooked the crime statistics to provide evidence of high clear-up rates. Blissett's candour about the mixed past of the CIB did not moderate his view of a threatening future when the 'State Commander, State Investigative Group' might respond to an emergency by seeking

> a miracle man from that register of informants to which they have given birth, or send a signal to Harvard, or some other seat of criminological study, seeking assistance from those who assisted in the disorganisation of an organised crime fighting unit.[6]

In spite of this bluster from the detectives, the realities of a fundamental re-organisation that might enhance the standing of everyday police duties have meant that the union has also played a role in promoting understanding of new agendas in policing. Most police, and thus members of the union, are not detectives, and have a different view of the priorities of policing, and of the realities of reward and status in the organisation. Stories like Blissett's about the heroic deeds of the CIB might prompt counter-thrusts by ex-coppers seeking to give 'a uniform version of what really took place', as did a former Kurri Kurri officer contesting Blissett's account of the arrest of a famous escapee of the 1960s.[7]

As much as it provides a voice to the disgruntled, a constructive union must also look to addressing the possibilities within an evolving agenda. In this context we can appreciate why the *Police News* simultaneously supported the resistance of the detectives while at the same time running stories on the new systems in policing. As might be expected, union executive members were invited, if belatedly, to briefings and discussions of community policing.[8] In December 1987, for example, the *Police News* ran an exploratory and reflective analysis of a new concept in community policing, 'total geographic responsibility', by the chief constable of Surrey. In advocating the development of a 'more interactive or proactive rather than solely a reactive or fire brigade service', the chief constable's analysis was on a par with Avery's reform programme — and a re-emphasis on the status and value of a constable on the beat. In response to such items there were many police correspondents who insisted that community policing was something they already did, or that there were other models internationally that were worth imitating.[9] The 'Mail-Bag' headlines on letters from working police tell the story, ' "Too much emphasis" on comm.policing' from 'another concerned member'; 'Community policing — fact or farce' from 'Sector Sergeant at a working Station'; and 'Community-Based Policing — or doing what comes naturally', from 'A named senior constable at Wallsend'.[10]

Such a role in advocacy and contestation of the new agendas in policing is of course secondary to the primary concern of the union — maintaining or improving fundamental pay and conditions. But as the fundamentals of police organisation change what are the implications for pay and conditions? The way in which new agendas become a bargaining chip is well illustrated at just this time, 1987, by negotiations over a claim for a 4% pay rise. The department sought to put a value on regionalisation and community policing as a rationale for award of the pay increase — but failed to achieve this. The Association found its position further eroded by the commissioner's attempt to bring in further work-place changes to offset against the pay increase — in particular the introduction of 'single unit patrols', which the Association and many members opposed on safety grounds.[11] In the upshot, with an election pending the pay rise was granted without a need to engage in sustained industrial action and concession.[12]

As an industrial demand, an increase in police numbers was not only linked to a perceived shortage of police in stations or on beats. At a more considered level police unions were increasingly likely to perceive a challenge coming from a shift in the balance of policing functions from public to private as a substantial challenge to future career opportunities. The changing external environment of policing was the focus, for example, of Police Federation representations to the Commonwealth government in 1986. Members of the New South Wales Association had the message highlighted for them under a headline in the August issue of the *Police News*, 'Police Federation acts on erosion of police functions':

> Policing on the cheap and the substitution of private security for traditional policing functions affects every police officer. A diminishing role for police limits, among other things, career development opportunities and can affect salary structures.

The Federation's case was set out in a letter from the secretary, Tom Rippon, of the Victorian Association to Special Minister of State Mick Young. He drew attention to the growth in private security agencies as well as the multiplication of public agencies such as the National Crime Authority, and various state bodies like the Victorian Road Traffic Authority. Security guards being employed at sporting functions were an additional aggravation. The 'difficulty with all non-professional organisations' Rippon charged, is that they were unaccountable, unlike the public police. Governments were avoiding responsibility for providing adequate public police.[13]

Police unions have been long concerned about the growth of private security. The concerns are elementary — the possibility that governments and private property owners will look to other means of security is a direct challenge to career opportunity. Over the last two decades of economic and managerial reform, governments have increasingly looked to a devolution of responsibilities away from government agencies wherever possible. The advantages and shortcomings were already canvassed in a Canberra seminar in 1982 when New South Wales Association secretary Bob Page, took a strong stand against the growth of private security, while explaining it in terms of government failure to provide sufficient numbers of public police. Ironically enough, in the light of Rippon's later charge against unaccountable private agencies, Page blamed government for 'legislative measures which had tended to reduce police effectiveness by holding officers more accountable for their actions'.[14] In addressing the growth of private policing the *Police News* adverted to an explanation of more substance canvassed by Canadian criminologists, Clifford Shearing and Philip Stenning, at the same seminar. Private police had advantages over public. They were more likely to focus on the prevention of future crimes rather than the detection of ones that had already been committed; and they had greater powers to the extent that they operated under the umbrella of private property interests.[15]

From this latter perspective it might be argued that a significant weakness of police unions during the policing reforms of the last two decades has been their frequently displayed reluctance to embrace alternative modes of policing. The iconic status of the cop who has been involved, not in community service functions, but in the tough and dangerous world of tracking down violent criminals has been reflected in the critical eye directed at innovative policing. The cynicism one finds displayed by some police union activists about initiatives in community policing, such as police education programmes or adopt-a-cop schemes, or neighbourhood watch, flows from a view which privileges reactive policing of a very traditional kind over the more mundane work that has in any case historically characterised policing. If an effect of this focusing of policing on thief catching is that private security with a crime prevention and order maintenance function is enhanced, then that has arguably been in part encouraged by police union priorities.

The analysis above has outlined some aspects of union reception of a philosophical and organisational re-framing of police work in the 1980s and after. There were other dimensions of change that were shaped by managerial innovation. These included changes in education and skills acquisition, as well as career mobility — and the two were brought together in the modern era by reforming commissioners seeking to develop police departments with well-qualified managers who had proved their capacities rather than just served their time. While the encouragement of police education was capable of inspiring all too predictable attacks on the irrelevance of academic knowledge to the real world of policing, it was less contentious politically and industrially than the issue of promotion. As we have seen earlier union members had seen promotion as one of the core grievances from the earliest days of police unionism. As a labour-intensive occupation with a large proportion of employees at the bottom of the organisational pyramid, policing constantly faces the problem of stalled career, and hence income, mobility. In 1997, the Wood Commission in New South Wales concluded that there were widespread perceptions that the system was unfair, 'a circumstance contributing to the attitude of cynicism and distrust that has pervaded sections of the Service'.[16] Along with wages, pensions and discipline/complaints procedures, promotions have been of fundamental concern to police unionists. As with the Victorian Association's conflict with Blamey in the 1920s, promotions have great potential to become a grievance that spills over into industrial and even political confrontation.

The heart of confrontation over promotions has been the contest between seniority and merit. On the face of it, merit would seem to have clear advantages for any efficient organisation. But the difficulty of the merit criterion in work where qualitative judgment is essential provokes the charge of favouritism or nepotism. The appeal of the alternative criterion of seniority, qualified as it usually was by the attainment of a basic skills level assessed by examination, was its avoidance of those charges. Seniority however had some considerable disadvantages — it frustrated police commissioners, and equally it frustrated able officers forced to wait decades for desired promotion. Add to these fundamental tensions the elements of competition, jealousy and envy, all encouraged by a promotion appeals system which fosters these traits and we can see why the union journals and conferences have a standing preoccupation with promotion issues.

The flavour of the contest is captured in the views of the disgruntled , or just the brutally frank. Take 'Sadly disillusioned' in 1994, having just unsuccessfully appealed against the promotion of another officer:

> How many of you remember when we used to get the Stud Book out and in quite poor taste, gleefully rule a line through so and so's name that had passed away, retired resigned etc to observe with immense satisfaction our immeasurable progress towards well-earned promotion. Sure, so some dickheads got to be bosses and even perhaps Commissioners, it did not matter really because, exam passes achieved, there was our career path stretched out in front like the F4 freeway — visible, tangible. The brown noses or those with patrons, could not beat this system. It may have been slow and ponderous but it was a darn sight fairer than this wonderful PROMOTION ON MERIT.[17]

'Sadly disillusioned' was not isolated in this expression of antagonism to a system already in place. An intensive study by Savery of attitudes in the Western Australian police to the proposed introduction of merit-based promotion in the mid-1990s showed widespread opposition at all ranks of the police.[18] Not surprisingly, a large number of the items contested by the Queensland Police Union under the Mundingburra MOU were concerned with promotion issues — as the union sought to roll back the merit-based promotion systems introduced in the reform period after 1989. The issue had been simmering throughout the later years of the Goss government, and was seen as closely linked with the complementary changes in personnel skills development. The introduction of a 'Competency Acquisition Program' (CAP) for example was tied to a pay rise, and was defended by the commissioner on the basis of its relation to competency and skills programmes in Australian employment generally. It was also evident that there was support in the union for the programme.[19] But the old rhetoric could assert itself. Attacked by executive member, later president, Gary Wilkinson in the union journal in 1993, the CAP was seen as a symptom of the divide in the police organisation, an imposition

> on those of us unfortunate enough not to be on the highest pay band of their respective ranks. It is interesting to note that Commissioned Officers need not undertake CAP for pay point progression. One might ask why the workers are being discriminated against?[20]

The CAP, along with promotion, emerged as one of the planks in the Wilkinson-led union list of demands that formed the basis of the Mundingburra MOU.

The level of ongoing aggravation in Queensland was little different to that experienced in other states undergoing significant managerial change — four of the six state union leaders identified merit-based promotion as a major concern in their statement of priority concerns going into the 1994 Federation conference. How was 'police merit' to be defined — 'what price, for example, street experience compared to degrees and diplomas?'[21] Beyond these conventional signs of resistance to a new order however the reasons for such a deep level of concern over changes in promotion have been tied to the changing workplace. Flatter management structures combined with an opening up of public sector positions to external applications have contributed to a significant contraction of the possibility of promotion, and a heightened sensitivity to a perceived unfairness of the system that blocks it. As a submission from the New South Wales Association put the case in 1993:

> One of the major concerns for constables eligible to apply for promotion to the rank of sergeant is the competitive nature of job applications combined with the reality of diminishing numbers of promotion positions available. Bearing in mind that a large number of those police eligible to seek promotion joined the service at a time when promotion was based on seniority and these police had a reasonable expectation of being promoted to the rank of sergeant, senior sergeant or, in most cases, commissioned rank. / It has been recognised for some time that an appropriate pay structure is needed to reward those police who continue to enhance their skills and competencies in their present position without promotion.[22]

Pay alone may not address the sense of grievance. The Australian police unions have also been aware of the larger context of changing promotional opportunities. The South Australian and Queensland union journals have for example given prominence to an American study emphasising the need for realism in police departments about the contracting promotional opportunities arising from managerial reform, and demographic shifts. Recognising the sense of personal failure that results from a lack of upward mobility, the authors noted that

> [t]o make matters worse, the impact of not being promoted within the law enforcement community is literally 'worn on the sleeve'. The paramilitary structure of law enforcement, with stripes and bars on uniforms denoting rank, makes officers keenly aware, on a daily basis, of their lack of promotion.

Their solution was to advise departments to enhance other dimensions of job satisfaction, including improved participation in decision-making and planning for a diversified range of policing functions.[23] The possibility of this vision becoming reality in Australian police forces seemed from the outside to be remote in the 1990s. As we note in the following pages the repeated endeavours of police commissioners to retrieve long lost powers to sack those suspected of misconduct spoke of a different sense of priorities.

7.2 Discipline and the commissioner's powers

What kind of impacts did the unions have on the freedoms of commissioners to pursue administrative change in police administration and operations during the period from the 1960s? The question was already being asked in Victoria in 1965. 'Very often', reported the secretary of the Victorian Police Association in August of that year,

> when the Association exerts pressure in an effort to win a particular point or support some specific cause, there is a tendency to criticise our activity on the basis that we are interfering unduly in "administrative affairs".

The simple defence was that almost every conceivable issue involving the Association was an administrative matter. In some cases the Association took up business which the commissioner or department chose not to prioritise — the publication of 'Case-Law Notes' in the union journal, the assistance to members in relief of bad debts through the 'Welfare Loan Fund' (thereby averting disciplinary charges against those not paying their lawful debts); the provision of legal assistance to police facing 'counter-summons' after arresting or charging someone. In others the Association advised members to pursue available administrative channels before seeking union advice. By the 1960s the bedrock of Association business was inevitably formed by practices of representation and advocacy of members' rights in the face of difficulties arising from their work. Yet from this time there was also a swell of change that threatened to roll back some of the achievements that the unions had won in the previous four decades.

Nothing appears to have provoked police unions as much as the threat of change to the commissioner's powers in order to re-establish managerial prerogatives of dismissal. As we have seen earlier in this book a signal achievement of Australian police unions in the first half century after the establishment of the police unions was the establishment of appeal mechanisms in personnel matters. It is conceivable that labour market forces might have improved police wages, shortened their hours and increased their leave and pensions rights over the decades after 1920. Without the unions however it seems unlikely that the appeal mechanisms in matters of promotion, transfer and dismissal would have been so readily adopted.

By the 1980s these procedures came under increased reform pressure. Reforming commissioners like Ray Whitrod in Queensland had already sought to re-establish commissioner authority in discipline matters, as a part of a broader commitment to wide-ranging administrative change in policing, and faced strong union resistance.[24] Essentially managerial inquiries such as that of Lusher in New South Wales provided another sign of change, and the struggle over implementation of Lusher's programme of reform would reach into the 1990s.

A later and publicly potent force for administrative change flowed from the corruption inquiries beginning with Fitzgerald (1987–9) and then Wood in New South Wales (1994–7). In each case an argument was developed that corrupt police had been protected by a system which was incapable of acting against them, even when their activities were known or strongly suspected by police administration. Part of that system had been the police unions themselves. As we have seen earlier, such was the depth of involvement of the unions that Fitzgerald had recommended that 'the Queensland Police Union revise its Rules to preclude any concern with police disciplinary matters other than as relevant to industrial relations'.[25] The reference was to that requirement in the union's Rules that 'any member making a "charge" against any other member do so in writing to the Honorary Secretary of the Union', a provision that Fitzgerald charged was 'an unwarranted intrusion by the Union into investigative processes'. A result was that on occasion the union 'has been both the means by which and the forum in which honest police have been dissuaded from doing their duty and reporting misconduct'.[26] Similarly Wood discerned in the role of the New South Wales Police Association in disciplinary matters a partial responsibility for protecting corrupt police.[27]

The forces for change then were cogent, and placed police unions under enormous pressure. A radical programme of work-place change that was affecting the public sector generally from the 1980s was inevitably going to affect police officers. The president of the Victorian Police Association warned members in 1985 about complaints by the chief commissioner that he had only limited powers of dismissal — there was a danger that police might be made more like private industry with the chief executive officer virtually having the right to dismiss at will.[28] The fears of the police unions were amplified by the overlapping on to the managerial reform programme of the political demand for police accountability, an expectation that a police force could no longer afford systems that protected corrupt or inefficient police under a rationale of employee rights to a fair hearing.

The diffusion of lessons from Fitzgerald and Wood into other states meant that the 1990s saw police elsewhere facing a demand for increased commissioner discretion in determining the fate of suspect officers. When the South Australian police commissioner called for the power to dismiss corrupt police in 1992, Federation secretary Bob Page responded with lessons from the recent past in which police had been dismissed or suspended, only to have their innocence established at a later date.[29] The South Australian commissioner persisted with his call for a change in the law, prompting Police Association debate at its 1994 conference. By May 1996 the union's members were being warned that the commissioner wished to obtain powers to dismiss officers about whose conduct he had reasonable grounds for suspicion — 'this draconian proposal is a fundamental erosion of police officers' employment and civil rights'. In spite of this oppositional rhetoric, the generally more measured politics of the South Australian union explain the moderate response of the union to the proposal, with 'a refusal to carry out certain police functions — as has been the case in previous disputes — ... unlikely to be the Association's approach in this matter'.[30]

Elsewhere the response of the unions appeared less qualified, but the possibility of achieving successful opposition to a politically demanded change was limited. Even in the face of the public disgrace brought on the police by the blatant evidence of corruption revealed in the Wood Commission, the unions reacted with great hostility to the government's speedy adoption of Wood's proposal to restore the Commissioner's power of summary dismissal. In the course of the commission the government legislated to enable the dismissal of certain officers named by the commission. Within the same year, in November 1996 the government went further — all police became liable to summary dismissal on loss of the 'commissioner's confidence', and their long held appeal rights were removed, appeal rights that had first been achieved through union pressure in the 1920s. A substantial campaign was engaged by the Police Association, with street demonstrations aimed at the government legislation and a range of other initiatives — 'political and legal action ... implemented on a District-by-District basis' as it was later described by the union president. By June 1997 the government reintroduced appeal rights. The Association president was in no doubt about the reason:

> The commitment to industrial action, the lobbying of politicians at local level and the provision of timely and accurate information presented a formidable and focused group that was not going to be denied.[31]

The attack on appeal rights as part of a process of enhancing commissioner disciplinary powers was only likely to enhance a police union sense of embattlement in an uneven struggle for equal rights of police as workers. In this context the police sense of grievance over the inroads of 'minority groups' had been highlighted from the 1970s on in the heavily ironic use of civil liberties standards in union demands on police administration. A sense of police being at sea in a changing world they barely comprehend is well conveyed in the aggravated comments in 1987 of the New South Wales detectives facing a philosophical re-orientation towards community policing:

> We suggest that, considering the lack of support from many sections of the presiding Government, which see fit to bend over backwards for any minority group one could name, including homosexuals,

> Aborigines, prisoner action groups and, in particular the civil liberation [sic] sector, the Police in this State carry out their duties in an admirable fashion under extremely difficult circumstances.[32]

The challenge posed by civil liberties reformers to police authority and autonomy was a perennial grievance from the 1960s and one we see also in debates about the policing of political dissent or the growth of law reform and civilian oversight bodies.

An alternative response went beyond reaction, and was to a degree continuous with the enhancement of police industrial and civil rights since the 1920s. This was to appropriate the language of civil liberties in dealing with police administration. While the rhetoric can be found in numerous complaints about police conditions from the 1970s it was given explicit form in the late 1970s over the question of disciplinary proceedings.

The 17th Biennial Conference of the Police Federation in 1979 adopted what was called a 'Bill of Rights for Police under interrogation in disciplinary matters'. The rights claimed were to include first and foremost a 'right to remain silent in all Departmental investigations'. Other matters covered included having another person of choice present, or a tape made of the interview, various claims for provision of documentation and other informations, and a limitation of time on the making a charge.[33] The 'Bill of Rights of Police' was a mirror to conventional civil liberties agendas on the rights of defendants in police interrogation. The fact that these latter rights were so commonly represented in the police union literature as an impediment to the effectiveness of policing and the justice of crime fighting were not matters highlighted in union discussions.[34]

The police union position was understandable, but the equation of the rights of police in internal inquiries with those of arrested persons facing police interrogation in relation to criminal offences was highly questionable. As we have seen earlier the issue of fairness and natural justice in police internal administration had been broached indirectly at least as early as 1932 in *Gibbons v Duffell*. Establishing a right to silence was of a different order altogether. The opportunity to establish whether the claim had legal substance emerged in 1984, when a Victorian police constable appealed internal charges laid against him, on the basis of common law standards.

Initially the police case gained judicial support. The Victorian Supreme Court decided that the privilege against self-incrimination applied to an internal inquiry in the police department and so a constable had been justified in refusing to answer questions put to him. The High Court saw it differently. Five judges delivered a decisive riposte to the claim that police had a right to silence. The union journals did not attempt to disguise the implications — both the Victorian and New South Wales journals ran complete transcripts of the judgment under the headline 'High Court decision on the Right to Silence' (unlike their response to another 'right to silence' case, that of the civilian *Williams*, a couple of years later, which attracted less attention[35]). The High Court found no justification in the *Police Act* to over-ride the expectation that police as employees in an organisation were subject to the requirements of the legislation overseeing their employment. The decision was a vital one in its affirmation of a commissioner's disciplinary powers over the police. It also appeared to define an important difference between Australian police and their counterparts in Britain where a Home Office proposal some years later to 'end a police officer's right to silence and legal representation at disciplinary hearings' was greeted with cries against this removal of allegedly 'basic human rights'.[36]

The High Court's decision was nevertheless also a matter of defining a threshold, over which the police unions continued to attempt to cross. The 'Bill of Rights' became a standard behind which Federation conferences repeatedly sought to establish an equivalence between the rights of police employees and those of the general public in criminal matters.[37] The urgency of the claim was stressed at the 1990 conference, at a time when police unions were feeling on the defensive from governments pursuing managerial reform and anti-corruption agendas. Conference condemned any moves by police administrations to 'introduce any process of administrative dismissal of Police based merely on suspicion of misconduct rather than substantive proof normally required at common law'. What the Federation really meant was that a criminal law rather than civil law standard of proof be adopted in disciplinary matters. The conference called on police commissioners and governments to provide police with 'a closely defined "Bill of Rights" to include all rights available to every member of the public'.[38] Not surprising was the police commmissioners' 1991 conference rejection of this call for a 'Bill of Rights' for police.[39] Into the 1990s commissioners continued to push for greater freedom in dealing with unsuitable, undisciplined or corrupt police, but were confronted predictably enough by union opposition to an extension of their powers in these domains.[40]

7.3 Operational issues — policy and practice

Much of the business we have examined in this chapter has related to the legal or institutional environment affecting policing from the 1970s. In respect of police administration it is evident that the unions continued to play a vital role in shaping or reacting to changing preferences in management process and style. But there were also operational issues emerging that were capable of inspiring fierce agitation by the unions. Chief among them in South Australia in the early 1980s was the policy on police handguns.

The availability and use of firearms in the community, and to the police, is understandably a sensitive issue. From the point of view of regulating the use of guns, the issues have been two-fold. There is a concern to restrict the availability of firearms to the general community, a concern accelerated in the last decade by several multiple shootings, culminating in the Port Arthur massacre in 1997. A different public issue emerges from time to time in the wake of police shootings — a matter highlighted in a succession of fatal events in Melbourne from 1988 leading to a major coronial inquiry and internal procedural review, but the focus of public criticism at many times over the years.[41]

We have already seen that as early as 1930 the Western Australian Police Union played a significant role in pressing for statutory controls over firearms. Over the succeeding decades the control of firearms, and their use by police, continued as union business. In 1939 for example the Victorian union was pursuing a repeal of clauses in the *Firearms Act* regarding restrictions on police access to firearms, at the same time as it was pushing for an issue of weapons to all police. Pressure continued during the 1940s and 1950s for the Victorian government to issue weapons to all police, the matter evidently being discussed in cabinet in 1953, without resolution, in part because the police department itself appears to have been opposed to a general issue. The new *Firearms Act*, enacted in June 1953, reflected the commissioner's opposition to the arming of police, based on his preference for English police practice.[42]

In 1969 following the deaths of two police constables in separate shootings, the Queensland Police Union sought government action to enhance the licensing of firearms. The union had already been active during this decade in securing a police right to carry concealable weapons. A few years later industrial action by the union led to the Queensland police being given a right 'to decide for themselves whether to wear handguns whilst on duty'.[43] Unions were not agreed that general arming of police was desirable — in 1980 the New South Wales *Police News* considered that the debate was equally convincing on both sides. What was agreed was that lax laws in some states represented a danger to both police and civilians — the shooting of a number of police in domestic violence incidents in New South Wales in the mid-1980s provoked strong demands by the New South Wales Association for tougher firearms laws.[44]

The 'handguns' dispute in South Australia captures much of the complex politics of the issue of armed police. This was a matter of operational policy, but quickly became the focus of public contention involving government, the political parties, and the labour movement. At its heart the issue was over the wearing of weapons in public — or conversely, the requirement to conceal personal weapons. For critics of police the visible wearing of weapons was an invitation to violence. To police themselves the question was alternatively one of law and order or occupational health and safety. To see how these issues related we need to consider briefly the genesis of the dispute and its capacity to provoke industrial confrontation.

From the union side the vulnerability of police under fire was highlighted by the shooting and wounding of two officers attending a domestic disturbance at Elizabeth in 1977. The Association had over the previous year been calling for firearms controls to be tightened in the light of claims of increasing incidence of their use.[45] The shooting of Constables Tappin and Jeffries however prompted an additional concern. This was whether police themselves were adequately armed in the event of being attacked. The Association called special general meetings in May 1977, resulting in resolutions to establish a firearms committee in conjunction with police department representatives, and with government support. The result was a recommendation for acquisition of new handguns, accurate and compact, reliable and readily used. As a contingency in the coming policy debate the committee appears to have commissioned a public opinion survey, which was said to support the visible wearing of handguns by police.

Subsequent controversy centred not only on the provision of personal issue handguns to police but especially on their being worn and visible. Following an ALP State Council resolution against the increased arming of police the government directed the commissioner that handguns were not to be exposed in 'designated sensitive areas', including public places like shopping malls and sporting events. The commissioner was a strong defender of the new policy at the 1978 PASA conference — not only would personal issue handguns be excessively costly but the dangers to police reputation of mishap or misuse were great.[46] The 'designated areas' policy continued but political concerns continued to be raised by critics of the police. These came to a head in 1983, after the return to government of the Labor Party. The June state conference of the party resulted in a resolution for the phasing out of exposed handguns, and the enforcement of existing policy on designated areas in the meantime. The Association response was almost instantaneous. A week later a special general meeting called by the executive at Morphettville racecourse was attended by about 1,100 police (about a third of the state's force). The meeting repudiated the ALP motion, and threatened industrial action through a ban on issuing of traffic tickets from 30 June, unless the government rejected the policy direction.

Before that date however the Association successfully brought the matter to an early resolution. Enlisting the assistance of the United Trades and Labour Council it met with the government and an agreement was reached to refer the matter to the Industrial Commission as an industrial dispute. Before the month was out the commission had directed that the threat of industrial action be withdrawn, but also that the police should be allowed to continue to wear on the hip the standard issue handgun, the .357 Smith and Wesson. Since the Association had insisted on this as the preferred weapon since the firearms committee recommendation of 1977 the ruling was a clear victory to the union.[47]

The merits of the debate over the wearing of handguns are not the central issue here, although it should be noted that police were able repeatedly to refer to the apparent freedom of private security officers to display weapons at any time. The handguns dispute was an important signal of the Association's capacity to carry the day on an issue that brought together a multitude of themes. Operational policy, which had resulted from government direction, had been gradually eroded by practice — and was now reversed through threatened industrial action. This had been possible in part through the occupational health and safety concerns raised by police in the wake of their colleagues being shot. Beyond this there was a political context — a burgeoning sensitivity to the criticism of police especially coming from the Labor Party and trade unions as well as other groups. South Australia it must be remembered was the state in which a government had twice taken on the police commissioner in the 1970s, the first time to require a change in the policing of demonstrations, the second to demand accountability for the failure to disclose to government the workings of the police Special Branch.[48] The political context flows through the rhetoric on both sides in the handguns dispute. But the central point remained — this was a matter in which police ownership of a certain territory of law-keeping was being challenged, a threat against which the members of the Police Association mobilised with great enthusiasm. Not surprising was it that the enactment soon after these events of the new police complaints mechanism in South Australia, inspiring a new round of union agitation, was interpreted by a *Police Journal* cartoon as payback for the union's win in the handgun dispute.[49]

Police operational practice involving access to and use of firearms was at stake in other jurisdictions in the years between the South Australian campaign and the Port Arthur massacre. Above all this was the case in Victoria where an extraordinary incidence of police shootings from 1988–93 provoked widespread concern, including successive coronial inquiries and eventually a review of training and procedure.[50] In such a context the Police Association was simultaneously forced into strong public defence of police, while also becoming involved in the change process. Association pressure resulted in the government providing financial reimbursement to the union for employment of senior counsel at the coronial inquiry into police shootings in 1990.[51] The generally conciliatory tone of union response to public concern in 1989 gave way in later years to a much more defensive and angry disposition. At the annual conference in 1992 the president invoked the usual charges over delayed justice to police: 'Well may we ask if any other group or member of the community would be forced to endure the stresses of such an inquiry for so long!' All the same the Association was positively involved in measures taken to address the excessive resort to firearms, recognising the weight of evidence against Victorian police — in 1994 the secretary suggested that the forthcoming review of firearms training might engage the help of a representative of the Royal Ulster Constabulary, which was reported to have a lower number of police shooting incidents than the Victoria Police Service. The union journal itself was a site of reflection —reprinting for example an article by a former police chief inspector that acknowledged the extent of the problem evident in the great disparities between the rate of Victorian police shootings and those in New South Wales or the United Kingdom.[52]

In this chapter we have explored some of the ways in which police unions have responded to the kinds of challenges, internal and external, that have shaped internal administration and police operational matters during recent decades. Their involvement has been characteristic of what one might expect of a major industrial union representing the interest of a sizeable workforce in a changing work environment. It does not follow that they are always successful — and we will take some stock of their influence in the concluding chapter. But it hardly demands re-statement that the range of union involvement in policing by the 1980s extended well beyond a simple concern with industrial relations issues. The administrative structures and resource allocations of police departments; the capacity of departments to exercise effective control over the actions of working police; the authority of the commissioner; the style of policing, whether armed or unarmed — all these matters have become over the decades areas in which the police unions will establish a claim, and pursue it with varying degrees of success. The implications of this involvement were the subject of quite conscious reflection and debate over the years in the police union movement, as we will consider in the final chapter.

Notes

1 *NSWPN*, Jun 1990, p19.

2 See eg, Barbara Etter and Mick Palmer, eds, *Police leadership in Australasia* (Leichhardt, NSW, 1995), David Dixon, ed, *A culture of corruption* (Sydney, 1999), Janet Chan, *Changing police culture: policing in a multicultural society* (Melbourne, 1997), George Lafferty and Jenny Fleming, "New management techniques and restructuring for accountability in Australian police organisations," *Policing : An International Journal of Police Strategies and Management* 23 (2000).

3 *NSWPN*, Jan 1988, p7.

4 *NSWPN*, Sep 1987, pp11–12.

5 *NSWPN*, Sep 1987, p13

6 *NSWPN*, Oct 1987, pp15–17; on 'Paddy's Book' see Philip Arantz, *A collusion of powers* (Dunedoo NSW, 1993), pp11–12, 18–20.

7 *NSWPN*, Mar 1988, p35 — this item, 'The True Facts', referred to the arrest of Kevin John Simmonds, which the correspondent suggests should have led to commendations of two constables and three civilians rather than the OIC of Detectives.

8 *NSWPN*, Oct 1987, pp11–12.
9 *NSWPN*, Dec 1987, pp13–17; Mar 1988, pp37–38.
10 *NSWPN*, Dec 1987, pp30–31.
11 *NSWPN*, Dec 1987, pp22–23.
12 *NSWPN*, Jun 1988, p14.
13 *NSWPN*, Aug 1986, p13.
14 *NSWPN*, Oct 1982, p12.
15 *NSWPN*, Oct 1982, p13. For the original paper see Clifford D Shearing and Philip C Stenning, "Private security and its implications: a North American perspective," in *Policing and private security*, ed A S Rees (Canberra, 1983) and for a more recent overview of the subject, Clifford D Shearing, "The Relation between Public and Private Policing," in *Modern Policing*, ed Michael Tonry and Norval Morris, Crime & Justice (Chicago, 1992).
16 Royal Commisison into the New South Wales Police Service, *Report*, 1997, Vol II, pp285–286.
17 *NSWPN*, Aug 1994, p37.
18 Lawson Savery, "Merit-based promotion system: police officers' view," *QPJ* (1994).
19 Eg *QPJ*, Sep 1994, pp22–23.
20 *QPJ*, Dec 1993, p59.
21 *NSWPN*, Aug 1994, p14.
22 *NSWPN*, Dec 1993, p17.
23 Ira Grossman and Jack Doherty, "On troubled waters: promotion and advancement in the 1990s," *Queensland Police Union Journal* (1995): 11–14. The article was published also in *The Police Journal* (SA), Oct 1994.
24 Bolen, *Reform in policing: lessons from the Whitrod era*, 4.4, 5.4.
25 Fitzgerald, "Report of a Commission of Inquiry into Possible Illegal Activities and Associated Misconduct".
26 Ibid, p287.
27 Royal Commisison into the New South Wales Police Service, *Report*, 1997, Vol II, pp531–532.
28 *VPJ*, Jun 1985, p7. This 1985 debate developed in the context of the High Court's decision in O'Rourke v Miller, 1985, which affirmed the Chief Commissioner's right to terminate the services of a probationary constable — *VPJ*, Jun 1985, pp15–31, 59.
29 *NSWPN*, Apr 1992, p14.
30 *SAPJ*, May 1996, pp4–5.
31 *NSWPN*, Aug 1997, p3; and see Feb 1997, pp5, 23; Mar 1997, p3.
32 *NSWPN*, Sep 1987, p13.
33 *NSWPN*, Sep 1979, p332. See commentary by Bruce Swanton, *NSWPN*, May 1982, p9, on the American origins of the police bill of rights rhetoric —Swanton noted that many of the bill of rights demands were in fact best covered as conditions of service under bargaining agreements.
34 Cf *VPJ*, Apr 1986, p11 on the proposed Australian Bill of Rights in which the proposals regarding suspects' rights are consistently questioned on the basis that they restrict or inhibit police procedure. And *SAPJ*, Dec 1991, p8 — 'Bill of Rights hampers NZ Police' (referring to a New Zealand Court of Appeal decision

that police be required to charge suspects promptly): 'whilst we have problems in Australia following the Williams High Court decision on questioning of suspects etc our colleagues across the Tasman have even bigger problems with their Bill of Rights'.

35 See eg *NSWPN*, Sep 1987, pp18–19: 'A Tasmanian bedevils the criminal justice system', which is nevertheless a considered response to the case. On the significance and uneven impact of the Williams case see Dixon, *Law in policing: legal regulation and police practices*, ch5.

36 *The Times*, 24 Sep 1993, p9.

37 *NSWPN*, Apr 1988, p26.

38 *VPJ*, Nov 1990, p39.

39 *NSWPN*, Apr 1991, p16.

40 *SAPJ*, May 1992, p10; Oct 1993, p6; Dec 1993, p8; Jan 1994, p8.

41 See Richard Harding, *Police killings in Australia* (Ringwood, Vic, 1970); Ian Freckelton, "Legal regulation of the police culture of violence," in *Violence and police culture*, ed Tony Coady, Seumas Miller, and Michael O'Keefe (Carlton, 2000); Jude McCulloch, *Blue army : paramilitary policing in Australia* (Carlton, 2001).

42 *VPJ*, Oct 1939, p254; Apr 1953, pp572–573, 580; Jun 1953, p613.

43 Johnston, *The long blue line: a history of the Queensland Police*, 320. Bruce Swanton and Garry Hannigan, eds, *Police Source Book 2* (Canberra, 1985), 182.

44 *NSWPN*, Aug 1980, p13; Nov 1986, p8.

45 Eg *SAPJ*, Mar 1976, p2; Nov 1976, p1.

46 *SAPJ*, May 1978, p13.

47 *SAPJ*, July 1983, pp8–12.

48 John Summers, "The Salisbury Affair," in *The Flinders History of South Australia: Political History*, ed Dean Jaensch (Netley, S A, 1987); Finnane, *Police and Government*, pp39–40.

49 *SAPJ*, Nov 1984, p21.

50 See especially McCulloch, *Blue army : paramilitary policing in Australia*, chs5–6.

51 *VPJ*, Sep 1990, p11.

52 *VPJ*, Jun 1994, p59; Oct 1992, p9; Sep 1994, p29.

8: Law and order

In the combative industrial relations environment of the 1990s police unions in Australia seemed to face enemies all around. After the challenges, above all political, to the authority of police in the 1970s and 1980s —embodied in the royal commissions and other official inquiries, but also in political dissent on the streets and the rising tide of complaints against police actions — the 1990s brought sometimes unexpected frustrations to the role of the police unions. In New South Wales police union delegates in 1990 found themselves having to attend annual conference in their own time — the first time so it was said since the Association had been formed.[1] In Queensland at the same time the union was attacking the Labor government's police minister for his refusal to allow payroll deductions for union dues.[2] The arrival of the Kennett government in Victoria in 1993 signalled a collapse of some conventional entitlements — such as the annual leave loading, and police unions found their members not exempt from such changes. In this changing climate police unions pondered both the possibilities of political and industrial action and its dangers. The political interventions that characterised the 1980s and 1990s had a longer history, as we have shown. In this concluding chapter we need to consider both how police unionists considered themselves as political actors by the end of the twentieth century, and how effective the unions have been over time as actors in the world of decisions and allocation of resources affecting the domain of law and order.

8.1 Political choices

It has been shown in this book that there has not been a decade since the 1920s when police unions in Australia have not sought in some way to influence electoral outcomes. Whether by 'quiet conversations', or by sustained and noisy publicity using a variety of media and many platforms, the police unions have asserted the claims of police to seek political advantage from a collective influence on the electoral process.

In the aftermath of Mundingburra there were few Queensland police unionists publicly questioning whether any boundaries had been crossed. Executive members were combative in their own defence. As it was put by one:

> Remember that the Mundingburra campaign was not a political campaign but a legitimate INDUSTRIAL campaign. I have a feeling that we will not be taken so cheaply by our masters in future.

The executive had been directed by the 1995 annual conference to undertake such an industrial campaign. Mundingburra was simply the earliest opportunity, 'such that we were guaranteed maximum effect for the effort expended'.

> Naturally we did not expect the Government of the day to be overjoyed but we did not expect to be subjected to all the dirty tricks and the strength of their hatred.[3]

Some might say if you can't stand the heat, get out of the kitchen. Is such an account of an innocent union simply taking part in an 'industrial' campaign disingenuous? Can this distinction between 'industrial' and 'political' be maintained in the real world of policing, or indeed of any other occupational area which is organised as a government service? Arguably such a distinction can only be sustained in the light of a very narrow definition of politics and the political.

When a police union asserts that it is not being political it means no more than that its primary object is something other than the acquisition of power and its perquisites by a specified political party or interest. On this definition of politics it is arguable also that many aspiring or successful politicians are not political in that their primary object is not the gaining of power as a personal interest, but its achievement in the service of some other purpose, for example to pursue changes in government policy, or the law, or perhaps simply to defend the existing order of things. Indeed we need to remember in this context that it is the attempt to characterise the 'political' as embodying only the personal and avaricious world of the politicians' or political parties' self interest that underlay much of the twentieth century's adventures in populist anti-politics. Under such banners marched and voted those who have sought and gained power in the name of not being 'political'.

If on the other hand we concede that the political pertains to those practices of social life in which choices are made, resources are allocated, powers are given or taken away, lives are harmed or benefited, then the claim that a police union's entry into an electoral contest is just 'a legitimate INDUSTRIAL campaign' collapses altogether. Our interest then becomes focused on what kind of political strategies a police union uses in pursuit of its industrial or any other objectives — and what part in those strategies might be played by engagement in the democratic electoral process.

Police union leaders considered these questions quite specifically in the last decades of the twentieth century. 'Should the Police Association of South Australia monitor the performance of politicians on "law and order" issues?' asked PASA member, Peter Parfitt in 1985. "Should the Association after having gained this intelligence present it to the public prior to an election?'. Parfitt's discriminating reflection sought to distinguish the parameters that might guide police unionists in this minefield. On citizenship and democratic grounds he concluded that there was no reason why politicians should not be monitored, but his subsequent arguments glossed over, as so often has become the case, the distinction between police and police unionist:

> ... to Parliament we — the police — are the public. Thus, if we present our findings to the public then we are essentially sharing information with fellow citizens.

There were obligations nevertheless bearing on the Association's activity in gathering information on

> the attitudes of various politicians and political parties, to questions which affect the policing of the community or the operation of the criminal justice system as it affects the community .... such information must be gathered objectively and impartially and be presented in the same manner.

The danger was that a partisan role would undermine the public credibility of the Association. This was especially the case where 'law and order' was concerned because that phrase had become 'historically identified with the conservative end of the political spectrum'.[4]

The dangers of political involvement were a live issue on other occasions for Parfitt. Writing in 1987 he reminded fellow unionists that

> in the past in this State, the police force has been unashamedly politically conservative. This was fine while conservative governments were in power, but it caused trouble when reformist governments took the reins.

Pragmatism was a value to be cultivated in changing political times — the kind of pragmatism which had driven the union executive in accommodating the government's objections to a 1975 pay increase, even against the condemnation of the rank and file. Parfitt's measured advice was that police should meddle in politics with care — there were dangers to a democratic society when a police force presumed 'to judge "good" law and "bad" law ... purely on the grounds of ideology'.[5]

The moderate message of a South Australian union secretary in the 1980s can be taken as lying at one end of a spectrum of union opinion. To assess its moderation we can contrast it with the unrestrained invective of the president of the Western Australian Police Union in 1992. For Mick Brennan, Australia was dominated by minority groups, 'community crazies', and self-interested career politicians. These combined forces have resulted in changes to laws and establishment of numerous watchdogs such that

> The wheel has now turned full circle and the handcuffs have now been taken off the criminals and placed on our Police Officers.
>
> .
>
> The streets have been handed over to the criminals by the people we have elected to guarantee the safety of all citizens. The avalanche of crime now overwhelming this country must be stopped, and the only effective method of achieving this is for the Police to "WIN BACK THE STREETS", supported by governments and the community at large.

Brennan's attack on the forces confronting police extended to governments which used budget constraint as an excuse for failing to maintain police budgets, and fooling the public through publicity campaigns 'to create a public feeling of well being'. Typical is the legislating of statutory rights for offenders, such as the *Crimes (Investigations of Commonwealth Offences) Act 1990* which 'can only serve as another nail in the coffin of justice'. In this world

> The Police Service is society's first and last line of defence against crime, and must therefore be maintained in adequate numbers, be properly equipped, and provided with the statutory powers to win back the streets instead of being expected to perform miracles with inadequate resources and authority.[6]

Behind such rhetorical posturing lies a determination to extend the police union's agenda into regions which have been seized away from police by minority interests. 'Winning back the streets' becomes an agenda which will not only secure to police the resources to which the union considers police are entitled — it will also avert the danger of seemingly constant challenges to the security of police work as an occupation authorised by its task of controlling the criminals. Perhaps it is not surprising to see such an outpouring from the boss of a union that had resisted so noisily and in so many forums the incursions of the 'watchdogs'.[7] But the slogan 'Win back the streets' was in fact a political rallying cry for police across the country at this time, if in less forthright terms than those of Brennan.[8]

A more measured but still defensive diagnosis of the state of policing was expressed about the same time by Tony Day, President of the Police Association of New South Wales. Day's message for the 1992 Federation conference was that 'governments have systematically undermined the independence of policing'. The 'police profession' was being undermined by the intrusion on the police domain of many other agencies, resulting in 'the loss of many traditional policing functions'.

> The creation of organisations such as State Crime Commissions, National Crime Authority, Criminal Justice Commission, Ombudsmen and so on was an attempt by Governments during the 1970s and 1980s to break the closed culture of police organisations. Unfortunately this has resulted in the loss of police autonomy through direct government intervention, interference and reduction of monies.

That the position is not simply reactionary is suggested by the concern Day expresses about the possibility of police becoming simply the tools of political interests at a time of 'rising unemployment and the devolution of the centralised system of industrial relations' — the police dilemma at Burnie in Tasmania in 1992, when resisting government and business expectations of more decisive intervention against picketing unionists,[9] was cited as a warning of the invidious position police might get into, one epitomised by the use of police by the Thatcher Government during the mining dispute. Day's answer to the challenge posed by such threats was to enhance police professional autonomy. This would require police unions going beyond traditional industrial issues towards 'having policing finally recognised and accepted as a true profession'.[10]

This range of views on the possibilities and limitations of police union activism captures the dilemma of the unions facing political choices.

Promoting an image of the police as a profession and the unions as associations of professionals draws a line of respectability around the police that is in tension with another mood that frequently dominates the discussions of union conferences — populist and labourist. Whether one or the other disposition is the more effective in the service of the police unions is a matter for debate. What is beyond doubt is that police unions have become increasingly convinced of the need to use all resources available to them in their industrial campaigns. If participation in electoral politics remains controversial, there is nevertheless no shrinking now from the message of police union history — being political works, at least for getting noticed. It can also work without getting involved directly in election campaigns.

So the more common political strategies are those of everyday political pressure, of political lobbying, of access to politicians and ministers, and of cultivation of the media. The international lessons mandate the need for political strategy. Hence, after attending the 1995 Police Federation of England and Wales annual conference, leading Australian police unionist, Peter Alexander, the president of Police Association of South Australia and the Police Federation, drew his own lessons:

> Recent discussions with Police union officials in both the UK and the USA indicate that the lack of political involvement by Police unions is the primary reason why they often do not achieve satisfactory results in the collective bargaining process or, as we call it, "Enterprise Bargaining". I have seen what has been achieved in the northern hemisphere by Police unions who have applied responsible political pressure.
>
> As members would be aware we would not have stopped the proposed changes to Police superannuation last year without political lobbying.
>
> To secure wage justice and fight against a reduced Police budget with the resultant hardship to our members and reduced service to the community we must now demand that our politicians declare themselves on Police issues.[11]

Well beyond elections then police unions have become active political lobbyists, at least on their own account. I consider in the next section the kinds of impacts police unions may or may not have had in terms of their own objectives and main areas of activity.

8.2 Taking stock

The problems of estimating the impact of police unions are equal to those of identifying the significance of other social factors in effecting policy or practice outcomes in any area of government. Police unions are very imperfect actors in the achievement of their fundamental objectives — inevitably so, since the range of factors determining outcomes in wages struggles, or numbers of police, or the powers available to them, includes so many outside the direct control of the unions. This can be shown historically in both the industrial and political arenas. How else do we explain the failure of police unions, even in conditions as friendly to the role of labour unions as most Australian jurisdictions have been, to achieve over long periods of time their treasured objectives — appeal rights that delivered desired outcomes to aggrieved members, resistance to merit as the core of promotion, wage outcomes that were better than those achievable in the general labour market, reform of laws that were seen as impeding police work? Yet simply to list these few areas of concern in this way is almost immediately to invite retorts that instead police unions have been very effective, and have won for their members gains that would otherwise be absent.

So could we as easily say, how do we explain the success of unions over long periods of time in changing conditions of employment to include appeal rights, to contain the spread of merit-based promotion or contract employment, to achieve law reforms or resist undesirable ones? How full is this glass, or how empty? Granted that we may be quite limited in reaching a definitive answer, in the following discussion we consider the possible areas of impact from two points of view. The first, given that we have sought throughout to identify the police union perspective, is to examine how well the unions have achieved what they set out to achieve. Second we want to consider what can be said about their impacts on the wider field of criminal justice.

The advantage of historical inquiry is that it enables a focus on cases, as well as patterns, that it does so over time, and that it seeks to understand both what actors said as well as what they did, in a context which they only partly controlled. In attempting to take stock we can review some of the achievements, as well as failures, against a background in earlier chapters of the examination of cases and processes whereby the police unions sought to effect or resist change, advance or contain the development of new ways of doing things. But most importantly we need also to make some estimation of the effectiveness of particular strategies of police unions in achieving those outcomes. The question of the implication of these strategies and effects for the political and social system will be left to the following section.

One way of estimating impacts of such organisations, favoured in American social science research especially, is quantitative. The large number of jurisdictions and police forces in the United States, for example, lends itself readily to an approach that might attempt to estimate the likelihood of particular factors, including the nature of police union activity, effecting particular outcomes. The small number of jurisdictions in Australia limits the application of such an approach here — a shortcoming that is arguably balanced by the advantages of the more detailed historical study of processes and dispositions enabled by this study. All the same it is notable that a recent quantitative study of American police unions and their effect on the police role lends support for the interpretation advanced here on the basis of this historical study of Australian unions. Studying 15 United States urban police departments Magenau and Hunt analysed the relationship between police unionisation and the police role. Their survey results suggested 'some support for a relationship between police unionization and greater emphasis on the law enforcement role'. While unions did play a role 'in shaping what the police do day-to-day', the effects were less than police chiefs and external commentators had feared a decade earlier. Predictably enough 'other factors, such as situational demands, tenure in the department, and regional preferences probably play a more important role than does unionization in shaping what a police officer does'.[12] Such conclusions from quantitative research suggest the value of understanding the local and historical contexts of policing.

Another approach to assessing the effectiveness of police unions might be to consider their effect in changing the overall deployment of resources in the total array of government services to the community. In the 1980s and 1990s the effectiveness and efficiency of government spending have been placed under increasing scrutiny, in turn producing new measures of performance. The now annual reports of the national Productivity Commission on the entire range of government services are the source of much data on comparative performance and resourcing of policing and other criminal justice system activities.

Does such data suggest any effect in the world of policing that might be related to an increased sensitivity to the kinds of political pressures that we have seen in the various states, related to the role of the police unions? The following table reproduces data on police spending during the 1990s, adjusted to the best levels of comparability possible, according to the Productivity Commission.[13]

Real recurrent expenditure on police services per head of population									
	NSW	**VIC**	**QLD**	**WA**	**SA**	**TAS**	**ACT**	**NT**	**Aust**
1993-94	171	168	141	190	176	149	174	344	168
1994-95	186	200	145	190	185	167	170	373	183
1995-96	193	212	143	205	193	179	177	396	191
1996-97	192	215	154	218	210	194	177	425	197
1997-98	200	207	164	224	192	204	189	454	199
1998-99	215	223	183	235	204	212	210	528	215
1999-2000	217	221	203	236	206	207	211	488	219
% change 1993-2000	**26.9**	**31.5**	**44.0**	**24.2**	**17.0**	**38.9**	**21.3**	**41.9**	**30.4**

Apart from highlighting the enormous cost of policing in the Northern Territory, and the continuing status of Queensland as still a state of low spending on public services, including police, the table might suggest that policing has been an area of increasing priority for government spending through the 1990s, at a time when expenditure on other government services has been declining. More interestingly it could suggest that Queensland, with a 44% increase in spending on police in seven years was particularly affected by law and order campaigns of the kind waged by the local police union in the middle of this period. Such an inference is however difficult to sustain in the context of other factors shaping government spending patterns — such as the very pressure associated with the Queensland government redressing over time its historically low spending on social service provisions, including law and order areas. In spite of the increase in spending, Queensland in 2000 was still below the national average in numbers of police personnel per head of population and in spite of being the only jurisdiction to have an increase in such numbers across these years. Data shortfalls make inter-jurisdictional comparisons difficult — and long time series are required before any valid inferences can be drawn, as we will consider below in relations to changes in income levels.

Beyond these gross comparisons, what should we look at in "taking stock" of police union wins and losses? Core industrial concerns are fundamental — they include wages, hours of work, leave, pension rights, promotion and transfer, discipline. All these matters pertain to the individual rewards of a police officer's career. There is a second level of industrial concerns that historically have interacted with these core areas. This includes numbers of police available for duty, and material resources available, including total budget as well as individual items (vehicles, firearms, safety clothing etc). Our historical inquiries have shown that in both of these industrial areas there was always potential for police unions to develop political strategies as well as pursue the matters internally within the police departments. But the political agendas have also come to address what we can alternatively characterise as *both* a third level of industrial issues, *and* as a first order of public political matters. Under this heading we would have to include such matters as law reform affecting police powers, but also those aspects of the political structures of policing such as appointments of commissioners and so on that have helped shape the kind of career that policing becomes. Arguably there is a further kind of political agenda however that is less directly industrial, and more ideological — and this concerns itself with a union intervention around matters of law and order, such as issues of sentencing and penalties. These are areas where the symbolic becomes more significant than the material outcomes — on occasion, however, no less vital for that. We can start however with the more mundane, and arguably central issue of wages and conditions of service.

The fickleness of external economic realities constantly play havoc with the achievements of labour unions in the wage market. Like other unions, police labour unions often seem to struggle to have an impact, and only at the margins — the bigger picture on wages is one determined largely by the state of the labour market and, in Australia, by the wage and economic policies of the government. Such contextual realities can confound the energies of the most ardent union campaigner. An interview with ACTU secretary Bill Kelty in 1996 brought praise of the police unions, and of Victoria Police Association secretary Danny Walsh, a person described by Kelty as 'very tough and industrial there is no nonsense about him'. Kelty's estimate of Walsh's impact flowed from evidence of a 25% increase in police wage rates in the previous five years, 'probably the biggest real wage increase in the history of the union movement'.[14]

Within a short time, by 1999, however, Victorian police were again languishing near the bottom of comparative pay scales among Australian police forces.[15] The explanation is only partly found in the different dates at which the now required enterprise bargaining settlements were achieved. The fact was that by 1999 it appeared that a number of years of fiscal conservatism and radical public sector downsizing had even had their effects in policing in Victoria, perhaps a partial explanation of the extent of dissatisfaction with the Kennett government in that year. The temptations of union officials to look to their best years as a mark of the success of the union is unable to disguise the longer-term reality that relativities in wage rates for public sector workers are largely stable, and that police wages are not immune from the effects of economic and policy changes. Thus when the Tasmanian Association boasted to its members in 1974 that it had won for its members the right to a 17½% annual leave loading, this was hardly an outstanding achievement in a national context where the federal government had taken the lead in introducing it some years before.[16] Concessions won in one decade can be taken in another — and just so did Kennett in Victoria remove the leave loading from police as from the rest of the public service in his attack on the budget deficit in 1993.[17]

Police unions themselves have understandably been inclined to look to their inter-state colleagues to assess their comparative worth. That was not always an approach welcomed by the wage setting authorities during the arbitration era — in Victoria in the 1960s the Police Classification Board was explicit in rejecting inter-state comparisons as a standard by which to judge police salaries.[18] Moreover a review of Western Australian police salaries over the two decades from 1974 has suggested that police in the various states may well suffer salary declines by attending too much to relative police wage rates, and not enough to comparative rates in other occupations and industries in their own jurisdictions.

Savery and Simpson claimed to find significant evidence of a decline in police salaries over two decades, with police performing particularly poorly during the period of the economic Accord under the Hawke Federal Labor government.[19] The requirement to demonstrate productivity improvements has proven especially difficult for occupations like policing and may have contributed to the decline during these years. Savery and Simpson concluded that greater attention to the performance of police in a local labour market might be needed to address declining police salaries. The extent of the problem however might be questioned. It should be noted that some of the extent of the decline noted derives from the authors' selecting as their benchmark 1975 (when the lowest police salary rate was 103% the level of average weekly earnings) rather than 1974, when it was 91% (and still higher than their end-of-series 88% in 1993).

The variable success in wages deals might suggest that the returns on members' investment in their union are limited, even disappointing. In other areas of working conditions the unions' efforts have been more rewarding. The road of advancing conditions had been been well worn before the police by other unions — but given the very real constraints on police work that prevailed one hundred years ago then we can see that the police unions have played an important role in bringing these improvements. This may especially be the case against international benchmarks. Returning from the 31st International Association of Women Police conference in Vancouver in 1994, an industrial officer from the New South Wales Association reported on her impressions after a meeting with 600 delegates from around the world:

> The conditions of employment within the New South Wales Police Service were by far superior to those in the USA in respect to annual leave, maternity leave (What maternity leave you may ask!), long service leave (what's that?), single unit patrols, limited payment for overtime etc. The New South Wales Police Association represented the greatest number of women at the conference. I was amazed at the disjointed approach to policing in the USA, the general lack of conditions, the difficulties experienced through the world in relation to EEO, sexual harassment. New South Wales Police are indeed fortunate in relation to all these issues and I believe should be held as world leaders in relation to EEO although there is still a long way to go'.[20]

The less than triumphant march towards gender equity in Australian police forces[21] makes such impressions about local achievements seen in a global context the more compelling. Simply to review the list of conditions included here is to become aware of the range of issues on which the police unions' primary role has been to follow where others in the Australian union movement have led before. This is not to belittle the importance of the rights thereby gained, but to understand that the context of the gain is one of changing social and economic policy, in which the police unions have largely sought to play catch up. All the same, to the extent that policing has become an occupation much like other occupations, sharing wage and leave entitlements, and bearing equity and other workplace obligations, that result has been one for which the Australian police unions may claim a good deal of credit.

As we have seen in examining the effects of the 1930s depression salary cuts, there were also occasions on which the police unions sought to uphold a notion of police occupational exceptionalism — but with only limited success. Inevitably the strategy of making police more like other workers has also brought with it the risk that the downside will not be avoided. Police, like other employees, and even while their employee status continued to be a matter of judicial dispute into the 1990s, were increasingly required to demonstrate productivity gains in justifying their salary claims in the 1980s, a decade in which their political clout seemed in other respects to be consolidated. Contract employment in the upper levels of the police services, and the possibility of lateral recruitment, were additional signs of changing employment conditions, which unions resisted, but again without holding back the tide. As enterprise bargaining replaced the old arbitration system in the 1990s, police again found that they were now much like other employees. Of course, by making them like other employees governments also increased the risk that police workers would be tempted to behave like other workers, especially with respect to industrial action. At a seminar convened by the Victorian Police Association in 1992, an industrial relations commissioner told police unionists that industrial action was a basic part of enterprise bargaining and should be allowed in essential services.[22] Having increasingly exposed police to the rigours of the labour market, governments can hardly be surprised when police employees take advantage of the options available to workers in any industry — go-slows, public protests and media campaigns, electoral activism.

A further sobering reminder of the forces swirling around policing can be seen in the steady, perhaps accelerating, growth in private policing. Again we have noted at different points in this book the police union role in jealously guarding police territory, against the pretensions of private operators, or even against the civilianisation of functions within public police agencies. While there may be occasional victories in such resistance, the capacity of the unions to significantly stem the flow of policing business into the private domain is very limited. A couple of pages of security guards and private agents listed in the Sydney Yellow Pages, noted by Gordon Hawkins in the mid-1960s, have swelled by the end of the century to an industry that is now double the personnel strength of public police.[23] New forms of regulation and policing that make public police redundant in ever-widening domains have become much more than a possibility — and now are consolidated as part of the permanent face of policing in society, while still less visible than the public police.[24] Against these trends the police unions have been of little effect.

If these observations are somewhat negative with respect to the capacity of police labour unions to affect the global conditions of police deployment and basic work entitlements, the outlook might appear more positive with respect to the impact on issues of police administration and management. In the area of appeals on discipline matters, transfers and promotions, there is little doubt that police unions were the driving force in the establishment of the relevant boards and processes. Yet, as with other public sector unions, the lesson remains that the larger political and industrial context determined whether these achievements came early (as in Queensland) or late (as in Victoria).[25] When these changes came, however, they certainly acted as a significant constraint on the ambit of police administrators. This was probably more the case with respect to discipline matters and transfers, but the unions' strong resistance to merit promotion schemes was also repaid by long delays in their implementation in all jurisdictions. Moreover, a symptom of the unions' success in rolling back disciplinary powers was the campaign of commissioners from the 1980s to reinstate summary dismissal on suspicion of misconduct. The limit of the unions' power in such matters was tested by various government responses along such lines, especially following corruption scandals, as in Queensland after 1989 and New South Wales after 1996. But the tide could turn even without a major corruption inquiry, as in Victoria in 1993 when the commissioner succeeded in rolling back the 1946 loss of autonomous disciplinary powers. The secretary of the VPA greeted the change with the headline, 'Discipline system: a ghost from the past?'[26]

The comments above suggest that in the core areas of union concern, the police labour unions have been influential in affecting, but far from determining the conditions of police work, which remain the product of conflicting political and economic forces, as well as of changing ways of governing and regulating social order. To say this much is already a significant indicator however of the importance of the unions. Beyond these core areas of workplace conditions what can we conclude about the impact and significance of the unions? How should we estimate the impact of the unions on those areas that constitute the field of criminal justice as a matter affecting the constitution of citizen rights, freedoms and obligations? In hazarding some general observations we can address a number of themes — law reform and legal regulation, police powers and their use and abuse, and criminal justice policy more generally, including issues of accountability as well as penal culture and alternative approaches to crime and justice.

The inevitable result of reflection on any of these matters is that police unions, like any interest group in a contested political environment, have only variable success. Our studies above have suggested what some of those successes might be, and what the failures. The unions have been active players in the law reform arena from the 1920s. This has not been their major concern — far from it. But there have been occasions when the unions played a formative role in bringing criminal law issues forward for the attention of government. In Queensland in 1931 and in New South Wales after 1979 this was notably the case. But there have been others where their pressure, and in a matter which was justifiably close to their direct interest, has been less successful — gun control being the notable instance. In spite of continuing agitation over many decades for stricter regulation of importation, sale and licensing of handguns and rifles, the unions had to wait until the Commonwealth government's post-Port Arthur legislation for significant intervention on this matter.

An alternative response involving law reform has been less proactive force, than reactive. A campaign developed by the Police Federation and pursued by the state unions during the late 1970s and early 1980s targeted the national government's proposed changes in criminal investigation. Not only did the unions face the changes with great hostility, seeing them as tipping the balance decisively in favour of criminals, but the mood of the campaign almost seamlessly linked this change to other prevailing issues, especially the police strength campaigns in a number of states. The idiom of the press advertisements conveyed the same message, regardless of the objective, whether fighting changes to criminal investigation or demanding more police — governments were seen as engaged in a planned assault on police work, rendering the streets and homes of ordinary Australians vulnerable to the assaults and invasions of common criminals.

While we have marshalled evidence to suggest that the long-term impact of such campaigns on law reform, or criminal justice resources, is very mixed in terms of police union objectives, the assessment of impact may need to take account of more subtle changes. There is some indication, for example, based on opinion poll research, of a reversal in recent decades of the 1960s liberalism which sustained an end to capital punishment in Australia.[27] To the extent that police unions have focused in their occasional single-issue campaigns on a sense of increasing risk and vulnerability then they may in turn have contributed to that wider change in mood. The risk for the unions, however, is that such campaigns in the longer term increase the attractions of other mechanisms for dealing with an increasing sense of vulnerability, especially a resort to alternative forms of regulation, and an increased resort to private policing. Such a result would in turn undermine police claims to identity with the interests of the community, and reinforce a narrower frame of reference for police as simply the instrument of last resort in the maintenance of a governable society.

Those risks I would suggest, in the light of the experience of the last two decades, as reviewed especially in chapters 6 and 7, are enhanced by the failure of some police unions to embrace the increased expectations and requirements of accountability. The analysis in those chapters of police union responses to the changed world of ombudsman's offices, complaints authorities, and royal commission inquiries targeting police corruption, suggests a difficulty, understandable as it may be, in countenancing a world in which police have become citizens, and now are expected to behave like them. Perhaps it is not surprising in this circumstance to find that talk of a retreat from public policing to embrace alternative means of social regulation, including forms of private policing, now comes from the left of the political spectrum, more familiar to us as friends of the public sector in government.[28]

8.3 Conclusion

It has been an argument of this book that the politics of policing have become important to the staging of political contests in Australia, but that they are far from determining outcomes, of elections, or policies. The reasons have to do not only with the adversarial structures of governmental organisation in Australia but also with a changing disposition of police unions. While the police unions have their origins in those circumstances they share with other employees, they have in recent decades asserted their determination to be independent of political loyalties to any side of politics. In the event they are as likely to disappoint, and in turn be disappointed by, Labor as non-Labor governments. Having won government in a law and order election in 1988, Liberal Premier Nick Greiner in New South Wales distanced himself from the union and turned it into an enemy.[29] His Labor tormenter of the early 80s, long-serving premier, Neville Wran, confessed in a lecture to the Fabian Society in 1986 that his biggest regret about a decade of reforming government had been the 'disobedience of police' — a charge he directed at them over their campaigns against his police complaints legislation, and the opposition to the repeal of the *Summary Offences Act*.[30] The more recent experiences of the Goss government in Queensland and the Kennett government in Victoria, both of which faced extremely hostile police union campaigns in their last year of office, appear to confirm the evidence of Australian police unions embracing a politics of confrontation wherever it may lead, and regardless of the political party affiliations of the government in power. In this sense the police unions can faithfully defend a claim that they remain, in the words of the New South Wales Police Association's rules adopted in the 1950s, 'non-political and non-sectarian'.

The history of the police unions shows however that only a very narrow conception of the political would allow us to affirm the proposition that the unions have been non-political. This is not only because they have become recently even more determined to embrace the political sphere. The truth is that in Australia a recognition of the political contexts of decision-making about fundamental police concerns, whether about pay and conditions or operations and law, has been an aspect of police union debates since the 1920s and earlier. In that regard then what are the implications, if any, for our conceptions of how policing should be regarded at the turn of century, and do these histories we have reviewed have any implications for democratic standards in an era of citizenship? A number of propositions might be advanced.

First, having conceded the right of employees of a core government service to organise in defence of basic industrial rights it can scarcely be contemplated that these might be taken away. Governments, and civil society, in countries like Australia have to live with the reality of police unionisation — but can legitimately expect that police unions will not enjoy rights greater than those granted to like bodies in other industries. In that context the special, and secretive, relationship fostered by the Queensland Police Union, first in the 1970s with the Bjelke-Peterson government, and then in 1996 with the prospective Borbidge government, rightly earned condemnation and political exposure.

Second, the advantages of unionisation need to be recognised. Not only does a labour union represent a form of civil association that should be protected in societies that claim to be free and democratic, but more pragmatically it can be seen as a mechanism by which grievances can be channelled, productively in terms of seeking solutions to legitimate concerns, perhaps preventively in terms of the institutional management of high levels of aggravation. It is a moot point, that is, whether a union might be seen as aggravating a level of industrial tension or containing it through the pressure of obtaining collective agreement on a particular issue.

Third, unions themselves need to acknowledge the constraints on their own power, and the potential of these organisations for producing positive transformations in the conditions of police work. Indeed recent years have seen contests in unions between those who have a strong interest in advancing the status of the unions as professional associations and those who see their organisations as predominantly defensive of employee rights.[31] The difficulties faced by either approach cannot be ignored. Policing might be seen as a profession by some — but the constitutional status of public police forces is a limit on professional autonomy. On the other hand, seeing the role of the union as only concerned with defending members' interests narrowly conceived runs the danger of failing to deal with the changing contours of a workplace under threat of change through the very reorganisation of policing.

In the development of a politics of law and order in Australia, the evidence of this book suggests the important role played by the police unions. Their capacity to determine the outcomes of such a politics is of course limited by the play of other influences, electoral, media, fiscal. Favourable political alliances in one generation collapse in another; internal political struggles over the direction a union should take have the capacity to undermine a union's potential influence. Media sympathy for the police case for extra numbers, more equipment, law reform, can evaporate in the storm of a corruption inquiry or evidence of maladministration. This is the course of politics — and the police unions have their part to play, not as the representatives of a public interest, but rather as one sectional interest among others.

Notes

1 *SAPJ*, Jul 1990, p5.
2 *SAPJ*, Mar 1991, p16.
3 *QPJ*, Apr 1996, p15.
4 *SAPJ*, Dec 1985, p19
5 *SAPJ*, Sep 1987, p16.
6 *WAPN*, Sep 1992, p1.
7 Wendy Bacon and Denis Hare, "The journalist who took on the police union," *Modern Times*, May 1992.
8 See the invited contributions on the theme by a range of union presidents in *VPJ*, Aug 1992, pp6–13.
9 Baker, "Trade unionism and the policing "accord": control and self-regulation of picketing during the 1998 Maritime Dispute".
10 *VPJ*, Aug 1992, p7.
11 *SAPJ*, Jun 1995, p2.
12 John M Magenau and Raymond G Hunt, "Police unions and the police role," *Human Relations* 49 (1996), p1331.
13 Data derived from Steering Committee for the Review of Commonwealth/State Service Provision, "Report on Government Services," (1999).
14 *VPJ*, Sep 1996, p6.
15 See *QPJ*, Jun 1999, pp7–8. The Victorian pay rises of 1999 were only to be paid from 1 December, whereas the higher Queensland pay rates were to be paid from 1 July.
16 *TPJ*, May 1974, pp2–3.
17 *VPJ*, Dec 1992, p49.
18 *VPJ*, Jan 1960, p2.
19 Lawson K Savery and Michael Simpson, "Western Australian Police Officers' Salaries ... the decline 1974–1993," *Queensland Police Union Journal* (1994), pp49–51.
20 *NSWPN*, Mar 1994, p36.
21 Tim Prenzler and Hennessey Hayes, "Measuring progress in gender equity in Australian policing," *Current Issues in Criminal Justice* 12 (2000).

22 *SAPJ*, Apr 1992, p7.
23 Gordon Hawkins, "Investigating the police: more BA's needed," *Victoria Police Journal* (1965), Tim Prenzler and Rick Sarre, "Regulating private security in Australia," (Canberra, 1998), 6.
24 John Braithwaite, "The new regulatory state and the transformation of criminology," *British Journal of Criminology* 40 (2000).
25 Thornwaite, "Regulating state employment in NSW, 1880–1980".
26 *VPJ*, Aug 1993, p3.
27 Jonathan Kelley and John Braithwaite, "Public opinion and the death penalty in Australia," *Justice Quarterly* 7 (1990), Mark Finnane, *Punishment in Australian Society* (Melbourne, 1997), 126–139.
28 See Braithwaite, "The new regulatory state and the transformation of criminology,"; Mike Brogden and Clifford Shearing, *Policing for a new South Africa* (London and New York, 1993), ch7.
29 *SAPJ*, Apr 1992, p5; May 1992, p11.
30 *SMH*, 12 Nov 1986.
31 A confusing picture that contributes to different evaluations of the role played by unions in managerial change by different authors in Etter and Palmer, eds, *Police leadership in Australasia*, 245, 296.

References

Amos, Keith. *The New Guard movement 1931–1935*. Carlton: Melbourne University Press, 1976.

Arantz, Philip. *A collusion of powers*. Dunedoo NSW: Philip Arantz, 1993.

Bacon, Wendy, and Hare, Denis. "The journalist who took on the police union." *Modern Times*, May 1992, 12–15.

Baker, David. "Avoiding "War on the Wharves": is the non-confrontational policing of major industrial disputues "Here to Stay"?" *International Employment Relations Review* 5, no. 2 (1999): 39–62.

———. "The evolving paradox of police unionism: employees or officers?" In *Unions 2000: Retrospect and Prospect*, edited by G Griffin, 22–43. Melbourne: Monash University, 2000.

———. "Police, pickets and politics: the policing of industrial disputes in Australia." PhD, Monash, 2000.

———. "Trade unionism and the policing "accord": control and self-regulation of picketing during the 1998 Maritime Dispute." *Labour & Industry* 9, no. 3 (1999): 123–137.

Balnave, Nikola. "Legislating for compulsory unionism: the New South Wales experience." *Labour History*, no. 72 (1997): 149–162.

Berliere, Jean-Marc. " "Quand un metayer veut etre bien garde, il nourrit ses chiens" La difficile naissance du syndicalisme policier: problemes et ambiguites (1900–1914)." *Le mouvement social*, no. 164 (1993): 25–51.

Bolen, Jill. *Reform in policing: lessons from the Whitrod era, The Institute of Criminology Monograph Series*. Sydney: Hawkins Press, 1997.

The Boston police strike: two reports. New York: Arno Press and the New York Times, 1971.

Braithwaite, John. "The new regulatory state and the transformation of criminology." *British Journal of Criminology* 40 (2000): 222–238.

Brien, Steve. *Serving the Force: 75 Years of the Police Association of New South Wales*. Sydney: Police Association of New South Wales, 1996.

Brogden, Mike, and Shearing, Clifford. *Policing for a new South Africa*. London and New York: Routledge, 1993.

Brown, Gavin, and Haldane, Robert. *Days of Violence: The 1923 police strike in Melbourne*. Melbourne: Hybrid Publishers, 1998.

Chan, Janet. *Changing police culture: policing in a multicultural society*. Melbourne: Cambridge University Press, 1997.

Chappell, Duncan, and Wilson, Paul R. *The Police and the Public in Australia and New Zealand*. St Lucia: University of Queensland Press, 1969.

Cunneen, Christopher. *William John McKell Boilermaker, Premier, Governor-General*. Kensington NSW: UNSW Press, 2000.

D'Arcy, Fergus. "The Dublin police strike of 1882." *Saothar* 23 (1998): 33–44.

Dickenson, Mary. *An unsentimental union: The NSW Nurses' Association, 1931–1992*. Sydney: Hale & Iremonger, 1993.

Dixon, David. *Law in policing: legal regulation and police practices, Clarendon studies in criminology*. Oxford: Clarendon Press, 1997.

———, ed. *A culture of corruption*. Sydney: Hawkins Press, 1999.

Egger, Sandra, and Findlay, Mark. "The politics of police discretion." In *Understanding Crime and Criminal Justice*, edited by Mark Findlay and Russell Hogg. Sydney: Law Book Company, 1988.

Emsley, Clive. *The English police: a political and social history*. Hemel Hempstead: Harvester Wheatsheaf, 1991.

———. "The policeman as worker: a comparative survey c. 1800–1940." *International Review of Social History* 45 (2000): 89–110.

Etter, Barbara, and Palmer, Mick, eds. *Police leadership in Australasia*. Leichhardt, NSW: Federation Press, 1995.

Finnane, Mark. *Police and government: histories of policing in Australia*. Melbourne: Oxford University Press, 1994.

———. "Police rules." *ANZ Journal of Criminology* 22 (1989): 95–108.

———. *Punishment in Australian Society*. Melbourne: Oxford University Press, 1997.

Fitzgerald, G E. *Report of a Commission of Inquiry into Possible Illegal Activities and Associated Misconduct*. Brisbane, 1989.

Fleming, Jenny. "By fair means or foul? The impact of police unionism in Queensland, 1915–1932." BA Hons, Griffith University, 1991.

———. "Power and Persuasion: Police Unionism and Law Reform in Queensland." *Queensland Review* 4, no. 2 (1997): 59–74.

———. "Shifting the emphasis: the impact of police unionism in Queensland, 1915–1925." *Labour History*, no. 68 (1995): 98–114.

Freckelton, Ian. "Legal regulation of the police culture of violence." In *Violence and police culture*, edited by Tony Coady, Seumas Miller and Michael O'Keefe, 140–181. Carlton: Melbourne University Press, 2000.

———. "Sensation and Symbiosis." In *Police in our society*, edited by Ian Freckelton and Hugh Selby. Sydney: Butterworths, 1988.

Gammage, Allen Z, and Sachs, Stanley L. *Police Unions*. Springfield, Ill: Charles C Thomas, 1972.

Gentel, William D, and Handman, Martha L. *Police strikes: causes and prevention*. Washington: US Department of Justice, 1980.

Godfrey, G F. "The police and the press." *Australian Police Journal* 11, no 4 (1957): 308–309.

Goldsmith, Andrew, ed. *Complaints against the police: the trend to external review*. Oxford: Clarendon Press, 1991.

Griffen-Foley, Bridget. *The house of Packer: the making of a media empire*. St Leonards, NSW: Allen & Unwin, 1999.

Grossman, Ira, and Doherty, Jack. "On troubled waters: promotion and advancement in the 1990s." *Queensland Police Union Journal*, no. February (1995): 11–14.

Haldane, Robert. *The people's force: a history of the Victoria Police*. Carlton: Melbourne University Press, 1986.

Harding, Richard. *Police killings in Australia*. Ringwood, Vic: Penguin Books, 1970.

Hawkins, Gordon. "Investigating the police: more BA's needed." *Victoria Police Journal*, no. May (1965): 249–253.

Higgs, P, and Betters, C. *To walk a fair beat: a history of the South Australian Women Police, 1915–1987*. Lockleys, SA: Past & Present Women Police Association, 1987.

Hogg, Russell, and Brown, David. *Rethinking law and order*. Annandale, NSW: Pluto Press, 1998.

Howe, Bruce. *The Blue Collar Workers' Union: a history of the Police Association of New South Wales*. [Sydney]: [Police Association of NSW (unpublished ms)], 1988.

Inglis, K S. *The Stuart Case*. Parkville: Melbourne University Press, 1961.

Jackson, R. "Police labour relations in Canada: a current perspective." In *Conflict and cooperation in police labour relations*, edited by Bryan M Downie and Richard L Jackson. Ottawa: Canadian Police College, 1980.

Johnston, W Ross. *The long blue line: a history of the Queensland Police*. Brisbane: Boolarong, 1992.

Kadziolka, Mark. "Masked man revealed." *Association News (PAT)*, June 2000, 11–17.

Kelley, Jonathan, and Braithwaite, John. "Public opinion and the death penalty in Australia." *Justice Quarterly* 7, no. 3 (1990): 529–563.

Kelling, George L, and Kliesmet, Robert B. "Police unions, police culture, and police use of force." In *Police violence: understanding and controlling police abuse of force*, edited by William A Geller and Hans Toch, 191–212. New Haven and London: Yale University Press, 1996.

Lafferty, George, and Fleming, Jenny. "New management techniques and restructuring for accountability in Australian police organisations." *Policing : An International Journal of Police Strategies and Management* 23, no. 2 (2000): 154–168.

Lewis, Colleen. *Complaints against police: the politics of reform.* Sydney: Hawkins Press, 1999.

Loos, Noel. *Invasion and Resistance: Aboriginal-European relations on the North Queensland frontier 1861–1897.* Canberra: ANU Press, 1982.

Lowe, W J. "The constabulary agitation of 1882." *Irish Historical Studies* xxxi, no. 121 (1998): 37–59.

Magenau, John M, and Hunt, Raymond G. "Police unions and the police role." *Human Relations* 49, no. 10 (1996): 1315–1343.

McCulloch, Jude. *Blue army : paramilitary policing in Australia.* Carlton: Melbourne University Press, 2001.

McGill, David. *No Right to Strike The History of the New Zealand Police Service Organizations.* Wellington: Silver Owl Press, 1992.

Moyle, Irene. "Union History 1915–1957 (3 parts)." (Manuscript held by Queensland Police Union of Employees).

Nasson, Bill. " "Messing with coloured people": the 1918 police strike in Cape Town, South Africa." *Journal of African History* 33 (1992): 301–319.

Peetz, David. *Unions in a contrary world: the future of the Australian trade union movement.* Sydney: Cambridge University Press, 1998.

Prenzler, Tim. "Women in Australian policing: an historical overview." *Journal of Australian Studies*, no. 42 (1994): 78–88.

Prenzler, Tim, and Hayes, Hennessey. "Measuring progress in gender equity in Australian policing." *Current Issues in Criminal Justice* 12, no. 1 (2000): 20–38.

Prenzler, Tim, and Sarre, Rick. *Regulating private security in Australia.* Canberra: AIC, 1998.

Reiner, Robert. *The Blue-Coated Worker: A sociological study of police unionism.* Cambridge: Cambridge University Press, 1978.

———. "Fuzzy thoughts; the police and law-and-order politics." *Sociological Review* 28, no. 2 (1980): 377–413.

Reynolds, Gerald W, and Judge, Anthony. *The night the police went on strike*. London: Weidenfeld and Nicolson, 1968.

Russell, Francis. *A city in terror: 1919, the Boston police strike*. New York: The Viking Press, 1975.

Sadler, Peter. "Sir John Gellibrand and the Victoria Police: a short, unhappy association." *Victorian Historical Journal* 66, no. 1 (1995): 58–77.

Savery, Lawson. "Merit-based promotion system: police officers' view." *Queensland Police Journal*, no. April (1994): 41–51.

Savery, Lawson K, and Simpson, Michael. "Western Australian Police Officers' Salaries ... the decline 1974–1993." *Queensland Police Union Journal*, no. September (1994): 45–53.

Seggie, Kevin. "Aspects of the role of the police force in New South Wales and its relation to the government 1900–1939." PhD, Macquarie University, 1988.

Shearing, Clifford D. "The Relation between Public and Private Policing." In *Modern Policing*, edited by Michael Tonry and Norval Morris, 399–434. Chicago: University of Chicago Press, 1992.

Shearing, Clifford D, and Stenning, Philip C. "Private security and its implications: a North American perspective." In *Policing and private security*, edited by A S Rees, 16–50. Canberra: Australian Institute of Criminology, 1983.

Sheridan, Tom. *Division of labour: industrial relations in the Chifley years, 1945–49*. Melbourne: Oxford University Press, 1989.

Spaull, Andrew, and Sullivan, Martin. *A history of the Queensland Teachers Union*. Sydney: Allen & Unwin, 1989.

Steering Committee for the Review of Commonwealth/State Service Provision. *Report on Government Services*, 1999, 2000.

Stenning, Philip C. "Police and politics: there and back and there again?" In *Police powers in Canada: the evolution and practice of authority*, edited by R Macleod and D Schneiderman, 209–240. Toronto: University of Toronto Press, 1994.

Summers, John. "The Salisbury Affair." In *The Flinders History of South Australia: Political History*, edited by Dean Jaensch. Netley, S A: Wakefield Press, 1987.

Swanton, Bruce. *Police employee representation in South Australia 1911–1963*. [unpublished]: [Australian Institute of Criminology Library], 1983.

Swanton, Bruce, and Hannigan, Garry, eds. *Police Source Book 2*. Canberra: Australian Institute of Criminology, 1985.

Swanton, Bruce, and Page, Robert W. "Police industrial dispute resolution processes and their implications for militancy." *Journal of Industrial Relations* 21 (1979): 399–417.

Templeton, Jacqueline. "Rebel Guardians: the Melbourne Police Strike of 1923." In *Strikes: studies in twentieth century Australian social history*, edited by John Merritt, John Iremonger and Graeme Osborne, 103–127. Sydney: Angus & Robertson and Australian Society for the Study of Labour History, 1973.

Thornwaite, Louise. "Regulating state employment in NSW, 1880–1980." *Labour History*, no. 68 (1995): 132–154.

Wilson, Sandra. "Police perceptions of protest: the Perth "Treasury Riot" of March 1931." *Labour History*, no. 52 (1987): 63–74.

Index

ACT (Australian Capital Territory), establishment of arbitration 61
ACTU 17, 128, 129, 146, 147, 229
ALP *see* Labor Party
Aborigines
  Aboriginal Legal Rights Movement 155
  Aboriginal Legal Service 178–179
  administration of (Qld) 70
  bail fund 155
  confessions 188
  deaths in custody 177, 178
  discriminatory use of criminal justice system 180
  Gundy, David 180
  land rights, demonstrations 161
  National Aboriginal Conference 178
  Pat, John 178
  police opposition to special rights 189
  rights under questioning 188, 189
  tent embassy 161
  unions, disposition concerning inquiries 180–181
  Western Australia, criminal justice issues 178
accommodation in police barracks 52
accountability of police 134, 192, 197, 202, 208, 233
"adopt-a-cop" schemes 203
advertising campaigns by police unions *see* police unions
Alexander, Peter 224
Alker, Foot Constable 53
Allan, Commissioner Norman 138, 165, 167, 168
American Federation of Labour 47, 48
Anderson, Peter 171, 172
appeal board decisions, whether binding 105
appeal boards 57, 60, 85, 100–107
appeal rights 9, 52, 84, 100–107, 207, 209, 225
appointments
  of commissioners 228
  of police 86
  of senior police 6, 9
arbitration
  access to 46, 52, 60, 61
  Arbitration Committee (NSW) 170
  compulsory 61
  courts 59
  federal 145
  industrial 60
  legal identity of police unions 64
  national police union agenda 128
  wages and conditions, impact on 74, 145
  workplace issues 59
armed forces
  analogy 28, 115, 146
  difference 94–96, 146
arming of police *see* firearms
arrest
  discretion of constable 115
  intimidatory tactics by police 72
  powers of police 72, 120
  see also civil litigation against police
Askin RW 15, 159, 166–169, 173, 193
assault *see* civil litigation against police
Australian Council of Trade Unions *see* ACTU
Australian Federal Police, management 19
Australian Journalists Association 135, 138, 141
Australian Law Reform Commission 161
Australian Workers Union 148
authority *see* discretion
Avery, Commissioner John 198, 200

bank robberies 171
Barry, Judge Redmond 30
bashings by police *see* police violence
Bavin, TR 67

Beattie government (Qld) 14
Bjelke-Petersen, Joh 185, 236
Black, George 42
"black Saturday" 53
Blamey, General Thomas 68, 78, 87, 107–110, 121, 135, 148, 203
Blisset, Superintendent Ray 200
Blogg, LJ 182
"blue flu" 19
Bonner, Senator Neville 188, 190
Borbidge, Rob 6, 14, 236
Brennan, Mick 222
Brooklyn police 18
Broughton, Fred 20
Bureau of Crime Statistics and Research (NSW) 161, 170
by-elections *see* elections

Cahill, Commissioner William 41, 42, 153
Cahill, JJ 140
Cain, John (snr) 68, 121, 122, 132
Cain, John (jnr) 173
Callaghan, Merv 154
Canada, right to unionise 27, 28
Canadian Charter of Rights 27
Canadian Congress of Labour 62
capital punishment, end to 234
career path *see* working conditions
Carney, Constable 113, 114
Carruthers Inquiry *see* royal commissions and inquiries
Carruthers, Kenneth 10
Chaffey, Captain 79, 80
Chifley Labor government 126, 142, 144
citizens, political interest of police as 132
civil and political rights of police 131
civil liberties groups 155, 161, 162, 209, 210
civil litigation against police 59, 71, 72, 118, 120, 136, 149, 154
civilian oversight of police actions 192–194, 197
Clair, Frank 11
class analysis of police politics 20–22, 24
classifications and appeals boards 60, 61, 100, 229
Cold War 143
Collier Labor government 61
combinations, prohibitions of 41
Combined Industrial Unions 148
Combined Law Enforcement Associations of Texas 20
commissioners *see* police commissioners
communism, response of police unions 151, 152
Communist Party 152
community based policing 198–201, 203, 209, 210
Competency Acquisition Program 204, 205
complaints
  appeal boards 57
  authority 1
  civilian oversight 192
  dissatisfaction (NSW) 170, 235
  hearings 6
  legislation 1
  Police Complaints Authority 193
  tribunal 161
  union response 215
compulsory unionism 65, 67, 68
conditions *see* working conditions
Connell, Commissioner 110
Connolly, Peter QC 11, 12
Constitution Act 1906 (Vic), s4 85
contract employment 231
Coolidge, Calvin 48
Cooper, Constable 99, 100
Cooper, Russell 6, 9, 10, 12
coronial inquiry into police shootings 212, 215
corrupt police, protection of 207, 208
corruption *see* royal commissions and inquiries
Cosgrove, Charles, general secretary (NSW) 73, 78, 97, 114, 119
Council for Civil Liberties 155
Country Party 166
county court judge, appeals from appeals boards 105
court attendances by police 17
Crimes (Investigation of Commonwealth Offences) Act 1990 222

criminal investigation
police powers 72
reform 188, 233
see also arrest
Criminal Investigation Bill 1977 190
Criminal Investigation Branch (NSW) 198-200
Criminal Justice Act (Qld) 10
criminal justice administration
Aboriginal issues (WA) 178
CJC (Qld) *see* Queensland
role of unions 2, 69, 117, 225-234
Criminal Justice Commission *see* Queensland
Curtin Labor government 144
Curtis, Police Chief (Boston) 47

Daily Telegraph newspaper 112
Day, Tony 223
de Groot, Captain 78
defamation *see* legal action
Delderfield, Commissioner (Tas) 68
DeLord, Ron 20
demonstrations 20, 152–154, 156, 161
demotion 101
depression (1929) 58, 73, 75, 77, 78, 81, 85, 92, 126, 142
detectives
decentralisation 198
functional divide 198
higher status 198, 199
non-membership of union (SA) 66
Diallo, Amadou 18, 19
discipline 6, 9, 14, 50, 59, 97, 100–104, 115, 122, 206–211, 228, 232
discretion
of commissioner 96
of constable to arrest and charge 115
of police in crime control and investigation 186
of senior officers 30, 59
discrimination
against Aborigines 180
against women 149, 150
dismissal
catalyst to strike (England) 49
commissioner, by 98, 100, 101, 207
Constable Foley 30
governor-in-council, by 98
right to be heard 30
strike, punishment for (Vic) 51
without hearing 30, 232
see also appeal boards
Dooley, James 42
Dovey, WR, 112
Downing, Mounted Police Constable George 39
Duffell, Inspector Thomas Alfred 94, 117
see also Gibbons v Duffell
Duncan, Dr George, inquiry into death 155
Duncan, Inspector 120
Dunedin (NZ), strike 31
Dunstan, Don 176, 177

education *see* training
eight hour day *see* working conditions
elections
by-elections 1, 12
campaigns by police union 1, 5, 6, 12, 83, 86, 159, 167, 168, 219
law and order elections 5–18, 168, 221, 227
Memorandum of Understanding, union-opposition leader (Qld) 6, 9–15
Mundingburra by-election (Qld) 2, 5–15, 134, 183, 185, 204, 205, 219
municipal councils, approach to 166, 168
police numbers (NSW) 167, 168
Electoral Act (Qld), s155 10
England, 19, 21, 24, 48, 49, 132, 211, 223, 224
enterprise bargaining 58, 231
entrapment 114
equal opportunity for women 149, 150
European Court of Human Rights 18

Fabian Society 235
Farthing, Mr 85
Federated Clerks Union 148
Federation movement 127, 144
Federation of Police Associations 139, 167

see also national union; Police Federation of Australia
Fenwick, Constable LB 66, 77, 143
firearms
 arming of police 122, 212–216
 Firearms Act 1953 (Vic) 122, 212
 multiple killings 187, 212
 police shootings 212–216
 reform of laws 70, 187, 212, 233
 regulation 187, 212, 233
 uniform legislation 187, 233
 visible wearing by police 213
Fitzgerald Inquiry *see* royal commissions and inquiries
Fitzpatrick, Brian 131
40-hour week *see* working conditions
France
 bureaucracy 132
 demonstration (1923) 34
 legitimation of unionism 33
 police violence 18
 Republican political ideals, affirmation of 33
 strike, Lyons (1905) 34
 syndicalism of police 33
Fraser Labour government (NZ) 91
Fraser, Malcolm 189

gambling, entrapment 114
Game, Sir Phillip 78
gang violence, policing of 141
gender *see* women
George, Lloyd 49
Germany 132
Gibbons v Duffell 93–98, 106, 117, 210
Gibbons, First Constable William Resolute 94, 117
Gosling, Mark 80, 81, 83
Goss government (Qld) 2, 5, 6, 8, 173, 204, 235
government
 accountability 161
 policy, union influence 7, 69, 70, 73, 81, 115, 186–191
 public relations offices 135
 see also ministers of police
Great Depression *see* depression
Great War *see* World War I
Greece, police union 27
Greiner, Nick 1, 15, 172, 235
Grigg, Constable 113, 114
Gundy, David 180
guns *see* firearms

habitual criminal legislation 73
handcuffs, use of 73
handguns *see* firearms
hangings, media interest in 134
Harbour Bridge *see* Sydney Harbour Bridge
Hawke, Bob 147, 230
Hawke-Keating years 127
Hawkins, Gordon 167
Hayden, Bill 133
Heffron, RJ 165
High Court of Australia 30, 95, 99, 115, 146, 210
Home Office, Britain 211
homosexual cases
 Dr Duncan inquiry 155
 entrapment 114
Howard League 176

immigration growth in Australia 132
immunity from prosecution, police 72, 94
indigenous peoples *see* Aborigines
industrial arbitration 60
Industrial Arbitration Act 1916 (Qld) 60
industrial court, action by police 84
industrial militancy by police 1, 16, 19
inflation, post-war 47
inquiries *see* royal commissions and inquiries
inspectors' reports, whether privilege attaches, 94–96
internal investigations 209, 210, 212
international environment 18–25, 33–35, 47–50, 161, 167, 168
interrogation
 law reform 190
 of police 210
 police powers 120
 practices 139
 right to silence by police 210

rights of Aborigines 188
 see also arrest
investigation *see* criminal investigation
Irish police 19, 24, 33, 34, 49, 215

Jackson, Commissioner (Vic) 181
job security 29, 30

Kaye Detective 100
Kelty, Bill 229
Kennett, Premier (Vic) 2, 148, 219, 229, 235
Keogh, Inspector 97
King, Rodney 23

Labor government 6, 32, 40, 42, 61, 62, 70, 133, 163
Labor Party 12, 14, 16, 17, 51, 62–64, 142, 148, 151, 184
labour movement
 links with police union 142–151
 split in 126
Land War (Ireland) 33
Lane, Don, Queensland Special Branch officer 152, 154, 189
Lang, Premier (NSW) 67, 78, 80, 83
Larkin, Ted 42
lateral recruitment 231
Lauer, Tony 170, 171
Laut, Frank 127, 128, 133, 145
Laver, Brian 153
law and order politics 5–18, 21, 192–194, 221, 227
 see also elections
law reform
 ALRC report into Criminal Investigation 188
 affecting police role 70, 81, 162, 187, 190, 228
 resistance by unions 185–191
 review of legislation by police unions 188
 role of police 59, 69, 70, 73, 187–191, 225
 see also Australian Law Reform Commission; firearms
Leane, Commissioner Brigadier 77, 84
leave *see* working conditions
legal action against police
 absolute privilege of senior police recommendation 94–96
 costs 119
 manslaughter 178
 privilege against self-incrimination 210
 prosecution 185
 union intercession 117, 174, 180
 union request for assistance 155
 see also civil litigation against police
legal action by police
 defamation 93, 97, 106, 113, 117
 libel 94, 137, 140
 success 98
 union support 98, 115, 180
Legal Defence Fund (Qld) 72, 117
Lewis, Commissioner (Qld) 184
libel *see* legal action
Liberal-Country Party 15, 159
Liberal Government 43
Liberal Party 166
Limerick (Ireland) 33
litigation *see* civil litigation
Louima, Abner 18
Lusher, review of policing (NSW) 162, 169
Lyons (France) strike (1905) 34

MacKay, Commissioner William 97, 98, 110–114, 120, 144, 184
McKell, WJ 111
McNally, Charles 111, 113
McNulty, Clarence Sydney 112
management *see* community based policing; organisational structure; personnel issues; working conditions
Manners, Robert 118, 136
Markell Royal Commission *see* royal commissions and inquiries
marriage of police officers 29
mass meeting (England) 19
 see also demonstration
Maurice Blackburn 86
Mayo, Herbert 76, 77, 105

media
access to police information 136
advertising campaigns by police unions *see* police unions
approach to unions 138, 139
bad publicity, complaints 136, 139
court proceedings, coverage of 134
criticism 140
information, attempt to manage flow 137, 138
interest in criminal justice 134
police misconduct, reporting of 136
police numbers, role in police campaign 164, 165, 168, 171, 172
police press passes 141
Press Liaison Office 136, 137
public comment by police 139, 140
Russell Street, information section 136, 137
union concerns about press coverage 139
use by unions 74, 122, 168
witness statements obtained by journalists 136
Mellish, Wally, house seige 138
Melville (MLC), Mrs 140
Menzies government, banning of Communist Party 152
merit *see* promotion
military *see* armed forces
ministers of police
final decision in appeal matters 104
sacking of 1
unions approaching directly 83, 121, 122
union role in selection of 183
minority groups
power of 222
progress of 209
misconduct *see* police misconduct
Monash, General Sir John 51
Muldoon, Prime Minister (NZ) 173
Mundingburra by-election *see* elections

NY Policemen's Benevolent Association 18
National Crime Authority 202, 223
National Party 6, 173
National Party (NZ) 173
national police union
advocacy of police interest 129
affiliation with state labour councils 128
agenda 128
conference 128
enhancement of professional image of police 129
formation 127–130
Industrial Charter 129
stimulus to formation 127
see also Federation of Police Associations; Police Federation of Australia
natural justice *see* procedural fairness
Neesham, review of policing (Vic) 162
Neighbourhood Watch 203
New Guard 78
New South Wales
appeal rights 100, 103
arbitration 61
classification appeal board 100
complaints legislation 1
conflict between unionists and government 1
corruption 119, 159, 169–170, 172
discipline appeal board 100
finality of appeals board decisions 106
formation of union 42
Liverpool union branch 140
New Guard 78
SWOS 180
summary offences powers 1
Teachers Federation 144
Trades and Labour Council 112, 142, 144
women police, conditions of employment 230
New South Wales Police Association
AJA, meeting with 141
affiliation 144
appeal rights 52, 103
arbitration 52
election, role in 15
extra police, campaign for 166–169

function of police, concerns over changing role 201, 202
handcuffs, use of 73
Minister, direct approach to 83
municipal councils, approach to 166, 168
national union 128
obedience to superior officer, repeal of rule 96
political role 84
preference to unionists 64, 66
promotion 205
strike, response to 53
wage reductions 78, 79
New Zealand 31, 91, 127, 130, 173
Newark race riots 154
Newnham, Noel 185
Northern Territory, arbitration 61

obedience 96
Offences in Public Places Act (NSW) 170
offenders' rights 222
"official misconduct" 10, 12
Ogilvie EJ (Tas) 63, 67
Oldfield, Constable 97
Oldfield v Keogh 111
Ombudsman 161, 170, 223
organisational structure
centralised structure 198
change 198–206, 212
detectives, general duty police, functional divide 198
effect on pay and conditions of change 201
regionalisation of Criminal Investigation Branch 198
unions, impact 232

Pacific Islanders, confessions 188
Packer, Frank 112
"Paddy's Book" era 200
Page, Bob 202, 208
Parfitt, Peter 221
Pat, John 178
pay
arbitration (SA) 46, 60
comparative scales 229
cuts 31, 75
Depression 75, 77, 78, 231
government objection to increase 221
increases (South Africa) 35
labour market forces, effect 207
organisational change, effect 201
Police Classification Board (Vic) 229
Premiers' Plan 76
Tasmanian Classifications and Appeals Board 61
union demands (Qld) 14, (Vic) 16, (Tas) 17, 18, (Ireland) 19
union impact 225, 228–234
women's wages 149, 150
payroll deduction of union dues *see* union dues
peace movement, demonstrations 161
pensions 35, 36, 50–52, 58, 61, 228
personnel issues, 94–96, 197, 207
see also working conditions
police administration
accountability 174
political interference in 7
procedural fairness 93
review of (Qld) 14
see also working conditions
Police Association of Tasmania 16, 44, 63, 67, 99, 103, 139, 163, 190, 229
police bashings *see* police violence
police commissioners
accountability 69, 98, 215
administration of resources 73, 206
appeals against decisions 100
appeals to county court judge 105
appointments 228
authority of 30, 91–93, 97, 115
effect of appeal rights on powers 102, 104–106
freedom to pursue administrative change 206
government's powers of intervention 98
power to demote or dismiss 98, 100, 115, 121, 122, 208, 209
relations with unions 91, 107–115

selection of 7, 183
union role in selection of 183
Police Federation of Australia 1, 17, 146, 151, 189, 197, 201, 210, 233
see also Federation of Police Associations; national police union
Police Federation of England and Wales 19, 20, 49, 52, 87, 224
police force
accountabilities 134, 162
age 162
hierarchical structure 162
police compared with other workers 142–151
professionalisation of 31, 223
respect for 155
role in repression of strikes 32
size 7
strength 163–174, 234
unionisation *see* unionisation of police
see also organisational structure; strikes; working conditions
police misconduct 1–5, 73, 136, 210
police numbers *see* working conditions
police offences 187
Police Offences Act (NSW), s36 119
Police Pension Fund 36
Police Pensions Act 1923 (Vic) 52
Police Regulation Act (Vic) 86, 146, 147
Police Rules (NSW) 114
police strikes *see* strikes
police unions
advertising campaigns 7, 13, 17, 73, 167, 168, 173, 187
affiliations 52, 62–63, 64, 70, 128, 129, 142–151
appeal rights of members 100–107
Bill of Rights of Police 210, 211
Case-Law notes 206
charitable activities 116
commissioners, conflict with 107–114
coverage of workforce 64, 69
discipline, role in 101, 115
freedom of action 121
independence of 49
independent force, emergence as 24
industrial strategies 16, 19, 214, 220
industrial v political action 7, 220
international comparison 18–25, 33–35, 47–50, 167
legal action, assistance to members 98, 115, 117, 174, 206
legitimacy, gaining of 82, 126, 236
limits 126, 142
media, approach by 138, 139
membership 67, 69
national union *see* national union
non-members 66
objectives 58
police strength campaigns 163–174, 234
political campaigns 69–73, 192-194, 220, 224
political power 2, 12, 18, 21, 33, 60, 69–74, 81–87, 102, 185, 220, 224, 228
politics, involvement in 82, 131, 132, 159–163, 235
promotional activities 116, 135
protest action 187
recruitment 50
registration 60, 64
representation on appeal board (Tas) 104
resistance to reform 185–191
safety concerns over single unit patrols 201
secretary position 57
selective law enforcement 187
steadying influence of 43
success 225–234
support for 49
unfinancial members 66, 67, 69
victims, police as 192–194
wages and conditions, impact on 74–81, 225, 228–234
Welfare Loan Fund 206
women, opposition to recruitment of 150
see also elections; New South Wales Police Association; Police Association of Tasmania; Police Federation

of Australia; preference; Queensland Police Union; unionisation of police; Victorian Police Association; Western Australian Police Union of Workers
police violence 1, 18, 23, 59, 99, 139, 140
policy *see* government
political rights of police 131–134
politicians, monitoring of performance by police union 221
population, police ratio 165–168
Port Arthur massacre 187, 212, 215, 233
power of police to shape conditions of employment 45, 60, 225
preference to union members 9, 64–69
Premiers' Plan 76–78
press *see* media; police unions
prisoners, release of habitual criminals 73
private police 59, 167, 201, 202, 214, 231, 232, 234
privilege *see* legal action
procedural fairness in police administration 93, 96, 97
Productivity Commission 226, 227
productivity improvements, need to show 230, 231
promotion
administration of 67, 108, 115, 121, 228
appeals against decisions of commissioners 100, 102–104
on merit 9, 100, 162, 184, 203–205, 225, 232
ranks, through 184, 203
proof in disciplinary matters 211
prostitution 16
protests 19, 31, 40, 152–156, 160, 161
see also demonstrations
Public Sector (Union Fees) Act 1992 (Vic) 2
public sector unions, support for police 44
public service, government attempts to align police (England) 19
publicity *see* media
Queensland
appeal board, establishment of 102, 104
appeals, success rate 106
Bingham Review 11
CIB 72
Carruthers Inquiry *see* royal commissions and inquiries
Cloncurry branch 96
commissioner, powers 101, 106
corruption 175
Criminal Justice Commission 6, 7, 9–11, 223
Fitzgerald Inquiry *see* royal commissions and inquiries
law reform 70
Legal Defence Fund 72, 117
Mundingburra by-election *see* elections
personnel practices 9
Public Sector Management Commission 9
Trades and Labour Council 148
Queensland Appeals Board 102
Queensland Police Union
appeals 106
arming of police 212
collaboration with other unions 148
criminal justice procedure, interest in 117, 131
founding, 42
government, relationship with 6, 14, 236
inquiries, support for 175
Legal Defence Fund 72
political power 8
promotion issues 204
strike, response to 52
women, equality of pay 149–150
Queensland Teachers' Union 102, 148

race riots, Newark 154
Raymond, Commissioner 38
recruitment, lateral 231
reform, union resistance 185–191
regionalisation of detectives 198–201
Renshaw, Jack 167

reports, whether privilege attaches, 94–96
resources spent on policing 15, 226–228
retirement of police 37, 40, 41
right to silence by police 210
right to unionise *see* unionisation of police
rights
  of offenders 222
  of police 131, 145
Rippon, Tom 162, 190, 202
road fatalities 171
Roper, Judge 113
Royal Australian Nurses Federation 148
Royal Canadian Mounted Police 27, 28
royal commissions and inquiries
  Aboriginal Deaths in Custody (WA) (1987–91) 177–180
  Beach Inquiry (Vic) 181, 185, 186, 191
  Carruthers Inquiry 10, 11, 14
  Connolly-Ryan Inquiry into the CJC 11, 12, 14
  coronial inquiry into police shootings 212, 215
  Fitzgerald Commission of Inquiry (Qld) 1, 5, 173, 181, 183–186, 207
  jurisdictional challenges 178, 180
  Lucas report into police investigations (Qld) 188
  Lusher, review of policing (NSW) 162, 169, 172, 207
  "McNally" summons 111
  Markell RC into SP betting 119, 120
  Neesham, review of policing (Vic) 162
  New Zealand 1898 31
  Queensland 1899 31, 93
  SP betting 116, 119
  South Australia 83, 176
  Stuart, Rupert Max 176
  union response 166, 174–186
  union role in criminal justice system 181–186
  United Kingdom Royal Commission into the Police 167
  Victoria 1906 31
  Wood RC (NSW) (1994–97) 8, 185, 186, 203, 207–209
Royal Ulster Constabulary 215
Russian Revolution 32
Ryan Ronald, prison escapee 137
Ryder v Foley (1906) 100

SP betting
  political protection of 175
  royal commission 116, 175
safety *see* working conditions
Sainsbury, Chief Commissioner 43, 44
St George and Sutherland Shire Leader 140
Scotland Yard, investigation into Victorian Police 120
Scott, Commissioner (NSW) 140
security guards 202
  see also private police
Selmouni, Ahmed 18
senior officers *see* appointments; discretion
sentencing
  leniency 73
  policy and practice 73
  union intervention 228
Sheahan, WF 112
Shearing, Clifford 202
sick leave 58
silence, right to 210, 211
Simmonds, Kevin John, arrest of 200, 216
sirens on police cars 122
Slater, William J 68, 108
Slater & Gordon 146
sly grog
  cases, entrapment 114
  political protection of 175
  traffic, suppression of 131
  traffic tickets, ban on issuing 214
  United Trades and Labour Council 214
socio-economic condition of police 45
South Africa 34, 35, 49
South Australia
  appeal board 104
  complaints legislation 1

Law Society 176
right of association 36
Trades and Labour Council 60, 143, 191
South Australian Police Association
affiliation with Trades and Labour Council 143
appeals 105
commissioner's powers, action to mitigate 98
early success 39
formation of association 36–38
mass resignation (1918) 46, 83–84
membership 68
non-members, treatment 66
objectives 37
pay cut, case against 75
political action 83
politicians, monitoring of performance of 221
royal commission, attitude to 177
rules 37, 38
traffic tickets, ban on issuing 214
wages claim 60
Special Weapons Operations Squad 180
Spencer, Robert Neal 117
spending on police services 226–228
"spooks" 50, 73
sporting functions, security guards 202
Springbok tour, protests 156, 161
staffing *see* working conditions
state Crime Commissions 223
state governments 164
State Services Union 148
Stenning, Philip 202
street offences 70
strikebreakers, police protection of 108
strikes
Boston (1919) 47, 49, 50
causes 50
division between unions 52, 84
effects of strike 45, 48, 51
France (1905) 34
Fremantle Docks 62
general strike, role of police 143
limited impact 47
London (1918) 46, 48–50
mass resignation (SA) (1918) 46, 47
Melbourne (1923) 28, 45, 47, 49–52, 73, 85, 183
mining dispute (England) 223
New Zealand 31
non-strike clause 10, 13
pensions 51
police role in repression 32
police strength, threats 171
punishment of strikers 31, 51
Queensland 31
South Africa (1918) 34, 49
Stuart case (SA) 139, 176, 177
Summary Offences Act (NSW) 170, 235
summary offences legislation 170, 187
superannuation 58, 224
Sydney Harbour Bridge, opening 78, 80
"syndicalism" of police (France) 33

Talty, Hugh 65, 66, 72, 131, 175
Tasmania
appeal rights 103, 104
appeals legislation 103, 104
arbitration rights 60
Budget 1990 16
Burnie dispute 223
classification board 60
discipline 103, 104
election 1989 16
Labor-Greens coalition 16
parity with Victoria 17
Police Discipline Board 104
Trades and Labour Council 146
work ban 16
see also Police Association of Tasmania
Tasmanian Classification and Appeals Board 60
teachers standing for election 133
Thatcher government 223
Torres Strait Islanders, confessions 188
traffic tickets, ban on issuing 214
training and education 162, 184, 215
transfers
administration of 67
appeals against decisions of commissioners 100

arbitrary 30, 97
punitive 7, 97
temporary transfer 97
union involvement in policy 115, 228, 232
Tremethick, Ralph 191

USA 20–24, 154, 224, 226
union dues
payroll deduction 2, 10, 68, 219
value for money 149
union journals, advertising revenue 83
unionisation of police
Canada, in 27
effects on police role 226
Greece, in 27
right to unionise 27–29
unions
anti-union legislation 153
compulsory unionism 65, 68
craft unions 32
impact on wages and conditions 74–81
legitimation 32
limits during Great Depression 78
membership 126
Queensland Teachers' Union 102
success in Australia 32
see also police unions; unionisation of police
Unsworth, Barrie 5, 15
uranium, sale, protests 161

vagrancy legislation 71–73, 187
Victoria
appeal rights 101
complaints legislation 1
Constitution, amendment 44
pensions bill 52
Police Classification Board 229
Police Service Board 170
Road Traffic Authority 202
Russell Street police depot 96
Scotland Yard, investigation into Victorian Police 120
strike committee 53
strike of 1923 28, 50–52, 85, 182
Trades Hall 44, 51, 53, 146, 148
Victorian Police Association
appeal board 101
communism, approach to 151–152
conflict with commissioner 107–110
conflict with state government 2
disaffiliation with Federation 146
donations to ACTU 147
Federation, membership of 132
formation 41, 43
illegality of organisation 109
legitimation 44, 122, 133
membership base 50
political action 85, 181
political affiliation 64, 70, 108, 133, 146
powers of police, demands for clarification 120
recruitment of police 164
restructure of 109
secretary, prosecution of 109
strike by 28, 50–52, 85, 182
threatened industrial action over pay 16
Vietnam War
protests 152–156, 161
role of police 141
violence *see* domestic violence; police violence; violence against police
violence against police 59, 73, 155
vocation, police work as 198

wages *see* pay; working conditions
Wainer, Dr Bertram 181
Walker, prison escapee 137
Wallis, FS 37, 38
Walsh, Danny 173, 229
Wanda Beach murders 166
war *see* Vietnam War; World War I
warrants, civil and distress 122
weapons *see* firearms
Welfare Loan Fund 206
Wellington (NZ), strike 31
Western Australia
Aboriginal criminal justice 178
affiliation with labour movement 61, 142, 145, 153

appeals board, establishment of 102, 103
basic wage cut 77
commissioner, union conflict 110
dangers of work 155
Fremantle Docks strike 62
law reform 70
legitimation of union 40
Port Hedland dispute 153
promotions 40, 103
Trades and Labour Council 153
Treasury riot (1932) 77
Western Australian Police Union of Workers 61, 62, 110, 145, 177, 178, 212, 222
Whitlam Labor government 161
Whitrod, Commissioner 150, 183–185, 207
Wilkinson, Gary 6, 9, 205
Williams 211
Williams, Edgar 148, 149
women
conditions 230
discrimination 149
employment as police officers 29
equal opportunity 149–150, 230
gender equity 230
International Association of Women Police conference 1994 230
non-membership of police union (SA) 66
recruitment 150, 184
role in police force 150
role in workplace 149
union membership 66, 149
wages 149, 150
Wood Royal Commission into the NSW Police Force *see* royal commissions and inquiries
work ban 16
work-to-rule campaign 1, 181–182
workers, police as 142–151
workers' compensation 58
working conditions 63
accommodation in police barracks 52
annual leave loading 219
career path 37, 203
Competency Acquisition Program 204, 205
discretion 61
drive to improve 35
education and training 162, 184, 203
eight hour day 32
factors affecting 233
40-hour week 128, 145, 164, 165
handguns carried by police 212–216
job satisfaction 205
leave 228
leave loading 229
managerial changes 162
national consideration 127, 128
organisational change, effect 201
police staff numbers 6, 8, 9, 13, 14, 16, 164–174, 190, 225, 234
power of police to shape 45, 74
rostering system 170
safety concerns of union 201
security of employment 29
single unit patrols 201
superannuation 58, 224
union impact 225, 228–234
vulnerability of police 213
working hours 32, 35, 164, 165, 228
workload, increase 165
see also discretion; organisational structure; pay; promotion; training; transfers
World War I 41, 45, 47
World War II 127, 151
Worrall, Constable 105
Wran, Neville 1, 15, 169, 235
wrongful arrest *see* civil litigation against police
wrongful imprisonment *see* civil litigation against police

Young, Mick 202